"In the Gospels and their own great traditions, America's mainline churches have wherewithal to heal our divided, broken politics. But do they have the will and spirit? Can they be missionaries for a Christian civic theology rooted in principles of Jesus and James Madison? In this wise, erudite, and readable book, Ray Roberts sketches a new path to revival and relevance for the church he loves."

—**Jonathan Rausch**, Senior Fellow, Brookings Institution

"Ray Roberts is deeply concerned about the health of our democracy and the state of mainline Protestantism. He argues that some of the concepts of theology can provide an intellectual foundation and basis for renewing commitment to liberal democracy. His intended audience is twofold: The mainline church, and also readers who do not share the theological framework, but who can understand the key concepts as relevant to their thought as a public theology."

—**Martin L. Cook**, Admiral Stockdale Professor of Professional Military Ethics Emeritus, US Naval War College

"In a moment when it seems that the only Christian alternative to evangelical nationalism is a progressivism not up to the task, *A Democratic and Republican Faith* calls mainline Christians to reclaim the 'thick' theological substance of our tradition to defend democratic life and restore the institutions necessary to form good Christian citizens. I heartily recommend this book for anyone concerned about the integrity of American Christianity or the health of our republic."

—**James Calvin Davis**, author of *The Character of a Nation: John Witherspoon and the Moral Foundation of the United States*

"As the great crisis theologians of the previous century saw all too well, societies are at risk when faith speaks on behalf of political factions instead of drawing from its own spiritual traditions to shape the faithful and impact the public sphere. In this worthy contribution to the conversation on public theology, Ray Roberts applies this insight to the current American moment of Protestant disarray and political fractioning, outlining a public theology that drinks deeply from the wells of the church's theological teachings in the interest of the common good."

—**Rachel Sophia Baard**, Assistant Professor of Theology and Ethics, Union Presbyterian Seminary

A Democratic and Republican Faith

A Democratic and Republican Faith

A Public Theology for a Church and Nation in Crisis

Raymond R. Roberts

Foreword by David P. Gushee

WIPF & STOCK · Eugene, Oregon

A DEMOCRATIC AND REPUBLICAN FAITH
A Public Theology for a Church and Nation in Crisis

Wipf & Stock
An Imprint of Wipf and Stock Publishers
199 W. 8th Ave., Suite 3
Eugene, OR 97401

www.wipfandstock.com

PAPERBACK ISBN: 979-8-3852-5142-1
HARDCOVER ISBN: 979-8-3852-5143-8
EBOOK ISBN: 979-8-3852-5144-5

VERSION NUMBER 04/23/26

For my grandchildren, Anne and George.

The greatest part of British America was peopled by men who . . . brought with them into the New World a form of Christianity which I cannot better describe than styling it a democratic and republican religion. This contributed powerfully to the establishment of a republic and a democracy in public affairs.

—Alexis de Tocqueville[1]

1. Tocqueville, *Democracy in America*, 300.

Contents

Foreword

We have reached the moment in US public life where many thoughtful people are asking the question, "What went wrong?" There is no question that there is something very wrong with not just our government but our culture. Even those who agree on very little can agree on that. But when it comes to discerning how we got to this wretched place, "what went wrong," the answers are only beginning to come in. Many of them have to do with the peculiar awfulness of the other side. For progressives, what went wrong is often described as Christian nationalism and Donald Trump. But such analysis is woefully partisan and superficial. We need to dig deeper.

In this searching book, Christian ethicist and pastor Ray Roberts answers the "what went wrong" question primarily by attending to what went wrong on his side of the religious and political fence; that is, what went wrong with "mainstream Protestantism." His analysis is acute and, in my view, correct. He describes mainstream (that is, mainline plus moderate evangelical) Protestants as having succumbed to decline, disestablishment, and disarray since the 1960s. This disaster has not only weakened these churches, but it has also led many to reject religion.

And it gets worse. Mainstream Protestant decline has created a denuded public square where the rich theological and moral resources of mainstream Christianity have lost their impact on US public life. Quoting with approval the famous line of John Adams—"Our Constitution was made only for a moral and religious People. It is wholly inadequate to the government of any other"[1]—Roberts then goes on to demonstrate the historic, now lost, still potentially constructive impact of Christian theological

1. Adams, "John Adams to Massachusetts Militia," para. 3.

beliefs, such as theocentrism, creation, *imago Dei*, natural law, sin, hope, vocation, covenant, freedom, and ecclesiology.

Roberts shows that these once widely held dimensions of Christian theology did lots of public work. People thought about life and exercised democratic authority within a thought- and life-world in which these concepts were formative and informative. They were load-bearing walls in American civic culture. Our contemporary crisis is best understood as what happens when these load-bearing walls collapse.

So, Roberts takes us back into these concepts and shows what they once contributed and could still contribute. To put as many of them as possible in one inadequate sentence, American political culture, at its best, was shaped by the idea that this is God's world, that all humans are made in God's image, that positive law should generally reflect the principles of natural law, that both personal and social sin must be accounted for and checked, that Christian eschatology offers a horizon of hope with implications for how we live now, that work is most dignified if understood as vocation, that the Constitution is a kind of national covenant to which all citizens are pledged, that our freedom of conscience and other freedoms must be respected by each other and by the state, and that the church has serious public responsibilities without state power.

Now imagine an American public life in which pretty much all of these ideas have disappeared, and neither top politicians nor average citizens have any idea of what these ideas are or what they mean. It's easy if you try. Because that is pretty much where we find ourselves today. What went wrong? That is a big part of what went wrong.

Join Ray Roberts now as he tells this sad story but then helps us retrieve what has been lost.

David P. Gushee

Preface

THROUGHOUT MY MINISTRY, I have been interested in the ways in which the church passes the values of Jesus Christ on to its members and how those values interact with the values of the larger culture. Sometimes, the church's values are compromised by sinful worldly values. Other times, though, the church's values have shaped worldly institutions and practices. I attended seminary following the civil rights era. The professors I studied with had lived through those tumultuous times and passed their sense of hope and responsibility on to me.

Early in my ministry, I wondered how the church's moral witness properly interacted in a religiously plural culture. I explored these questions in my doctoral studies and in my first book, *Whose Kids Are They Anyway?: Religion, Morality, and America's Public Schools.* I came to appreciate that the church, if it is to be faithful and maintain a distinct identity, must be self-consciously shaped by gospel values. It must know that it marches to a different drummer. I also learned how many of the church's principles influenced the trajectory of Western culture as it developed through the centuries. While these influences were never unambiguous or without sin, they also have had been largely forgotten. This amnesia diminishes the church's witness. In this connection, I came to see that, as historian Larry Siedentop summarizes, "secularism is Christianity's gift to the world."[1] Religious freedom and the pluralism it enables not only represent Christian values, but it provides an opportunity for the church to reclaim its distinctive voice.

The ideas in this book developed in fits and starts over forty years of pastoral work and sermon writing. The invitation to serve on the Presbyterian (USA) Advisory Committee for Social Witness Policy gave me an

1. Siedentop, *Inventing the Individual*, 360.

opportunity to begin developing them in a more systematic way. In this connection, I am grateful to Christian Iosso and Steven Webb for their responses to predecessor papers that addressed several of this book's central themes. I am particularly grateful for their arranging a 2018 panel discussion in Washington, DC, on a paper on global order that contained the seeds of this book. Thanks also to Philip Woods, who followed up on this initial work by asking me to present a paper responding to the decline in liberal democracy at a global mission conference in 2019 in Bangkok. That paper germinated the seed of this book, introducing me to literature on the democratic decline since 2008 and raising my awareness of anti-democratic developments in the United States.

I am very grateful to James Calvin Davis, Douglas Ottati, Hal Breitenberg, Rosemary Mitchel, David Foltz, Rachel Baard, Jack Haberer, and Roger Gench for reading early drafts of the book proposal. Their criticisms and encouragement sharpened my argument, helping the book take form.

I owe a great debt to Martin Cook for commenting on drafts of the manuscript and making numerous valuable suggestions. I am also grateful to James Calvin Davis for his comments on the chapter on religious freedom, to Rachel Baard for her suggestions on the chapter on hope, and Chris Iosso for his suggestions on chapter 13.

Words cannot express my gratitude to Tom Jakob for being a sounding board and offering editorial suggestions. The book would look very different without his suggestions and grammatical eye. The shortcomings, of course, belong to me.

Few people could ever be as supportive as my partner in life, Sallie Roberts. She has created space and time to write. Without the structure she has brought to my life, I would never have had time to read, think, and pursue this book. One. Four. Three. Let's now go do something fun!

Introduction

> I began bending my ear to warnings that Christianity's crisis is democracy's, too. I came to realize that in American civic life, Christianity is a load bearing wall. When it buckles, all the institutions around it come under stress and some of them buckle too.
>
> —Jonathan Rauch[1]

Experts warn that America's democratic political culture is in crisis and that the United States is slouching toward authoritarianism. Studies find growing acceptance of political violence on both sides of the political divide.[2] US Capitol Police estimate that in 2025, they worked through 14,000 threat assessment cases involving members of Congress.[3] Rachel Kleinfeld observes,

> Between 2016 and 2021, threats against members of Congress rose tenfold. . . . Threats to federal judges have doubled since 2021. And in recent quarterly polls, a fifth of local elected officials—such as school board members and county commissioners—report that they have received violent threats.[4]

1. Rauch, *Cross Purposes*, 35.

2. Pape, "January 2023 Survey Report"; PRRI, "Americans See Democracy at Risk"; Kleinfeld, "Rise of Political Violence"; Wintemute et al., "Views of American Democracy."

3. Wong et al., "People Are Scared to Death."

4. Kleinfeld, "Rising Tide of Political Violence," para. 2.

Polls show that faith in democracy's superiority to autocracy is flagging, particularly among younger voters.[5] The Democracy Fund found wavering support for democracy in a longitudinal study of the attitudes of a representative cohort of US voters. They say that only 8 percent of those surveyed provide a consistent "pro-democracy response across the battery of questions over time." They characterize this vacillation as a "partisan double standard" or "democracy hypocrisy." That is, while the majority claim to support democratic principles, they disregard these principles "when their side's agenda is slowed by political opposition, their leaders say that they know best, or their preferred candidate claims a rigged election." The researchers conclude that "a significant segment of the population . . . may be willing to embrace or accept the cause of authoritarian figures if and when it is in their partisan and political interests."[6]

Another study by the Institute for the Advanced Studies in Culture sounds similar alarms. They conclude that while democratic institutions seem robust,

> underneath and within that sturdy frame is the substance of democracy, which, at its best, is constituted by high-minded ideals, rich governing philosophies, capable leaders who give fresh voice to those ideals, practices of civility in the face of bitter disagreement, and a knowledgeable and virtuous citizenry. The substance has not disappeared, but there is no question that it has been depleted—to the point, some would say, of being all but hollowed out.[7]

One reason people are losing faith in democracy is that government is not solving people's problems. Sometimes, it seems that every sphere of society is hampered by dysfunction and inefficiency or has been captured and derailed by special interests. The U.S. health care system spends a significantly greater percentage of GDP on healthcare than any other nation on earth (nearly 18 percent). Despite this largess, it regularly bankrupts people who get sick and produces worse net outcomes than peer nations.[8] In 2024, 27.2 million people (8 percent of the US population) still did not have health insurance.[9]

5. Harvard Public Opinion Project "Harvard Youth Poll."
6. Goldman et al. "Democracy Hypocrisy," para. 5–6.
7. Hunter and Brown, *Vanishing Center of American Democracy*, 61.
8. Wagner et al., "What Drives Health Spending."
9. NCHS Press Room, "Uninsured Rate Drops."

The economy is incredibly productive, but it is also saddled with monopolies that choke entrepreneurialism, limit social mobility, and erode the income of the working and middle classes. The average cost of housing used to be less than five times the median annual income. Today, it is seven times the median annual income.[10] The median age of first-time homebuyers was twenty-nine in 1981. In 2025, it is forty.[11] Many do not think the economy works for them.

Responsible journalism is in crisis. The consolidation of media companies, the movement from print to online platforms, the failure to find sustainable journalistic business models, and the polarization of the media have undercut the quality of reporting and political discourse. During this same time, the public has become increasingly distrustful of responsible journalistic voices. The invisible algorithms of a handful of social media platforms contribute to the spread of misinformation, disinformation, and extremist views.[12]

Since 1980, the cost of higher education has increased four times faster than the Consumer Price Index. Graduates are saddled with mountains of debt. Today, institutions of higher learning are managing federal and state funding cuts, state and federal governmental interference in the curriculum, administrative bloat, and the advent of online education.[13] In response, universities are eliminating majors and colleges are closing.[14]

Americans used to brag about the nation's low incarceration rate. However, over the past four decades, the prison population exploded, even as violent crime declined. The US, which accounts for 4 percent of the world's total population, incarcerates 20 percent of the world's prisoners.[15] Studies indicate that the US spends more than $88.6 billion annually on incarceration.[16][17] This does not include costs to families, lost economic opportunity costs, or the impact of incarceration on diminished employment prospects, earning potential, or marriage possibilities.[18] Mass incarceration,

10. Long Term Trends, "Home Price to Income Ratio."
11. National Association of Realtors, "First-Time Home Buyer Share."
12. Rauch, *Constitution of Knowledge.*
13. Curry, "Gutting of the Liberal Arts."
14. Thompson, "What Universities Are For."
15. Stuntz, *Collapse of American Criminal Justice.*
16. USAFacts, "How Much Do States Spend."
17. Horowitz, "Local Spending on Jails."
18. Advisory Committee for Social Witness Policy, "Report on Drug Policy Reform."

economic factors, and unhelpful cultural values have contributed to the disappearance of marriage among the poor and working classes.[19] This is correlated with detrimental economic and social impacts, particularly for men and children.[20]

Put together, the negative trends impacting healthcare, higher education, the economy, the criminal justice system, and the family have made life much harder for many, perhaps the majority of people. While many have bemoaned these trends, the deterioration has persisted unaddressed. Government has not constructively responded to these developments. And the things the US government has done, such as the military adventures following the 9/11 terror attack, have further undermined confidence. Little wonder that people have lost faith in institutions, in elites, in each other, and in the hope that the future will be better than the past.[21]

While democratic norms have been deteriorating for some time, the election and reelection of Donald Trump has accelerated the unraveling. The work of repairing the damage that has been done will take time and broad-based commitment. In short, it will require a renewal of democratic culture.

Religion and the Crisis of Culture

Then there is the dysfunction that besets American religion. Over the past decade, numerous authors have described the threats that Protestant Christian nationalism and Catholic integralism pose to democracy. While illiberal Christianity's sins of commission have been widely studied, mainstream Protestant sins of omission have received less attention. Mainstream Protestantism has been in disarray for two generations. The consequences extend far beyond surveys showing that increasing numbers of people do not identify with any religious institution. It changed the culture. By failing to impart their values to their members, mainstream Protestants contributed to the depletion of the cultural and moral resources on which democracy depends. John Compton reminds us that for much of the twentieth century, mainline Protestants advocated the adoption of an expanded social safety net and civil rights for all. He says that the decline of mainline

19. Fry and Parker, "Rising Share of U.S. Adults."

20. Reeves and Pulliam, "Middle Class Marriage."

21. Deane, "Americans' Deepening Mistrust of Institutions"; Daniller, "Americans Take a Dim View."

Protestantism, beginning in the 1960s, led to an erosion of empathy and shared moral commitment among white Protestants.[22]

James Davison Hunter claims that America's democratic crisis is caused by the depletion of cultural and moral resources that were rooted in America's hybrid religious-secular enlightenment. Without these resources, the public lacks the language to navigate their differences and find common purpose. As a result, he says, they have lost a sense of solidarity.[23]

Jonathan Rauch makes the connection between mainstream Protestant disarray and democratic deterioration explicit. Mainstream Protestantism, he says, was once "a load bearing wall" for democracy.[24] He worries that it can no longer provide the spiritual and communal anchors that democracy requires. This is a problem because, he says, "There is no secular substitute for the meaning and moral grounding which religious life provides. . . . Christianity seems less and less able to keep up its end of an implicit bargain with liberal democracy."[25] If Rauch is correct, the public needs to recover religious principles that support liberal democracy and that can guide them in addressing the dysfunctions that plague society.

Mainstream Protestants have rich theological resources and a tradition of supporting democratic and republican government. This suggests that if mainstream Protestants were to recover the wisdom of their theological tradition, recommit themselves to spreading their ideas, and find effective ways of supporting a deeper commitment to their core theological principles, they could help replenish the cultural resources on which democracy and a just and healthy society depend.

This book seeks to strengthen democratic commitment by renewing the church's theological and moral resources. Toward this end, it articulates the practical implications of nine principles of a public theology—theocentrism, creation, *imago Dei* (image of God), natural law, sin, hope, vocation, covenant, and ecclesiology.[26] Rediscovering the wisdom of these principles promises to help Protestants find renewed purpose.

22. Compton, *End of Empathy*, 5.

23. Hunter, *Democracy and Solidarity*, 378.

24. Rauch, *Cross Purposes*, 35.

25. Rauch, *Cross Purposes*, 39.

26. This book was inspired by, though it does not follow, the ten principles of public theology outlined by Max Stackhouse. Stackhouse, *Public Theology and Political Economy*, 17–35.

Protestants may also discover that recovering their theological language has an influence beyond their own membership. Many of these doctrines continue to circulate in common parlance. Although they have been shorn of transcendent meaning and need to be refreshed, these principles serve as a kind of public theology. Even outside ecclesiastical settings, they still have the capacity to interpret the noisy data of experience, describe human nature, frame issues, call attention to practicalities we would be wise to consider, and ground moral principles in something "more."

These principles remain relevant because they evolved alongside and helped shape the ideas, institutions, philosophies, and practices of Western civilization. Biblical convictions about human dignity contributed to the development of human rights. Christian natural law theology, which borrowed from both biblical and pagan Greek sources, shaped the development of the Western legal tradition. The covenantal theological tradition gave rise to federalist political philosophy. These doctrines or principles have left an indelible imprint on secular understandings of liberalism, federalism, constitutionalism, human rights, corporations, the separation of powers, freedom of conscience, and the rule of law. Arguably, these principles and their contributions constitute Christianity's greatest legacy. Recovering these core tenets promises to renew principles that are often considered secular and that frequently require a thicker rationale than liberalism can or should provide on its own.

Although this book begins by describing the complicated connection between mainstream Protestant disarray and the crisis in American democracy and closes with thoughts about how the church may reorder itself for effective mission, its heart lies in the exploration of the principles or doctrines that were designed to guide the faithful in a way of life. They serve as lenses to bring the world into focus and shape a disposition toward it.

As the church developed the practical implications of these doctrines, they came to serve as guiding principles, verbal shorthand for a posture toward the world and a cluster of moral commitments. Refreshing the meaning of these core principles is a pressing need at a time when mainstream Protestants are besieged by a loss of identity and institutional drift. It has new urgency at a time when the public needs to deepen democratic commitment.

Two Caveats

Any Christian project to renew American democratic culture requires two caveats. First, American democracy does not require a Protestant or even Christian culture. Democracies have existed in states with pagan Greek, Jewish, Indian, Japanese, and Islamic cultures. Although the political culture of the United States has retained a Protestant cast for most of its history, Jews, Catholics, atheists, and others have all drawn on their metaphysical and moral resources to understand and contribute to the principles and practices of republican government. Replenishing cultural resources will require many religious groups to renew thick accounts of democratic and republican principles. That said, given Protestants' outsized influence in American history, the rise of Christian nationalism, and the way Christian concepts still resonate in this culture, it is incumbent on Protestants to get their ecclesiastical house in order.

Second, and more importantly, this book should not be construed as advocating what H. Richard Niebuhr called "Utilitarian Christianity."[27] Utilitarian Christianity values Christianity for its perceived usefulness. The Christian's first loyalty is to God, not to the United States or any particular form of government. Christians should view republican government, in its many forms, as immensely beneficial, yet they should also beware of turning democracy into a false religion. The principles of public theology outlined in this book lend support to democratic political institutions. At the same time, they judge every institution as falling short and have the power to inspire efforts to reform these institutions to make them more just. For this reason, they inform a democratic and republican faith. While this book addresses the crisis of depleted cultural resources, it does not aim to make better Americans but better Christians.

Chapter Outline

Chapter 1 surveys Protestant disarray as it is exhibited by its neglect of institutions for Christian formation and spreading its ideas. It then looks at ways that this dysfunction is connected to the breakdown of other cultural spheres.

Chapter 2 looks at the positive role religion can play in a pluralistic democracy. It explores Alexis de Tocqueville's observations concerning the

27. Niebuhr, "Utilitarian Christianity," 3.

contribution of democratic and republican religion to democracy, taking time to note two types of undemocratic religions, Protestant Christian nationalism and Catholic integralism. Drawing on Michael Walzer's distinction between thick and thin moral arguments, the chapter shows how a moral consensus forms in pluralistic democracies and how religious groups can contribute to this consensus without insisting on being the dominant voice.

The third chapter addresses the concept of public theology. It shows how theological doctrines speak to perennial human questions and offer a practical wisdom that enable them to serve as moral principles. It explains that while theological doctrines carry thin but significant public meaning apart from explicit Christian commitment, the church needs to continually renew their meaning for them to remain relevant.

Chapter 4 observes that human beings organize their lives around centers of value that vie for loyalty and become objects that we trust and serve. This raises a perennial question: "What is most important?" Drawing on the work of Jonathan Edwards, H. Richard Niebuhr, and James M. Gustafson, the chapter examines the implications of theocentrism and its related prohibitions against idolatry.

Chapter 5 correlates the doctrine of creation with the question, "Why is there something, not nothing?" It explores the implications of the doctrine's differentiation between creation and creator and what this suggests regarding the rational ordering of the world, life's goodness, and the nature of evil.

The sixth chapter correlates *imago Dei* with questions about the value and place of human beings in the cosmos. It examines how the image of God upholds human dignity, underwriting human rights, and how, as a vocation, it calls humans to mirror God's care for all creatures.

Chapter 7 begins with two related perennial questions. Is there a right and wrong? And can people know it? Natural law answers both questions in the affirmative, insisting that every human being has a moral sense. This chapter surveys the far-reaching implications of a belief in this universal moral capacity. It also discusses the relationship between natural and positive law (or human law) as well as the possibilities and limits of human law in light of John Calvin's three uses of the law.

The eighth chapter starts with a question that is only asked by those who can distinguish right from wrong: Why are human beings inhumane? The principle of sin stresses that every human being shares a chronic tendency to corruption. Furthermore, sin has a social dimension as evil becomes embedded in society, corrupting institutions, and encouraging sinful behavior. This chapter looks at how sin continues to provide wisdom for anticipating and minimizing the damage sinners inevitably cause.

Chapter 9 opens with a question asked by the weary: must the brokenness, dysfunction, and death associated with sin and evil be our destiny? It observes that assessments of the possibility of change rest on how people imagine that the forces of goodness are related to the forces of evil. After surveying ways that humans have considered the possibilities of history, the chapter outlines how Christians have approached the possibilities of history and encouraged a posture of hopeful realism.

Chapter 10 begins with a question asked by individuals, groups, institutions, and nations: What are we to do? This chapter examines how vocation answers this question by placing it in a theocentric framework in which every person and institution finds its purpose by serving God's creative and redeeming purposes. This larger purpose gives us wisdom to navigate competing purposes and to clarify what is important.

The next chapter explains how covenant answers the perennial question: How do we form communities of mutual responsibility, regard, and support? It details covenant's consideration of the social dimensions of human nature and contrasts it with other ideologies. We also consider the wisdom of the covenant tradition for attending to sometimes neglected features of family, political, and economic life.

The twelfth chapter asks how religion should be institutionalized in society. It shows how the fight for religious freedom was inspired by religious conviction, tracing it from the church's beginning as a distinct body in society, to its absorption into the state, and then subsequent separation from state support. The chapter responds to the illiberalism of Christian nationalism and integralism. It shows how liberalism, including religious freedom, is a second-order worldview.

The final chapter briefly reflects on the work that will be required to restore a democratic culture and the church's role in this process. It invites mainstream Protestants to repudiate their massive despair, reclaim their distinctive voice, gather their resources, and become intentional about forming a thicker faith.

Chapter One

Mainstream Protestant Disarray

Democracy is a culture, not just a legal system. All cultures have norms. If these norms are functioning effectively, they do not often need to be discussed. It is only when norms are being violated or weakened that we remember that they are there and why they are there.

—David P. Gushee[1]

Early in the nineteenth century, French diplomat Alexis de Tocqueville made an extended visit throughout the United States. He shared his reflections about American culture and government in what has become a classic book, *Democracy in America*. Among his observations was that the origin and success of American democracy was owed due to a unique form of religion brought to the Americas by the settlers. He termed this religion "a democratic and republican faith." The churches, he said, formed republican sensibilities, teaching equality, moral responsibility, and civic duty, which were essential for democracy to flourish.

Throughout US history, churches and other religious institutions of varying convictions transmitted this faith to successive generations. They built religious schools, colleges, and other institutions to educate their

1. Gushee, *Defending Democracy*, 36.

members and lay leaders. They created broadsheets, publishing houses, and other organs to communicate their ideas with members and other citizens. They formed voluntary associations, the original non-governmental organizations, with goals that ranged from charitable work to societal reform. These included abolitionist groups, missions to the unhoused, children's homes for at-risk kids, prison reform movements, settlement houses for immigrants, and social gospel efforts to confront the challenges of immigration, urbanization, and industrialization. These also included temperance movements (originally focused on temperance, not prohibition), just and durable peace conferences to build public support for international institutions capable of maintaining a tranquil global order following World War I and World War II, and the civil rights movement. This faith adapted, in fits and starts, to America's growing pluralism, intellectual developments, technological changes, and globalization.

Today, this heritage is at risk. Mainstream Protestant churches are in disarray. They have lost significant numbers of members, and the cultural resources they once helped steward have eroded. Without these resources to lend legitimacy to republican government and help Americans work through their differences, democracy teeters.

Mainstream Protestant Disarray

By "mainstream Protestant," I mean a broad range of Christian denominations and churches. While I am keenly interested in the historic role that "mainline Protestants" played in championing moral causes and shepherding democratic sensibilities, I have chosen the term "mainstream" because the current disarray is not limited to mainline Protestants. Moderate evangelicals and other Protestant denominations display similar weakness and confusion.

Peter Williams identifies mainline Protestants with seven denominational clusters, including American Baptist, Congregational (UCC), Disciples of Christ, Episcopal, Lutheran, Methodist, and Presbyterian. Many of these denominations consist chiefly of middle and upper-middle-class people of Northwest European descent, with some having roots in the colonial or founding era of American life.[2] Wade Clark Roof and William McKinney defined "mainline Protestantism" in terms of their influence, saying that they are the dominant, culturally established faiths held by the majority of Americans "that occupy the religious and cultural center of

2. Williams, *America's Religions*, 356.

American life."[3] Some claim that the decline in membership and influence of these congregations means that we should view the remnants as "sideline," "oldline," or even "deceased."[4]

John Compton observes that for a time during the late nineteenth and twentieth centuries, mainline Protestants were strong enough to "enforce" empathetic and costly political behavior. They embraced the social gospel in an effort to humanize capitalism, promote workers' rights and safety, eradicate political corruption, and protect food safety and public health. They supported US leadership in creating international institutions to preserve a just and durable peace after WWII. They organized to advance civil rights. And then, beginning in the 1960s, mainline Protestantism lost its ability to shape the beliefs and behavior of members.

Compton blames much of this weakness on the rise of evangelical Protestantism. The evangelical movement has roots in the fundamentalist movement, formed by Protestants who rejected Darwinism and higher biblical criticism and split from the Protestant mainline. While initially socially moderate, their alienation from intellectual currents easily transferred to opposition to women's rights and civil rights. Over time, they balanced these oppositional stances with a general endorsement of "traditional American values" and became evangelicals. Following World War II, people migrating to the suburbs sought out congregations that confirmed their attitudes and found evangelical congregations attractive. Mainline Protestant congregations competed by ignoring denominational pronouncements and spiritualizing the gospel. Later, when evangelical leaders tried to shape their church's values on issues such as climate change, they discovered that their institutions were not strong enough to discipline pastors or members. Recent declines in evangelical membership remind us that they also suffer from disarray.[5]

Decline

The predicament of the mainline and other mainstream Protestants is frequently described as a "decline." This signifies the devastating drop in membership and giving among the mainline, and now among evangelicals.[6]

3. Roof and McKinney, *American Mainline Religion*; Baltzell, *Protestant Establishment.*
4. Jones, *White Christian America.*
5. Compton, *End of Empathy.*
6. Rauch, *Cross Purposes*, 8.

Estimates vary, but some claim that mainstream denominations have dropped from thirty-one million members in 1965 to twelve or thirteen million in 2023. During this time, giving shrank, ministries were shuttered, congregations folded, seminaries closed, and denominational offices entered endless cycles of restructuring.

Compton notes that funding cuts ended local and regional council conferences of the National Council of Churches. A predecessor organization, the Federal Council of Churches had held similar meetings in conjunction with the Just and Durable Peace Conferences to build support for international institutions following World War II. The National Council of Churches relied on these meetings in its work promoting civil rights. One should remember that the information conveyed in these meetings went both ways, allowing top church leadership and members to stay in touch with each other. The curtailment of these conferences enabled distrust to grow between top church leadership and the pew. This distrust affected both sides and undermined the moral authority of the mainline church.[7]

Disestablishment

The mainstream predicament is also frequently described as a "disestablishment." This points to cultural developments that marginalized its once influential voice. Put succinctly, mainline Protestants were unable to preserve an ecology of institutions that once assisted them in forming members and spreading their ideas.[8] Protestants founded a remarkable number of colleges and universities at home and abroad because they believed that training leaders for church and society was an effective way to engage the world with their values.

Over the course of the nineteenth and twentieth centuries, large numbers of American colleges and universities associated with mainline Protestantism shed their denominational distinctiveness. Historian George Marsden says that liberal Protestant values of "freedom, democracy, benevolence, justice, reform, inclusiveness, brotherhood, and service" were used to marginalize the thicker particularities of the faith, leading to "the virtual exclusion of religious perspectives from the most influential centers of American life."[9]

7. Compton, *End of Empathy.*
8. Coalter et al., "Presbyterian Presence."
9. Marsden, *Soul of the University*, 5.

Another observer, Douglas Sloan, places more blame on the church. He reminds us that early twentieth-century neo-orthodoxy spurred significant engagement with higher education. During the post-World War II college boom, mainstream denominations launched numerous campus ministry efforts. The National Council of Churches sponsored ecumenical religious awareness days, bringing young clergy to campuses around the country to build student interest in religious groups. In 1953, the National Council of Churches launched *The Christian Scholar*, a journal that examined the intersection of Christian faith and academic disciplines. By 1970, these efforts largely ceased, a victim of budget cuts, anger at campus ministers' opposition to the Vietnam War, and a regrettable myopia. Sloan says,

> The passing of neo-orthodoxy [and its mid-twentieth century engagement with higher education] was part of a larger phenomenon that involved the decline in cultural influence of the whole of mainline Protestantism itself. The abandonment of the engagement with the university was accompanied by a stunning loss of members by mainstream Protestant churches.[10]

One cannot understand the disestablishment of mainstream Protestants without reckoning with changes in their approach to the media, as well as massive changes to the media itself, that fractured the network monopolies that mainline Protestants once dominated. Early in the twentieth century, radio and, later, television networks were required to offer free public service programming as a way to honor the idea of public ownership of the airways. The networks offered much of this programming to mainline Protestants in recognition of their place in society. This access was not afforded to minority, poor, non-credentialed, or fundamentalist churches. To coordinate efforts, the Federal Council of Churches established a Radio Commission and a Film Commission. These were merged into the Broadcast and Film Commission when the Federal Council of Churches joined other denominations and formed the National Council of Churches in 1950.

As commitment to the principle of public ownership of airways receded, the requirement for free public service programming was abolished. This was followed by the elimination of fairness doctrines. Mainstream Protestants did not join their evangelical coreligionists in buying airtime and began disengaging from public media. Indeed, they were pleased not to be involved in the money-grubbing, scandals, and message deterioration

10. Sloan, *Faith and Knowledge*, 226.

that plagued evangelical media. In 1978, the Broadcast and Film Commission was eliminated. It would take decades before the National Council of Churches would realize the significance of their apathy.[11]

Disarray

Although "decline" and "disestablishment" describe aspects of the mainstream predicament, it may also be described as "disarray." Disarray names the ineffectiveness of denominations that do not know how to organize for effective ministry. It describes their neglect of institutions for Christian formation, organs for spreading their ideas, and systems for sustaining commitment. This neglect has contributed to cycles of denominational deterioration.

Mainstream Protestants are not alone in their disarray. Ira Rifkin observes, in connection with the announcement that Hebrew Union College in Cincinnati will cease ordaining rabbis, "The bottom line in this saga is that Reform Judaism is in a demographic downswing. The same may be said for Conservative Judaism, the more centrist of America's three main Jewish congregational movements."[12]

Characterizing the mainstream Protestant situation as disarray holds the possibility for reformation and renewal. Unlike disestablishment, it does not locate the problems externally and therefore beyond their reach. Unlike decline, disarray calls them to look beyond their grief at shrinking members, budgets, and influence. It denies that demographics are destiny. It suggests that congregations and denominations need to regather themselves, reclaim their mission, and focus their efforts.

The Sociological Impact of Mainstream Disarray

Mainstream Protestantism has been unraveling for two generations, and the sociological, cultural, and political fallout has become clear. Perhaps the most obvious result is the growing number of people who, when asked to identify their religious group, check "none of the above." While mainline Protestants made a direct gift of their own lapsed members, they also made an indirect contribution. By failing to provide an effective, visible

11. Voskuil, "Reaching Out," 72.

12. Rifkin, "Decline Closes Reform Jewish Seminary," para. 24.

alternative to the rising Christian right, they helped produce the conditions that have led many to reject all religion. Jonathan Rauch observes how a loss of members shapes the culture: "A culture that used to be Christian, just like a person who used to be one, carries much of the past along with it. Yet even that muscle memory of Christianity will fade as more children and grandchildren of 'nones' grow up without inherited knowledge of Christianity."[13]

Studies show a correlation between regular worship attendance and voting, participation in service clubs, volunteering, and blood donation. They suggest that a decline in mainstream Protestant worship attendance may be one factor that has contributed to flagging civic engagement.[14] The Center for Inclusion and Belonging at the American Immigration Council notes that belonging to a religious institution is also associated with better individual outcomes, such as "better general health, increased life satisfaction, decreased pain, stress, and loneliness," as well as better social outcomes, including improved social cohesion, increased trust of one's neighbors, more openness to diversity, and greater satisfaction with and support for democracy.[15] People cast adrift from the ritual of weekly community find the community and meaning-making hard to replace.[16] The loss of religious communities and other voluntary associations has eroded what Robert Putnam calls "social capital" and contributed to an epidemic of loneliness and deteriorating mental health.[17]

The afflictions of loneliness are not solely personal. Loneliness burdens society. Political philosopher, Hannah Arendt, observed that totalitarianism bases itself on loneliness.[18] Jay Frankel explains how this works, observing that lonely people identify with authoritarian figures or groups in the same way that abandoned children tend to identify with abusive aggressors in hopes that they will continue to belong.[19] Senator Chris Murphy concurs, observing that "the isolated become easy targets for demagogues

13. Rauch, *Cross Purposes*, 10.

14. Lipka, "Religious Americans' Lives Are Different"; Beyerlein, "Religion on Blood Donation."

15. Argo and Sheikh, "Belonging Barometer."

16. Thompson, "True Cost of Churchgoing Bust."

17. Putnam, *Bowling Alone*; Hill, "20-Somethings Are in Trouble"; Frist, "Youth Mental Health Is Worsening"; Murphy, "Spiritual Unspooling of America," para. 11.

18. Arendt, *Origins of Totalitarianism*, 623–29.

19. Finkel, "Narcissistic Dynamics of Submission."

and movements built on division. Loneliness quickly becomes the father of political instability," pushing people to look for meaningful connection in "dark, dangerous places."[20]

Churches, like other religious organizations and voluntary associations, frequently served as "cross-ideological institutions." Mainstream congregations brought people of different political persuasions together to worship, organize, debate, teach, and care for one another through life's trials and transitions. The decline of mainstream Protestantism and the more recent sorting of purple churches into red and blue congregations has accompanied a marked decrease in social trust and a hollowing out of the political center, particularly on the center right.

While the disappearance of caring communities that encouraged civic engagement and facilitated trans-ideological engagement has injured public morals, the withering of mainstream Protestantism has had another, more direct and destructive impact on public morals: it has contributed to the deterioration of democratic and republican culture. Understanding the constructive role religion can play in a pluralistic democracy is key to replenishing a common civic culture. It is to this we now turn.

20. Murphy, "Spiritual Unspooling of America," para. 11; Illing, "Everything's a Cult Now."

Chapter Two

Religion and Republican Virtue

Our Constitution was made only for a moral and religious People. It is wholly inadequate to the government of any other.

—John Adams[1]

The American founders knew that republics were fragile. They sought to mitigate the antidemocratic threats that had sabotaged previous republics by designing a constitution that established the rule of law, separated powers, set interest against interest, and instituted checks and balances. At the same time, they understood that the structures of government did not run themselves. Sinful human beings must do the checking and balancing. Government of and by the people could only succeed if the people embodied "republican virtues," which they broadly identified as restraint, a passion for the public good, and a principled commitment to democratic processes and the rule of law.[2] This recognition inspired John Adams's observation: "Our Constitution was made only for a moral and religious People. It is wholly inadequate to the government of any other."

1. Adams, "John Adams to Massachusetts Militia," para. 3

2. Hutson, *Religion and the Founding*, 62; Durham et al., *Virginia Founders and Religious Freedom*, 70.

Adams's framing of the relationship between the Constitution and religion and morality raises complicated questions for a society that values freedom of religion and conscience. Which principles are normative? Why isn't morality sufficient? What does religion contribute to public virtue? Who is responsible for forming these virtues? How does this work in a free society?

Throughout history, most Americans have held that the government bore some responsibility for forming democratic citizens. They commonly viewed public schools as "nurseries of democracy," tasked with inculcating citizenship and teaching a shared, public morality. Though the content of this moral instruction has frequently been contested—as is to be expected in a free society—at its best, public schools have provided a forum in which the many voices of civil society speak and coalesce.[3]

Even while believing that public schools play an essential role in the formation of citizens for a liberal democracy, most have not viewed or wanted public education to be the sole institution of moral formation, replacing families, religious groups, or voluntary associations, such as Scouting. This is because a moral and democratic society requires citizens who possess thicker moral sensibilities than public schools can or *should* foster.

Adams did not define religion. Notably, he didn't single out the Christian religion. This has not stopped people from projecting their own agendas onto his remark. Christian nationalists claim he is endorsing their own religious traditions, while cultured despisers of religion dismiss Adams as nonsensical.

The French diplomat Alexis de Tocqueville may give us a more nuanced way to interpret Adams's meaning. Arriving in America shortly after Adams's death, he observed, in a manner reminiscent of Adams, that democracy in antebellum America rested on habits of the heart formed largely in Protestant congregations. He went on to say that these congregations encouraged "a form of Christianity, which I cannot better describe, than by styling it a democratic and republican religion." He believed that these congregations were the principal source of public attitudes concerning freedom and equality and claimed that they "contributed powerfully to the establishment of a republic and a democracy in public affairs."[4]

3. Roberts, *Whose Kids?*

4. Tocqueville, *Democracy in America*, 300.

Anti-Democratic Religion

By identifying "democratic and republican religion" as the source of virtue rather than religion generally, Tocqueville both qualified and broadened Adams's remark. First, the qualification—Tocqueville did not think that all religion was democratic. He was aware of anti-democratic forms of Christianity. "In France," he wrote, "I had seen the spirits of religion and freedom almost always marching in opposite directions."[5] Tocqueville also commented on the contradictions between slavery and Christianity's tenets.[6] Adams would have concurred with both observations.

Tocqueville explained illiberal religion this way: Christianity's view that all people are equal in God's sight encourages the republican ideal that all citizens are equal before the law. Yet, he noted, "By a singular concourse of events, religion is entangled in those institutions which democracy assails, and [religion] is not unfrequently brought to reject the equality it loves, and to curse that cause of liberty as a foe which it might hallow by its alliance."[7] Tocqueville gives the alliance between the clergy and the aristocracy in France as an example.

Unsurprisingly, American history bears the mark of undemocratic religion.[8] Mainstream Protestantism, like every human organization, has never been a consistent embodiment of or advocate for democratic and republican values. Whenever Protestants have addressed injustice, the forces of undemocratic religion have reacted from within the denominations themselves, as splits over slavery, civil rights, and gender equality remind us. In the late nineteenth century, Protestants inspired by the social gospel created the Federal Council of Churches and addressed problems associated with urbanization and industrialization. This provoked accusations that they had abandoned the church's calling to save souls from damnation. In the 1950s, the National Council of Churches supported Supreme Court decisions prohibiting prayer and Bible reading in public schools and worked to address chronic poverty and extend civil rights to blacks, women, and, later, gender-minorities. In the 1960s, they opposed the Vietnam War. Illiberal Protestants denounced these policies at every turn, accusing mainstream Protestants of heresy and of harboring communist

5. Tocqueville, *Democracy in America*, 308.

6. Gershman, "Alexis de Tocqueville and Slavery"; Maussen, "Post-Colonial Reading."

7. Tocqueville, *Democracy in America*, 12; Pierson, *Tocqueville in America*, 416.

8. Kagan, *Rebellion*.

sympathies.[9] Sensing their cultural marginalization, conservative dissenters from mainstream denominations created alternative educational institutions and media outlets. These would later facilitate the Christian right's rise to prominence and power.

Christian Nationalism

Today, a diverse group of undemocratic Christians wants to do more than spread their moral and religious viewpoints. Portions of the Protestant right seeks to dominate positions of power to restore a mythical, evangelical national founding. They cite Adams's remark about religion as evidence that the United States was inaugurated as a Christian nation. WallBuilders, a Christian nationalist group run by David Barton, cites Adams's remark with the explanation that "to our Founders, 'religion' meant Christianity; 'morality' or 'virtue' meant Biblical character."[10]

A number of groups have articulated Christian nationalist goals. The 2023 "Statement on Christian Nationalism and the Gospel" calls for the nation "formally to acknowledge the Lordship of Christ"[11] and claims that "nations are commanded to honor God by officially affirming the orthodox Christian faith as historically and universally defined and affirmed."[12] The statement "National Conservatism: A Statement of Principles" declares that "public life should be rooted in Christianity and its moral vision, which should be honored by the state and other institutions both public and private."[13]

Stephen Wolfe, a fundamentalist Presbyterian, defines Christian nationalism as the "totality of national action, consisting of civil laws and social customs, conducted by a Christian nation as a Christian nation, in order to procure for itself both earthly and heavenly good in Christ."[14] Wolfe says, "Let us passionately assert that Christian nationalism is the recovery of a Christian *megolothymia*—a collective will for Christian domination of

9. Zubovich, *Before the Religious Right.*
10. WallBuilders, "Lesson 4," para. 1.
11. Silberman and Devers, "Statement on Christian Nationalism," article 10, para. 1.
12. Silberman and Devers, "Statement on Christian Nationalism," article 2, para. 1.
13. Chamberlain et al., "National Conservatism," no. 4.
14. Wolfe, *Case for Christian Nationalism*, 9.

the world."[15] Thymia, is a pagan virtue that is in deep tension with the New Testament virtue of humility.

Wolfe alleges that we are living under "liberal totalitarianism" that compels atheistic beliefs and immorality, like gay marriage. In other places, he claims that America is ruled by "gynocracy"—rule by women—that oppresses men.[16] In the face of this, he asserts that it is time for Christians to say, "No, this is ours and we're not going to take any more and we're going to go fight for it."[17] Wolfe asserts that God entrusts magistrates with the responsibility to uphold "true" religion and suppress disbelief and heresy. At the same time, he understands that Christians need to exercise prudence, saying, "I would be okay with, like, atheists being, I guess, suppressed in a way. But I just mean just the willingness to say, 'We're not going to allow degeneracy. There's not going to be the drag queen thing. No, you're not going to have a pride parade.'"[18] Wolfe believes that Christians await a "theocratic Caesar," a "prince" who will bring "a Christian people to self-consciousness" and "restore their will for their good."[19] Although he does not currently see a *man* who meets his criteria, he adds that society threatens to fall into anarchy, and things can change quickly.

Doug Wilson, author of *Mere Christendom*, defines "Christian nationalism" as "nation-states that basically claim Jesus rose from the dead."[20] He says that, like Stephen Wolfe and others, "I do believe in the continuing validity of the first table of the law. If someone says, 'Do you want to see blasphemy eradicated? Do you want to see limitations on blasphemy and restrictions on blasphemy?' Yes, I do very much, and I do think that should be something that is done constitutionally and via the law."[21] Wilson clarifies that Scripture frequently portrays government as the biggest blasphemer. While he eventually wants to "deal" with the "village atheist sitting outside his cottage and yelling at the moon,"[22] he is more interested in dealing with government blas-

15. Wolfe, *Case for Christian Nationalism*, 448.
16. Wolfe et al., "Interview with Stephen Wolfe."
17. Wolfe et al., "Interview with Stephen Wolfe," para. 77.
18. Wolfe et al., "Interview with Stephen Wolfe, para. 120."
19. Wolfe, *Case for Christian Nationalism*, 279.
20. Wilson, "Interview with Doug Wilson," para. 82.
21. Wilson, "Interview with Doug Wilson," para. 68.
22. Wilson, "Interview with Doug Wilson," para. 77.

phemy and its embrace of legalized abortion and homosexuality. "We should hunt the dragon first and then deal with the garden snakes."[23]

Catholic Integralism

Catholic integralists take a different approach. They seek to overthrow the founders' vision for America and replace it with a model of integrated religious and political authority based on medieval Christendom.[24] Patrick Deneen, for example, calls for "regime change" and for ending the "so called separation of church and state," which he claims, echoing Wolfe, is a "totalitarian undertaking."[25] Other thinkers in the integralist movement, including Edmund Waldstein, Thomas Pink, Sohrab Ahmari, and Gladden Pappin, endorse the claim that government neutrality in religion is impossible and religious freedom is a myth. Rather than giving us religious freedom, they contend, the founders established the religion of nonbelief.

Instead of the separation of church and state, Edmund Waldstein claims, "I want to defend the authoritative ideal of the relation of temporal and spiritual power taught by popes such as St. Gregory VII and Innocent III."[26] According to this vision, spiritual authority rules over temporal and political authority and directs them to their proper ends. The integralist website Josias explains, "Since man has both a temporal and an eternal end, we hold that he ought to be ruled by two powers: a temporal power and a spiritual power. And since man's temporal end is subordinated to his eternal end, temporal power must be subordinated to the spiritual power."[27] This does not mean that church leaders exercise temporal authority, running the government. Rather, it means that temporal authorities recognize that they are under the spiritual authority of the church and have a responsibility to ensure that the state serves God's purposes.

Adrian Vermeule, a professor of law at Harvard, provides legal cover, claiming that the Constitution has been misread to "protect liberty, maximize individual autonomy, and minimize the abuse of power." This approach suppressed the law's function as parent, wise teacher, and inculcator

23. Wolfe et al., "Interview with Stephen Wolfe," para. 89.

24. Millies, "What Is Catholic Integralism?"

25. Deneen, *Regime Change*, 228.

26. Troutner, "Integralist Mirroring of Liberal Ideals," para. 22; Waldstein, "Logic of the Cross."

27. Tveit and Barnas, "What Is the Josias?," para. 1.

of good habits. It undercut the power rulers require to rule well. That is, "for the good of the subject, even against the subjects' own perceptions of what is best for them—perceptions that may change over time anyway, as the law teaches, habituates, and re-forms them."[28] This begs many questions about the consent of the governed in a democratic republic. Some integralists go further, calling for the establishment of confessional states capable of enforcing orthodoxy, predicting that one would be Mormon and the rest would either be Protestant or Catholic.[29] It is important to note that many, perhaps most, Catholics oppose this movement.[30]

Whereas their Protestant counterparts dismiss concerns about religious freedom by saying that it has been three hundred years since people have been persecuted for religion in the United States, integralists never explore how this will impact religious minorities and nonbelievers.[31] Neither do they address the European wars of religion, nineteenth-century Protestant nativism, and other examples of religious intolerance. Neither group foresees how enacting their visions will corrode the character of privileged religious institutions.

Protestant Christian nationalism and Catholic integralism have inspired efforts to introduce religion to public schools, compel public religious observance in the armed forces, and undermine religious freedom in other ways.

Democratic Religions

Tocqueville's identification of democratic and republican religion qualifies Adams's blanket endorsement of religion by acknowledging the existence of undemocratic religion. He also broadened Adams's confidence. While Tocqueville was impressed by the contributions of American Protestants, he did not think any sect cornered the market on democratic and republican religion. In fact, he contended that since Catholic priests in the United States were no longer allied with an aristocracy, Catholics were "naturally more disposed" to transmit democratic attitudes of equality and freedom that are at the heart of Christian faith.[32] Catholic "allegiance to the

28. Vermeule, "Beyond Originalism," para. 8.

29. Schaetzel, "Bring Back the Confessional State."

30. Vallier, *All the Kingdoms.*

31. Walzer, "Notes on a Dangerous Mistake," 32.

32. Tocqueville, *Democracy in America*, 300.

American attitude" persisted despite nineteenth-century nativist hostility and papal writings condemning democracy.[33]

Tocqueville's optimism about the possibility of ecumenical, interfaith democratic religion is also part of the American tradition. One sees it in the nation's founding. It was expressed by voluntary associations that sprang up in the early republic. These associations, like anti-dueling societies, temperance, and abolition movements, united religiously diverse groups in promoting moral improvement.[34]

During the twentieth century, the claim that the United States was the bearer of "Judeo-Christian values" supplied an inclusive sense of purpose in the nation's struggle against fascism and, later, in its struggle against "godless" communism. In the 1950s, Will Herberg cast an inclusive vision of religious pluralism in American life in his sociological study *Protestant, Catholic, Jew*.[35] If Herberg were writing today, he would need to cast his net wider to encompass America's religious diversity.[36] President Eisenhower expressed gratitude for democratic and republican religion when he said, "Our government makes no sense unless it is founded on a deeply felt religious faith—and I don't care what it is."[37]

Necessary Thickness

James Hutson claims that John Adams's observation is typical of his time, saying that the comment "imprinted itself so strongly on the minds of the founders that it became a cliché: religion promoted virtue; virtue promoted republicanism; religion promoted, and was indispensable for, republicanism."[38] Today, many are less certain of this connection. Indeed, some point to the destructive influence of anti-democratic religion to argue that all religion is pernicious.

Michael Walzer's distinction between thick and thin moral arguments helps us imagine how a religiously pluralistic society may coalesce in support of a thin, shared public morality. It also helps us to see how mainstream disarray contributed to the deterioration of our shared morality and how

33. Berg, *Religious Liberty*, 133.
34. Adams, *Voluntary Associations*, 171.
35. Herberg, *Protestant, Catholic, Jew*; Murray, *Religious Liberty*.
36. Dionne, *Souled Out*, 191.
37. Pluralism Project, "A Three Religion Country?"
38. Hutson, *Religion and the Founding*, 62.

it may be amended.[39] Walzer defines thick moral arguments as maximalist, thick with religious and cultural references that supply the rationale for principles and policies. By contrast, thin moral arguments are minimalist, detached from religious and cultural particularities.[40]

It is important to note that Walzer's distinction between thick and thin moral arguments is not a binary but a polarity. It points to a continuum from thick to thin. It allows that the thickness of what is shared in the broader community and between subcommunities can shift over time. Consider that in 1989, Chinese protesters in Tiananmen Square carried signs saying, "Liberty or death," echoing Patrick Henry's famous statement at St. John's Church in Richmond, Virginia. These signs succeeded in eliciting support from many Americans.

Yet, if you asked a Chinese protester and an American sympathizer to define "liberty," their thick description of the "what" and "why" of freedom would likely be rooted in widely different religious, cultural, and historical narratives. The overlap between Chinese and American understandings of liberty would likely be thinner than the overlap of any two Americans who share thicker narratives about Patrick Henry's speech, the American Revolution, and subsequent First Amendment freedoms. That said, if you press two Americans deeper, their accounts may diverge on important points. One might point to libertarian philosophies, such as Ayn Rand's objectivism, while the other might point to the Exodus liberation in the Bible, the experience of enslavement, and advances made during the civil rights era.

Lest we think that religious beliefs are thick and secular beliefs are thin, Walzer helps us appreciate that religious people can be united in thin agreement on important points while holding thick, contradictory views of their significance. We have seen how people who agree that Jesus is the Christ draw classically liberal conclusions, while others draw illiberal conclusions. A shared commitment to a thin point makes it possible to have conversations about its thick significance. This suggests that mainstream Protestants need to become better acquainted with their religious traditions so they may better engage their illiberal coreligionists.

Perhaps because Walzer is Jewish and a member of a minority religious group, he does not expect or desire society to share a single thick religious perspective. This makes him different from Christian nationalists and integralists who seek moral and spiritual renewal by imposing thick versions

39. Hetherington, *Why Trust Matters.*

40. Walzer, *Thick and Thin.*

of their beliefs. For Walzer, it is enough that diverse thick viewpoints find thin resonance. In this way, his distinction between thick and thin is similar to John Rawls' notion of an "overlapping consensus."[41] Neither does Walzer require a single, thin moral statement that everyone approaches from their unique thick religious perspective. A rigid approach to the content of any moral consensus is unnecessary. All that is needed is for a working majority of people to share moral principles so a pluralistic society may function. Although thick rationales may not align, thin agreement on guiding principles can enable diverse people to find common cause on matters of public concern. Furthermore, when thin moral arguments connect, even if they do not carry the day, it encourages the sort of trust required for democracy to function in a pluralistic society.[42]

Walzer reminds us that the recovery of thick and compelling morality requires the renewal of particular thick traditions, including theological traditions. Principles shorn of thick substance lack sufficient weight to be compelling. This runs counter to the temptation to point to thin resonances between traditions and conclude that everybody really believes the same thing. It is at odds with the view that the thin resonances comprise the essential, important part of traditions and that the thick particularities of religious and cultural traditions are ephemeral, easily detached, and, perhaps, should be discarded for the greater good. Moral reasoning is most compelling when it is thick.

As we consider how people acquire thick meaning, we should not allow Walzer's insight to become disembodied from institutions, rituals, and relationships. Strong religious institutions do more than pass on religious information; they foster relationships, encourage habits, support an ethos, and form identities that reinforce their values. These make thin principles compelling. People's moral understandings are not simply cognitive but shaped by group dynamics and social pressures.

Walzer's distinction between thick and thin moral reasoning helps us understand how mainstream Protestant disarray contributed to the deterioration of public morals. By neglecting educational and media institutions for spreading their ideas, mainstream Protestants allowed their members to lose touch with thick reasons for supporting democratic and republican principles. When thick rationales for principles grow thin, they lose their force. While thin, secular principles supporting, say, religious freedom and

41. Rawls, *Political Liberalism*, 133.

42. Hetherington, *Why Trust Matters*.

government neutrality in religion are indispensable, thick religious reasons for supporting religious freedom will always be more compelling to members of those traditions. When weakly held principles require sacrifice or fail to deliver desired outcomes, people abandon them. When a sufficient portion of a community loses thick reasons for upholding moral principles, the community lacks antibodies to protect it from those who encourage us to forsake these principles. The predictable result is the growth of illiberal religion and the "democracy hypocrisy" we discussed earlier.

Other Views on the Thinning of Our Shared Morality

Others have connected the current moral drift with a loss of thick rationale. James Simpson provides a complementary way to think about the loss of thick meaning. Drawing on a different set of metaphors, he notes that liberalism is criticized for being "hollow," meaning that it cannot produce its own thick rationale. He says it is unfair for critics to call this hollowness a "failure" because liberalism was always intended to be hollow. This is because it is a *second-order belief system*, not a *first-order belief system.* Liberalism and its mediating mechanisms—which include the division of powers, separation of church and state, equality before the law, toleration of minorities, freedom of association, respect for liberty of conscience, etc.—were invented by Protestants in their struggle against illiberal Protestants.[43] Liberalism was developed as a tool for managing first-order belief systems, which can be intolerant and violent. It was never meant for Protestants alone. Precisely because it is a second-order belief system, "it can be supported by any first-order belief system."[44] Simpson suggests how, as the thick, first-order beliefs of liberal Protestants receded in our culture, support for liberalism was hollowed out and lost its force.

Philosopher Charles Taylor comments on this loss of meaning from yet another angle. He observes that "high standards need strong sources." That is, we need good, thick reasons to do necessary but difficult things. Taylor worries that we are "living beyond our moral means" and are losing reasons to "support our far-reaching moral commitments of benevolence and justice."[45]

43. Simpson, *Permanent Revolution*, 349.

44. Simpson, *Permanent Revolution*, 350.

45. Taylor, *Sources of the Self*, 516.

Jonathan Rauch echoes concern about a loss of thick rationale. He says that polls correlating Americans' growing secularity with growing cynicism about politics, disdain for institutions, and discontent with public life are "evidence of the inadequacy of secular liberalism to provide meaning, exaltation, spirituality, and morality anchored in more than the self."[46] They point to a vacuum in public life that used to be filled by faith.

E. J. Dionne, a liberal Catholic, also mentions this vacuum. He describes the impact of mainstream Protestantism's disarray this way:

> There is still a tug toward a public moral sense, a communitarian sense, if you will, that provides public moral values within a context of liberty . . . a search for a common public moral language. This quest for a new public language has become all the more urgent with the disestablishment of mainline Protestantism as the dominant discourse in American public life. Most Americans welcome the advances in religious liberty made over the last four decades. And yet we also notice the absence of the civic glue that the old Protestant values provided.[47]

Dionne, like Rauch, calls on believers to renew "what might be called a theology of democracy," noting that this will "require work across traditions and within traditions."[48]

46. Rauch, *Cross Purposes*, 15.

47. Dionne, "Keynote Address," 13; Dionne, "End of White Christian America."

48. Dionne, *Souled Out*, 190.

Chapter Three

Public Wisdom

> Nearly all the wisdom we possess, that is to say, true and sound wisdom, consists of two parts: the knowledge of God and of ourselves. But, while joined by many bonds, which one precedes and brings forth the other is not easy to discern.
>
> —John Calvin[1]

It is a truism that while knowledge has vastly increased, wisdom has not. We know much more about the cosmos and the quantum universe, but it has not made us better at addressing perennial human questions: What should take priority in our lives? How shall we organize our common life? Can we trust "good" people with power? What do we owe the weak who are useless to us or enemies who threaten us? Is there a right or wrong? Does the universe care? Does justice have a chance against entrenched evil?

Wisdom is related to knowledge because it seeks to see things as they are. Wisdom *wants* to be rooted in reality. If it knows the road is icy, it it would be foolish to speed. But wisdom also sees beneath the surface of things to perceive deeper realities. For example, while wisdom appreciates what it takes to get ahead in life, it also knows that a fulfilling life is about more than accumulation and self-advancement. Wisdom knows what's truly valuable and important. Wisdom can locate the self in the world. It

1. Calvin, *Institutes of the Christian Religion*, 35.

knows who and what we depend on and appreciates what we owe to others. It understands human nature, its grandeur and potential, as well as its limits and flaws.

Theology as Wisdom

John Calvin observed that all wisdom consists chiefly of the knowledge of God and knowledge of the self, and that these are so entwined that one can scarcely tell which one gives rise to the other. Most people probably agree that wisdom involves knowing the purpose, capacities, and nature of the self. But the notion that the knowledge of God is a source of wisdom or that it is deeply entwined with knowledge of the self likely seems strange to people who are uncertain about God's existence. This idea is not helped by the fact that so many religious people seem to act like fools.

Calvin gave two illustrations to make his point. His first was that if we truly know ourselves, we know that we are not self-made. We recognize that we rely on many others—other people and creatures—and beyond them on biological, climatological, and even cosmological systems. We have received many gifts. He goes on to observe that if we trace these gifts back to their source, it is like tracing rivulets back to a spring, to God, the fountain of life. In this way, knowledge of our dependence leads to knowledge of God.

It works the other way, too. Knowing that God is the giver of life's rich abundance prompts us to count our blessings, appreciate life's profusion, consider our place in God's world, and weigh our responsibilities. There is wisdom in this knowledge. The foolish ungratefully imagine that they are self-made, forget that they depend on others, and ignore their obligations.

Calvin's second illustration linked knowledge of sin with knowledge of God. Knowledge of God's perfection, he noted, strips away our pretenses, confronting us with our "wretchedness." When we perceive God's justice and benevolence, we sense how far all people have fallen from what God intends for every creature and for the glory of the whole creation.

Conversely, knowledge of our sinfulness leads us to the knowledge of God. This is because we do not serenely accept the injustice, depravity, and corruption endemic to the human condition. Rather we are "stung" by our misery. Sin's oppression, waste, and futility weigh on us. We sense that things have gone awry. Life falls short of its glorious promise. In these ways,

Calvin believed that the unhappiness associated with sin forces us to "turn our eyes upwards" and indicates some knowledge of God.[2]

There is wisdom in knowing that people are sinners, lest we foolishly give them unfettered power. There also is wisdom in knowing how far we have fallen from the perfections of God's justice and love. On the one hand, if we neglect God's justice, we become complacent in the face of evil. On the other hand, if we neglect God's love, we become harsh and forget that, as Jesus said, "God sends rain on the just and the unjust" (Matt 5:45).

All church teaching about God has bearing on how we understand the human self, just as all knowledge of the human self has theological implications. This is because we can only understand God in relationship with ourselves and the world. By contrast, claims about the inner workings of God that do not touch the world of experience tend to become speculative and run a significant risk of being projections. When we view ourselves in relationship with God, aspects of the self are revealed. It's not that we can't sense these realities apart from God. They are realities after all. However, the lens of faith brings them into focus and imparts wisdom.

Wisdom is singular because all things connect with each other. This means that theological wisdom is more powerfully conveyed when the principles work in concert with each other. In this book, we shall see that some doctrines sound notes that reinforce or complete another doctrine. Other times, a doctrine may seem to contradict another doctrine, establishing a paradox. Whether the notes harmonize or are discordant, they suggest overtones of meaning and nuance that none quite carries by itself.

Principles of Public Theology

When we talk about "*principles* of public theology," we refer to the practical wisdom carried by a set of nine theological doctrines: theocentrism, creation, *imago Dei*, natural law, sin, hope, vocation, covenant, and ecclesiology. These doctrines, or teachings, which is what the word "doctrine" means, were created to instruct the faithful. They carry wisdom that shape our sense of the world's goodness, human dignity, our capacity to know right and wrong, the human tendency to corruption, the possibility of hope, human purpose, human community, and the importance of religious freedom.

We call them "principles" to highlight their capacity to provide normative guidance for the church in its witness on matters of ecclesial and

2. Calvin, *Institutes of the Christian Religion*, 35.

public moral concern.[3] They have the capacity to inform a way of life and add substance to public, moral commitments. As first-order religious principles, they stand over and judge every political polity. This includes liberalism as a second-order concept, as well as American Constitutionalism in its every historical embodiment. While it does not deny the relative justice of political orders, it does deny that the American experiment (or any other era) ever had a golden age to which we should return. Movements for social reform are frequently rooted in first-order religious language because it has the capacity to transcend the current order.

Theologians and thoughtful readers may notice that there are many more things that could be said about each of these principles. The treatment of covenant, for example, does not address how the concept describes a believer's relationship with God. Neither does the principle of vocation explore the general calling to follow Christ. There are many more things that should be said than can be said in a short book that addresses a broad audience.

We should not reduce these principles to moralism. Their first purpose is descriptive. They were developed to help people notice and attend to realities in their lives. Normative, moral judgments follow from this. It will help if we remember that these principles derive from fuller theological accounts that include other doctrines, including revelation, Christology, soteriology, pneumatology, the Trinity, the atonement, and such. While these other doctrines also convey wisdom, they do not carry the same public, linguistic currency and may seem esoteric for people unacquainted with theology. By contrast, the principles of public theology stand out for offering practical wisdom for a public that is navigating questions of democracy and life together. That said, the fullness of their meaning is found in concert with other doctrines.

We can also resist the slide into moralism by remembering that the full power of theological imagination is released when these principles are supported by a rich personal and communal spiritual life. Although "to pray" in popular culture has come to mean "to make a request," the New Testament word *proseuché* means to make a vow or commit oneself. This meaning is clearer in Latin, which translates *proseuché* using the word *votum,* which has given us the English words "devotion" and "voting." A personal and communal devotional life that attends to the theological dimensions of life can give these principles heart and strength.

3. Stackhouse, *Public Theology and Political Economy*, 17–35.

The first audience for all theology is believers. But when we talk about *public* theology, we point to a broader audience, which potentially includes everyone involved in political, economic, and social life.[4] While the term "public theology" has lately become popular in the church, it is not always clear what is meant. Sometimes it seems to mean ethics, other times social engagement, and still other times the shared beliefs of civil religion.[5] By public theology, we mean presenting theological concepts in terms the public can understand in the anticipation and hope that the non-believing, non-practicing public will turn to these principles for wisdom and guidance. The most powerful evidence of this possibility is when nonbelievers criticize the church for failing to exhibit a life that aligns with what Christians claim to believe.

The possibility of shared public meaning is also supported by the fact that the history of ideas is mostly one of promiscuous borrowing and adapting. New ideas do come along, but individuals and communities seldom invent them out of thin air. New ideas are always explained in terms of existing ideas. The early Christian movement did not invent all its concepts but drew on its Hebraic roots and other ideas circulating in first-century Mediterranean cultures. Again, as we will see in chapter 7, the eleventh-century theologians who developed the doctrine of natural law borrowed from pagan understandings of natural law as they interpreted Rom 2:14–15. Such borrowing and adaptation reinforce the idea that religious symbols and language can communicate meaning that is accessible to nonbelievers. It also prepares us for the likelihood that believers and nonbelievers alike may appropriate and reinterpret ideas they find useful and disregard those they do not.

These principles convey meaning outside explicitly theological contexts. They are part of the language and culture by which believers and nonbelievers alike understand what is on one another's minds. Sometimes theology identifies realities that might otherwise escape our attention. In the chapter on covenant, for example, we will see that covenant calls attention to the way in which our lives are bound to others. Other times, theology reframes realities, as when it recasts a career as a calling. In naming realities of the self in relation to God, it encourages postures or attitudes toward these realities. Viewing one's work as a "calling" rather than a job evokes an attitude of service.

4. Tracy, *Analogical Imagination*, 3.

5. Breitenberg, "To Tell the Truth," 55–96

David Hollenbach observes that in the face of a fragmented pluralism, the "common pursuit of a shared vision of the good life is a work of intellectual solidarity."[6] The *public* theology offered here seeks to build bridges with a broader, diverse public for the sake of making a meaningful life together. It celebrates correlations with and insights from other religious and secular viewpoints. It believes that "thin" agreement on moral principles is important for pluralistic societies. While it accepts that "thin" agreement does not obscure "thicker" differences of religion and worldview, it also anticipates the possibility of voluntarily embraced, thicker, shared meaning. For example, it hopes that a broader appreciation that human beings are chronically flawed "sinners," whether or not everyone understands this theologically, would make the public suspicious of unchecked power.

Why It Matters

Recovering a public theology is important for Christians because the logic of Christian faith requires it. The church exists to bear witness to the word by its life together and by sharing its wisdom with the world. Recovering a public theology is important because it is hard to see how these principles continue to inform the public if they cease to inform the church. Huston Smith observed that institutions give ideas "traction in history."[7] Mainstream Protestants need to rehabilitate existing institutions and build new institutions if they are to spread their ideas to others and fulfill their calling to be salt and light to the world. If the church were to gain a new appreciation of the valuable, practical wisdom contained in its theological heritage, it would cease to be demoralized. It would sense urgency and energy for the long, difficult work that lies ahead.

Recovering the principles of public theology is also important because it is hard to see how a public moral consensus can be renewed without thicker moral language. The principles of public theology evolved alongside the institutions, political philosophies, practices, and sensibilities of our society and public culture. The principles that helped shape their development hold the potential to rejuvenate them. Finally, recovering a public theology matters because without the church's witness, people may not have the language to see the depths of reality. They may fall into the despair of believing that "might makes right," that using others is the best

6. Hollenbach, *Common Good*, 137–70.

7. Smith, *World's Religions*, 5.

way to get ahead, that those who suffer have no champion or succor, and that those who abuse others answer to an indifferent universe.

Not Neutral

By now, most readers have likely picked up on the fact that the principles of public theology are not morally, politically, or economically neutral. They are valuable precisely because they have "spin." They encourage a posture toward the world. For example, as we shall see, the claim that humans bear the image of God not only names the dignity of every person but, by extension, rebukes the indignities of dehumanization and exploitation that would deface the divine image. The claim that every person bears God's image should prompt us to side with those who suffer, to oppose their mistreatment, and challenge oppressors.

Even as these principles guide the church in engaging the world, there are occasions when circumspection about public policy implications is warranted. Many aspects of life are not immediately theological but technical, scientific, and prudential. Theologian Emil Brunner reminds us that many aspects of life do not "spring from faith":

> A Christian who is called to be a statesman [*sic*] is not called to "govern as a Christian," but—and just because he is a Christian, he ought to know this—as a good statesman. A scientist is not to conduct his research work as a Christian, but as a scientist, a Christian engineer does not build "Christian bridges" but solid bridges.[8]

Sometimes the church is silent because it perceives that theology does not address every detail of a policy. Silence can reflect an appropriate humility and wisdom, including a laudatory concern to avoid division on non-essential matters. There is wisdom in recognizing that people can have good reasons to disagree. There is also wisdom in appreciating that the church usually makes its greatest impact not when it is issuing prophetic statements but when it forms virtuous people who bring their values to bear on their vocations and participate in life as Christians.

Other times, however, circumspection reflects an unethical impulse. Church leaders and followers sacrifice their callings to avoid conflict. Sometimes the aforementioned wisdom is misused to justify cowardice. Sometimes the church's silence has been rationalized by a theology that

8. Brunner, *Divine Imperative*, 263.

crisply distinguishes politics from religion. Southern Presbyterians, for example, frequently talked about the "spirituality of the church" and limited the church's purpose to cultivating a relationship with God, encouraging spiritual practices, and preparing people for their eternal destiny. James Henley Thornwell, a nineteenth-century professor of theology, justified the church's quietism in the face of slavery by stating that the church "has no commission to construct society afresh . . . to change the forms of its political constitutions. . . . The problems, which the anomalies of our fallen state are continually forcing on philanthropy, the Church has no right to solve."[9] In recent years, the inclination for the church to remain silent on matters of public morality has been encouraged by the emergence of more privatized theology that Christian Smith and Melania Lundquist Denton identify as "therapeutic, moralistic deism."[10] History condemns the church's silence and apathy in the face of slavery and Jim Crow.[11] Future generations will be just as critical of the church's complacency in the face of the looming ecological crisis that threatens life on this planet.

Against limited construals of responsibility, public theology insists that the subject matter of all theology is this: God in relationship with all things and all things in relationship with God. Such a theology can guide us in answering perennial human questions. Its wisdom will be more disruptive than quietists prefer. Its theocentrism will challenge every idol of culture.

9. Thornwell, *Collected Writings*, 382–84; Thompson, *Spirituality of the Church*.

10. Smith and Denton, *Soul Searching*.

11. King, *Testament of Hope*, 289.

Chapter Four

God, Gods, and Human Valuing

You shall have no other gods before me.

—EXODUS 20:3

AFTER THE TERRORIST ATTACKS of September 11, 2001, Pat Tillman left a lucrative career as a quarterback for the Phoenix Cardinals to enlist in the US Army. We can imagine any number of considerations that likely informed this decision: the welfare of his family, his sense of financial security, as well as his calculation of the relative risks of injury and death. We cannot know how he assessed all these matters, but we are probably safe in assuming that his love for country outweighed his love for football.

People are always making judgments about the relative value of things. Does a soccer coach give the weak players game experience or keep the better players in and try to win one for the team? Does a parent answer work emails while on vacation? How should a nation balance spending on the military, education, and foreign aid?

The necessity of organizing our lives raises perennial questions: What is going to take priority? What is most important? As well as an inescapable related question, what must be sacrificed? As people answer these questions, they wind up organizing their lives around the things they deem most precious: they love their families, are loyal to their friends, are dedicated to their work, trust their doctors, pursue hobbies, pledge allegiance to the flag, support human rights, donate to charity, and worship God. Of course, among the things they value is the self, though it is not always the object they value most.

The most important things, the things that take top priority, become "centers of value." They give value to other things. Perhaps we deem other things "useful" relative to them. A parent, for example, may value a minivan for ferrying around the family. Perhaps a situation arises that forces us to rank one object as having higher value relative to other things, as a family may deplete its wealth to pay for a medical procedure that will save a child's life.

A Matter of Faith

Our priorities are always an expression of faith.[1] What we believe about objects can inspire lots of reactions: respect and repulsion, desire and loathing, marvel and indifference. As it relates to an object's value, faith generally involves confidence and fidelity. Both English words come from the Latin word for faith, *fide*.

Imagine you are in a position to consider purchasing a Rembrandt painting. You might ask what confidence you have in its authenticity. Is the art dealer trustworthy? If the painting is a forgery, what *intrinsic* value does it have for you as a work of art? Do you find it delightful or excellent, even though it is a relatively worthless fake? We value the things we enjoy for their intrinsic value. The intrinsic value can be symbolic. For example, a person may value a wedding ring far beyond its weight in gold. All of this has to do with an object's intrinsic value. Perhaps a Rembrandt's excellence awakens a loyalty to the public, and you think it should hang in a gallery where others can appreciate it.

We can also have confidence in an object's *extrinsic* value, trusting that we will find it useful for something we value more. When we value something for its extrinsic value, we pass over its value as art to consider what it might be good for. Perhaps upon discovering that it is forgery, you find that it no longer brings you joy. You begin to measure its value in more utilitarian ways. Perhaps you speculate on its future value, anticipating that the market for well-executed Rembrandt forgeries will grow, even though they are still making them. Perhaps you sell it to purchase something you

1. Niebuhr, *Radical Monotheism*.

value more, say, a piece of "real" art or a bicycle for a child. Perhaps, upon learning that it is worthless, you use it to block the door and keep the chickens in the coop.

We cannot know how Pat Tillman valued football. Maybe he loved it for its intrinsic virtues, its strategy, choreography, graceful athleticism, physicality, the camaraderie of being on the team, or hanging out with fans. Perhaps he found the practice, travel, and physical brutality so onerous that he lost sight of the game's intrinsic virtues but tolerated it for extrinsic reasons, perhaps the lucrative pay. We can value things for a mixture of intrinsic and extrinsic reasons. Both are expressions of confidence.

In addition to confidence, faith in an object's value is expressed in the active side of faith, fidelity. If you think you have a real Rembrandt, you may feel obliged to conserve it, repair a tear in the canvas, or have it cleaned. Fidelity to a friend may inspire costly loyalty that they can never repay. Returning to Pat Tillman, the terrorist attack of 9/11 seems to have awakened a sense of fidelity to the nation, inspiring him to sacrifice his football career.

Faith as confidence and fidelity shapes our moral values in complex ways. James Gustafson recalls starkly different reactions to an early paper on human genetic engineering. Some, whom he calls "hawks," favored the vigorous pursuit of the emerging genetic technology. Others, whom he calls "doves," viewed genetic research and intervention with deep foreboding. He notes that these reactions were not about matters of hard science but had a religious character. The hawks viewed the possibility of ridding humanity of genetic scourges and enhancing human life as a sort of salvation. By contrast, the doves dreaded an apocalyptic annihilation of the human race. Different objects of trust were advanced in the debate. The hawks encouraged people to trust scientists and the politicians and government workers who would oversee their work with the power to interfere in the evolutionary process. The doves preferred to trust the evolutionary process with minimal intervention. The differences not only reflected competing faiths about desirable ends but also differing levels of trust in the human capacity to exercise stewardship over the technology.[2]

The language of confidence, fidelity, and sacrifice suggests that our valuing has religious overtones even when religion is not explicit. Faith can lead us to trust someone's word or, if we trust contradicting witnesses more, to doubt them. Faith may lead us beyond merely believing someone

2. Gustafson, "Theology Confronts Technology."

to the deeper trust we call "believing *in* someone" (or in something, or in a cause). This involves entrusting ourselves to their innate goodness, worth, and ability.

Pat Tillman offers lessons about the inevitability of trust and the possibility that it may be misplaced. Tillman's confidence in the nation seems to have been shaken. After serving in Iraq, he characterized the war as "so fucking illegal." He was then transferred to Afghanistan, where his platoon mates killed him with three shots to the forehead at close range, under conditions of good visibility. The questionable details of his death, the cover-up by the military and the George W. Bush administration, and the exploitation of his sacrifice to shame protesters and boost the war effort point to the uncertainty inherent in all faiths.[3] Misplaced faith is an inevitable feature of human existence.

We love the things we value most. We invest our hopes in them, trusting them to carry our dreams and secure the destinies of the people we love. We enjoy them. We worship, revere, and celebrate their excellence. We feel attached to them and incorporate them into our identity. Fidelity may inspire us to offer sacrifices to advance an object's cause.

All of this suggests that while faith is a part of religion, it is not limited to religion. It pervades the human experience. Religious faith differs only in the object it takes.

Henotheistic Theocentrism

The faith that informs our priorities and drives the universe of competing centers of value looks different when viewed through the lens of henotheistic theocentrism and its prohibitions of idolatry. Henotheism, like monotheism, literally means "one God." Unlike monotheism, henotheism accepts the existence of other gods. Unlike polytheism, which accords each god a unique realm of agency, authority, and honor within a larger narrative or theological community, henotheism is theocentric. Henotheism believes that one God should be given primacy over all other gods in every instance. In this context, idolatry means giving some other object, or "god," greater priority, reverence, or centrality in our valuing than the one God.

The Bible expresses henotheistic theocentrism in a number of places. Psalm 82 portrays God as presiding over a great assembly of the gods, which we may assume refers to pagan deities. Psalm 86 claims that no other god

3. Collier, "Family Demands the Truth"; Krakauer, *Where Men Win Glory*.

compares with Yahweh, while Ps 96 declares that Yahweh is the most to be revered of all the gods. The clearest statement of henotheism and theocentrism in the Bible is found in the first directive in the Ten Commandments, which declares, "You shall have no other gods before me" (Exod 20:3). The command assumes that although other gods compete for primacy, God should be first.

There are parallels between common value centers and the ancient Near Eastern gods of the Bible. Although many of the ancient gods represented powers and vitalities on which humans depended and were worshipped for utilitarian reasons (to ensure fertility, rain, etc.), other deities represented loyalty to a craft, the family, and the ancestors. Jesus singled out mammon as the personification of "greed," and portrayed it as a false idol (Matt 6:24). The Roman Caesar cult, whose temple Jesus doubtlessly encountered in Caesarea Philippi, reinforced fidelity to the state and its ruler (Mark 8:27–29).

Henotheism tracks with the understanding of valuing and faith outlined here. Everyone has faith and sets priorities. Human beings place their confidence in objects to secure their existence. They worship objects that they find excellent and find purpose in serving objects they trust are more important than themselves. An atheist who denies the existence of God and the gods, who would never worship at the temple of the Caesar cult, may offer the nation other tributes to protect, enhance, and enrich it. When they hesitate to make a sacrifice, say they oppose the genocidal sacrifice of a civilian population to advance a national interest, it likely reflects their confidence that some other center of value, perhaps the value of humanity broadly conceived, is more sacred. Just as priorities and faith are inevitable parts of the human experience, so are the gods.

Like every other object, our understanding of God's existence, nature, and character is shaped by faith. We will have more to say about God's character in the following chapters. For now, we note that, according to developed theological traditions, God is not merely another object in a world of objects, or even another god ruling a pantheon of gods. God is beyond existence, making existence possible. As such, we can only know God's nature through God's works of creation and redemption.

The whole community of being originates with God. This includes the vitalities thought to be represented by the gods. Whereas the followers of ancient Canaanite religion thought Ba'al personally controlled the rains on which they depended, weather systems are mere creatures and do not have an independent basis of existence. As henotheism questioned the reality of other gods, it evolved into monotheism.

In addition to creating all things, the biblical tradition claims that God cares for all things. In Genesis, for example, God is shown as repeatedly surveying creation and calling it "good." The gospel of John says, "God loves the world." Biblical religion marshals a collage of images to portray God's relationship with the world: Creator, Governor, Judge, Liberator, Redeemer, and Friend. These images express multiple ways that God values the world, its parts and the whole. According to this vision, theocentric ethics means living life so that we honor God and God's purpose for all things.

Valuing the Other

Theocentrism has practical ethical implications. When we put other value centers before God, we lose sight of the value of other people and objects. Consider the New Orleans Saints bounty scandal in which the football team paid bonuses to players who deliberately injured opposing players.[4] Although the program may have helped them win the Super Bowl in 2009, it illustrates how a non-inclusive center of value cannot account for the good of others—in this instance, players on opposing teams. When one places top priority on one's own team or winning, other people are expendable and may be sacrificed.

Theologian Jonathan Edwards explores this phenomenon in his essay "The Nature of True Virtue." He notes that in the same way that beauty suits a larger situation, we consider actions virtuous when they are fitting—that is, appropriate—to the context. Something that seems virtuous from the perspective of a limited context may seem unvirtuous when viewed from a more expansive setting. To put this in the language of value centers, something that seems virtuous from the perspective of a less-inclusive value center may seem to lack virtue when viewed from the perspective of a more inclusive center of value.

For instance, we frequently judge the morality of actions from the perspective of the family. Yet, fidelity to the family, like loyalty to a team, can foster blindness. In 2019, for instance, a college admissions bribery scandal came to light, known as "Operation Varsity Blues."[5] It found a number of wealthy parents and celebrities guilty of bribing coaches, school officials,

4. ESPN, "Saints Bounty Scandal."

5. Hatfield, "Varsity Blues Scandal Explained."

and college entrance exam administrators to ensure their children's admission to elite universities. These parents harmed the college admissions process, injured the prospects of other college applicants, and sacrificed their own integrity to give their children an edge. They were following the logic of putting family first.

Edwards says that in order to evaluate whether an action is truly virtuous, we must view the action "comprehensively and universally, with regard to all its tendencies and its connections with everything it stands related to."[6] That is, not just in relation to its immediate context but in relation to the totality of being that flows from God. Only this maximally inclusive context, he claims, will help us rightly value all the impacted objects and determine whether something is truly virtuous, fitting, or moral.

If Edwards is right, it follows that we cannot finally judge the virtue of even the most prosaic things that parents do solely from the perspective of family devotion. Consider a parent who changes their plans so they can attend their child's concert. From the limited perspective of the family, it would appear laudable. Yet, most people would consider it irresponsible for a political leader to cancel peace talks that would prevent an imminent military conflict so that he or she could attend their child's concert. This is because they view national security and the lives at stake as a more inclusive center of value and, thus, a higher priority.

While national security and well-being are more inclusive than the family, they are hardly inclusive of all things either. Like the family, nationalism can inspire efforts we deem moral, like universal education. It can also inspire horrific things, like genocide. If we want to truly evaluate whether an action is moral, we must evaluate things in relation to a yet more inclusive center of value.

Finding a Center of Value

Some doubt whether God provides the most inclusive value center. They encourage us to value objects and judge actions in terms of whether they are beneficial for humanity. These critics observe that a lot of religion does not honor the humanity of others. We shall return to this point in a moment. For now, we acknowledge that humanism or anthropocentrism (human-centeredness) provides a more inclusive value center than national interest and some religious expressions.

6. Edwards, *Ethical Writings*, 540.

Although theists should make common cause with humanists on a host of issues, it is hard to concede that humanity represents the highest, most inclusive good by which we should evaluate the morality of our actions. For one thing, the growing ecological crisis suggests that we have not properly valued nature but treated it as expendable in the service of human wants and desires. For another, as theologian James Gustafson observes, advances in science make it hard to imagine that humanity is the chief reason for all existence.[7] Humanity has existed for the briefest spark of cosmological time on the tiniest speck of a planet in a universe of unimaginable perpetuity and immensity. It is hard to believe that everything exists and finds its purpose and should be valued solely for how it benefits humanity. Science suggests that humanism cannot be the most inclusive center of value.

H. Richard Niebuhr reminds us that Albert Schweitzer sought to make reverence for life his value center. While reverence for life is more inclusive than humanism, Niebuhr observes that theocentrism would also include an appropriate reverence for the dead, for things that are inorganic, and for ideas. He concludes that theocentrism "dethrones all absolutes short of the principle of being itself, while at the same time reverencing every relative existent."[8]

Responsibilities to Those Near to Us

Theocentrism has parallels with other universalisms, such as Stoic cosmopolitanism. Epictetus, a Stoic philosopher, encouraged his followers to never say, "'I am Athenian,' or 'I am Corinthian,' but 'I am a citizen of the universe.'"[9] This is a noble thought, especially during times of hypernationalism and xenophobia. Yet, like other universalisms, including theocentrism, it begs the question of how one balances one's universal responsibilities with one's obligations to family, work, neighborhood, city, country, etc. Hierocles, a later Stoic, integrated cosmopolitanism with our other responsibilities by means of ten concentric circles of concern. At the center was one's mind, then one's body and what's needed to sustain the body; one's immediate family, then uncles and aunts, then fellow citizens; and so on, in continually expanding circles until the circle includes

7. Gustafson, *Ethics from a Theocentric Perspective*, 87–112.

8. Niebuhr, *Radical Monotheism*, 37.

9. Epictetus, *Discourses*, 63.

all humanity.[10] To draw the circles tighter, he encouraged his followers to call strangers "brother" and "sister." Marcus Aurelius integrated his view of Stoic cosmopolitanism with his responsibilities as a Roman emperor, who was fighting wars by way of this aphorism: "My city and my country, as I am Antoninus, is Rome; as I am a human being, it is the world."[11]

Theologian Thomas Aquinas integrated one's higher love for God with duties to others near us by talking about orders of love. According to this vision, God is loved most, then the self, and then others based on their similarity to God and their proximity to us. Love for those close to us cannot be exclusionary but must be integrated into the wider scope of God's justice and love.[12]

The theocentrism offered here differs from both visions. It differs from the Stoic vision of concentric circles of responsibility in that it places love for God at the center. This reorders one's love for self and others. Rather than Aquinas' orders of love, we will be using the concept of covenant to integrate our proximate responsibilities into a theocentric vision. Covenant envisions human beings as participating in many overlapping communities. Covenantal circles of concern are not necessarily concentric, running from proximate to distant, and may demand different obligations according to how the community serves God's purpose. We will explore this in greater length in chapter 11.

Political Equality

Theocentrism is able to ground political equality because it reveres every person regardless of who they are. We see this in the Declaration of Independence, which states that it is self-evident that all people are created equal. Of course, human equality is anything but self-evident. Experience shows us that people are manifestly unequal in terms of their talent, mental capacity, beauty, fertility, privileges, skills, knowledge, wealth, and charisma. A football team would be foolish to recruit players without regard to their size, strength, smarts, and ability to excel at the game. By contrast, a law firm would be foolish to use a football team's criteria to recruit new attorneys. The need to differentiate between the good football players and the good lawyers illustrates how such discrimination is always relative to

10. Wedgewood, "Hierocles' Concentric Circles," 4.

11. Aurelius, *Meditations*, 6.44.

12. Aquinas, *Summa Theologica*, 1289.

some finite center of value. While differentiation based on job criteria is acceptable in limited contexts, such as football teams and law firms, political equality is critically important for upholding human and democratic rights as well as maintaining equality before the law.

Because questions of political equality generally involve state power, there is a perennial temptation to rank privileges and prioritize human and democratic rights using the political community as the value center (or in illiberal regimes, an authoritarian ruler). We have seen how non-inclusive value centers blind us to the worth of those outside the community, whether it be the team or a family.

While it is one thing to distinguish between citizens and non-citizens so a democratic nation can function politically, it is another thing to deny human and legal rights to citizens or immigrants. For example, in the United States, some claim that it is in the national interest to deny asylum to people fleeing persecution, treat immigrants cruelly, and violate immigrants' rights to due process. The idea that all people are equal in their relationship with the Creator provides powerful grounding for a prophetic critique of the nationalistic tendency to deny the humanity of others.

Notice, also, that when we affirm that all people are created equal, we are denying that the state is the source of human dignity and political rights. H. Richard Niebuhr makes a related observation regarding the way theocentrism frames questions of religious freedom. Religious freedom, he says, is necessary not because religion is a private, other-worldly affair, but because it concerns (or should concern) an "allegiance to a sovereignty and community more immediate, more inclusive, and more fateful than the political commonwealth."[13] From this perspective, religious freedom is not a grant from the state but an acknowledgement of the state's limited sovereignty relative to God. If one believes that loyalty to God should transcend loyalty to country, it follows that one should demand religious freedom for everyone. The bloody history of religious persecution reinforces this wisdom. We return to the topic of religious freedom in chapter 12.

Ethical Theocentrism in the Bible

Unsurprisingly, the ethical concerns attached to theocentrism inform the Bible's moral sensibilities. In the Exodus story, when God appears to Moses in the burning bush, God says that he's heard the Hebrew slaves' cries and

13. Niebuhr, *Radical Monotheism*, 70.

seen their suffering. While it is not clear how the Egyptians denied or rationalized the Hebrew's misery, God noticed. The Sabbath commands instruct the faithful to give everyone, immigrants, servants, children, and animals, a Sabbath so they may rest "as you do" (Deut 5:12–15). God's universal care lies at the root of the biblical prophets' concerns for people who are perennially treated as useless or expendable, foreigners, the poor, widows, and orphans.

God's inclusive concern is the central theme of the Jonah saga. The story shows God confronting Jonah's prejudice against the Ninevites. At one point, a worm destroys a plant that is shading Jonah. When Jonah becomes bitter about the plant's dying, God chastises him, "You're concerned about the plant, should I not also be concerned about Nineveh, that great city with people who don't know right from wrong and also many cattle" (paraphrase of Jonah 4:11). Notice that God's concern is not limited to humans.

Isaiah speaks for God when he says, "My thoughts and ways are higher than your thoughts and ways" (Isa 55:8–9). This counsel protects theocentrism by cautioning us not to presume that God endorses our projects or to imagine that our thoughts about God share the same reality as God.

Jesus' life and teachings reflect a similar theocentrism. His central message was a call to reorient our lives and live under God's rule, thereby placing all life, including loyalty to the state, under the inclusive rule of the realm of God's rule (Mark 1:15). His instruction that no one can follow him unless he "hates his father and mother, wife and children" (Luke 14:26) placed revolutionary limits on familial loyalty. Jesus continually lifted up "the least of these" (Matt 25), those considered unimportant or unacceptable. He ate with sinners and touched the unclean. He criticized his faith tradition's loss of theocentric focus when he portrayed religious leaders as being more concerned about their personal righteousness than their neighbors' well-being in the parable of the good Samaritan (Luke 10:25–37). He overturned tables in the temple, claiming that they betrayed the temple's prayerful focus. Jesus' prayer in the garden of Gethsemane before he went to the cross is an exemplary, theocentric personal petition. He asked, "Let this cup pass from me," and then rededicated himself to God's cause: "Nevertheless, not my will but yours be done" (Luke 22:42). Jesus' call to love our enemies and his pardoning of his enemies on the cross show the extent of his universal, theocentric concern.

When Jesus commissioned the apostles to make disciples of all nations (Matt 25), he did not intend to create a new "Christian nation" out of all the nations, ethnicities, and peoples of the world. Rather, Jesus intended for his followers to reorient their national and ethnic identities according to his theocentric teaching. His commission echoes Isaiah's messianic vision of all nations streaming to the mountain of the Lord (Isa 2). Each nation retains its identity even as they beat their swords into plowshares and learn the ways of peace.

Historian Tom Holland notes that Christianity grew rapidly among the poorest in society because it insisted, contrary to other voices, that they mattered to God. The value of the lowly was demonstrated by Jesus' life and death. When God's son came to earth, he did not act like the pagan deities. He was born among the humble, manifested the attitude of a servant, lifted the lowly, and was crucified on a Roman cross. The success of Christianity among the lowest classes led some early observers, like the second-century writer Celsus, to dismiss Christianity as the religion of women and slaves.[14] Christianity's theocentric vision, when it is not corrupted by loyalties to other idols, continues to challenge images of wealth, power, and masculinity that endorse dominating and abusing others. It does this by fostering a theocentric ethic.

Idolatry and Religion

We have discussed the most obvious type of idolatry, literal gods who represent the vitalities of life. We've also talked about the idolatry of allowing faith in a finite value center to obscure the value of others. But there are other ways that idolatry gets tangled up in religion.

Much idolatry is packaged as utilitarian religion. Some religious systems promote devotion as a technology for managing mysteries that are beyond our control and influencing the gods. According to the value theory we have discussed here, when the gods are valued for their usefulness for healing, protection in battle, fertility, fortune, power, etc., the real thing being worshiped is the object we want them to serve.

Christian forms of utilitarian religion can be subtle. They can make a show of encouraging devotion and standing for orthodoxy, yet be as idolatrous as the paganism of old. Utilitarian Christianity values God and faith as a means to some end. Take, for example, the adage, "The family that

14. Origen, *Contra Celsus*, 482.

prays together, stays together." That *feels* true enough, though the bonds of family life rest on a host of dynamics and practices besides shared prayer. The trouble is that it encourages prayer as a means for corralling the family rather than conforming our will to God's will (as in Jesus' theocentric prayer in Gethsemane, "not my will, but yours be done"). When prayer is promoted for family togetherness, it becomes a technique to control God and manipulate spouses and children. This can cause oceans of harm.

Utilitarian religion is usually a response to anxiety and a sense of powerlessness. Consider religious leaders who call people to turn to Christianity to "save the nation." Anxiety rooted in fears, perhaps brought on by changes in the economy, immigration, or culture, is named as the explicit motivation. When religion is valued for its utility to benefit the nation, it becomes distorted. Rather than helping people live into God's purpose for all nations and people, it privileges one nation over others. It also tends to view the religious group as the "real citizens" of that nation and smear others as a threat. This inevitably leads to ethical blindness.

This book could easily fall into this sneaky sort of idolatry. It is occasioned by the crisis in American democracy and encourages a revival of democratic and republican faith to "save the nation." While it differs from Christian nationalisms in honoring pluralism as a way to protect the integrity of the faith, there can be no guarantee that we will avoid idolatry. That's how sin is. This is why we are saved, not because we get it right but because God is gracious.

The best we can do is intentionally seek to maintain a theocentric focus. Such a focus enjoys and celebrates God's excellence for the sake of God's inherent excellence. It views service to God's greatness, justice, and love as the highest and greatest good for all people, nations, institutions, and things. It understands that humans, their families, work, economics, politics, and religious communities exist to serve God's glorious purposes revealed in creation and redemption. It knows that the chief purpose of human beings is to glorify and enjoy God forever.

Theocentrism and the Other Principles

Every other principle of public theology we examine in the coming chapters reflects theocentric assumptions. *Imago Dei* suggests a way to affirm human dignity and purpose without falling into anthropocentrism. Natural law points to God's moral order, which transcends temporal laws and systems of morality. Sin is frequently viewed as being rooted in idolatry. Hope in God centers us in the midst of sin, evil, and death. Vocation insists that individuals and institutions are called to a larger, theocentric purpose. Covenant casts familial, political, and other obligations in a theocentric perspective. Religious freedom honors the individual and communal responsibility to faithfully follow God. Creation explores God's purpose in creating the world. It is to this topic we now turn.

Chapter Five

Creation as Gift and Task

> It is enough for the Christian to believe that the only cause of created things, whether in heaven or on earth, visible or invisible, is nothing other than the goodness of the Creator who is the one true God, and there is nothing that is not either himself or from him.
>
> —Augustine[1]

Humans are always asking questions: Where did we come from? Why is there something, not nothing? What *is* this something, anyway? How shall we make sense of the threats to human existence, such as evil and death? Does existence have a purpose or rationale?

The church has answered these questions with the doctrine of creation. The doctrine of creation is based on observations about the world as well as reflections on the biblical witness, particularly the two foundational creation myths that are linked together in the book of Genesis. The church has interpreted these stories in ways that prompt and intensify a distinctive set of attitudes toward the world. This is what makes creation not only a doctrine or teaching of the church but a guiding principle of public theology.

1. Augustine, *Enchiridion*, 240.

Inevitable Myths

Myths are an inevitable feature of human existence. By myths, we do not mean false beliefs, as when people talk about the mythical Loch Ness Monster. Rather, they are tales that help us see the deeper truths that lie beneath the surface of things. People, ancient and modern, are always creating myths to make sense of the world they inhabit. They tell myths to invite people into a story. Myths locate us in a narrative. They shape our attitudes about the things of this world. They give us a mission and a sense of responsibility. Consider how a biographer's account of the life of a saint, founding father, or other great figure differs from hagiography (a holy biography), which fashions a legend worthy of emulation, or how a historian's dispassionate, objective, impartial chronicle of the nation's past differs from myths of national greatness. Myths shape our beliefs, values, loyalties, and identity. This is why many are threatened when their myths are challenged.

The two myths linked together in Genesis are hardly the only creation myths. Indeed, comparing the biblical account with ancient and modern myths can help us discern parallels and contrasts. It may also help us see what the authors and editors of Genesis were trying to convey by creating these myths and linking them together.

Enuma Elish

The biblical authors likely encountered a number of ancient Near Eastern myths, including the "Enuma Elish." Scholars think it was written around 1300 BCE, six hundred years before Genesis.[2] This may explain resemblances between the accounts. For example, in both, light is created before the sun and the stars. Both also begin in watery chaos and involve a separation of the waters above and below the earth, though they differ on how the separation takes place. In the Bible's first creation account (Gen 1:1—2:3), God's Spirit hovers over what is called in Hebrew *tohu va bohu,* sometimes translated as "the dark, deep" or "the formless void." Scholars disagree on the exact meaning of this phrase as well as its implications for theology, but it seems to refer to primordial chaos or a featureless emptiness.

The Babylonian creation myth also begins with watery chaos until the waters separate into freshwater (the god Apsu) and saltwater (the goddess Tiamat). Soon after Apsu and Tiamat give birth to other gods, a great

2. Mark, "Enuma Elish," para. 2.

struggle ensues. It starts with Apsu's irritation at the younger gods' behavior and escalates into patricide. After they kill Apsu, a battle of the gods ensues. It ends in an act of self-defense/domination, with Marduk (a god) killing Tiamat (his mother) and creating the universe from her body. As part of that work, he fashions human beings from the blood of the slain rebel god Qingu, who had been Tiamat's consort and leader of her army. In this way, Marduk brings order out of chaos and the world is born.[3]

The Babylonian creation myth's battle and slaying stand in stark contrast with the first Biblical creation account (Gen 1:1—2:3), which portrays God speaking the world into being. The effortless move from divine mind to speech to existence suggests a God of a different order than the skirmishing deities of the Babylonian epic.

Differences in the myths also suggest divergent views of the place of violence in life. "Enuma Elish" implies that violence may be inherent to life. Since killing Tiamat was a precondition for creating the world, one is left with the impression that violence may be a necessary good, a natural means of creation and order. By contrast, violence only appears in the biblical account after creation is finished, when Cain kills Abel. It is portrayed as a deep disturbance in creation. Abel's blood cries to God from the ground (Gen 4:10). God responds by holding Cain accountable in a way that invites humans to emulate God's justice and mercy.

The myths have radically different takes on the role of humans in relation to God. Theologian Rachel Baard observes that in the "Enuma Elish," humans exist to feed the gods and relieve them of their labor. Scholars think that this arrangement reinforced peasant submission in the emerging Babylonian empire.[4] Just as Marduk rules the heavens, so political elites rule on earth.

By contrast, in Genesis, God does not depend on humans or anything else in creation. In fact, God provides food for the humans (Gen 1:29). This idea is explored further in Ps 104, the Bible's most significant meditation on creation. It praises God for providing food and shelter to God's creatures, who all look to God "for their food in due time" (Ps 104:27). God's provision reinforces that life is a gift.

3. Mark, "Enuma Elish."

4. Rachel Baard delivered a sermon at River Road Presbyterian Church in 2023. Her thoughts prompted this investigation.

Neo-Darwinian Myths

The ancients are not unique in creating origin myths. Philosopher Mary Midgely, an atheist, has observed the tendency of modern writers to go beyond the science of life's origins and turn evolution into a religion.[5] Richard Dawkins casts evolution as a myth about "selfish genes." Ignoring numerous counter examples (monasticism, heroic sacrifice, birth control, and other wasted opportunities to procreate), Dawkins tells us that human beings are "robot vehicles" designed and programmed by genes for the purpose of carrying the genes to the next generation. The result is endless competition that forces the genes to build ever more effective "gene machines." In this fierce environment, the genes have become "ruthlessly selfish" so that they "resemble nothing so much as Chicago gangsters."[6]

Dawkins is uncomfortable with the amoral implications of his myth and seeks to to rescue morality: "We have the power to defy the selfish genes of our birth. . . .We can even discuss ways of deliberately cultivating and nurturing pure, disinterested altruism—something that has no place in nature, something that has never existed before in the whole history of the world. We are built as gene machines . . . but we have the power to turn against our creators. We, alone on earth, can rebel against the tyranny of the selfish replicators."[7] Dawkins encourages us to rebel against our creators, the genes. Yet one wonders how "machines," built and programmed by selfish genes, have the agency to violate their programing and do something that "has no place in nature" and "has never existed before in the whole history of the world." Whether or not one finds this myth coherent, no one can doubt that it presents a different portrait of reality than Genesis's depiction of a generous God who graciously bestows the gift of life.

Whereas Dawkins invites us to reject the implications of the selfish gene myth, M. T. Ghiselin leans into them. He claims that biologically-rooted selfishness proves the appropriateness of social Darwinism:

> The economy of nature is competitive from beginning to end . . . what passes for cooperation turns out to be a mixture of opportunism and exploitation. The impulses that lead one animal to sacrifice himself for another turn out to have their ultimate rationale in gaining advantage over a third, and acts for the good

5. Midgely, *Evolution as a Religion*.
6. Dawkins, *Selfish Gene*, 2.
7. Dawkins, *Selfish Gene*, 201.

> of one society turn out to be performed for the detriment of the rest. Where it is in his own interest, every organism may reasonably be expected to aid his fellows. Where he has no alternative, he submits to the yoke of servitude. Yet, given a full chance to act in his own interest, nothing but expediency will strain him from brutalizing, from maiming, from murdering. . . . Scratch an altruist and watch a hypocrite bleed.[8]

Ghiselin portrays life as a bleak competition driven by the necessity to reproduce. Altruism is not rebellion; it is deception, a ploy. Expediency, he claims, is the only thing that prevents us from brutalizing, maiming, and murdering others to advance our interests. According to Ghiselin, Dawkins is a hypocrite.

Ghiselin's myth sharply contrasts with Genesis's depiction of murder as a disturbance in creation that cries to God for justice. One wonders whether Ghiselin ever encountered a soldier who suffers from the form of PTSD called "moral harm," the crippling sense that, having brutalized, maimed, and murdered others, they have done something really, really bad. They have violated the moral order of things. They sense blood crying out from the ground.

Like all myths, myths of selfish genes shape a disposition toward the world. The selfish gene myth developed at a historical moment loaded with portraits of human nature that explain behavior in terms of selfishness and utility maximization. Such depictions are reductive. They differ significantly from an observation made by the founder of modern economics, Adam Smith, who opened *The Theory of Moral Sentiments* by calling attention to decidedly unselfish behavior: "How selfish soever man may be supposed, there are evidently some principles in his nature, which interest him in the fortune of others, and render their happiness necessary to him, though he derives nothing from except the pleasure of seeing it."[9] Whatever one makes of the contributions of the broader culture to the selfish gene myth, it seems safe to assume that all human behavior expresses human genetics, not just selfishness.[10] Furthermore, it is not clear that selfishness always serves reproduction or that altruism always hinders it. It is mythology, not biology, that reduces human agency to selfish genes and the natural order to brutal competition.

8. Ghiselin, *Economy of Nature*, 247.
9. Smith, *Theory of Moral Sentiments*, 1.
10. Pinker, *Better Angels*.

God the Source

The doctrine of creation maintains that all life and all things have their source in God. The implication is that the whole world is God's handiwork. This differs from myths that view the sun or the stars as divine and the source of life.[11] Viewing creation as God's handiwork gives us perspective on how we understand the destruction and use of creation for food and other human needs. On the one hand, it differs from animistic views and neo-pagan romanticism that perceive human productivity as an attack on God or God's sacred body.[12] On the other hand, creation's theocentrism differs from human-centered views that do not properly value creation and its creatures.

In this connection, it is important to note that human beings are not made *ex nihilo*, out of nothing. In the second creation account (Gen 2:4–25), God gets his hands dirty, fashioning the first human, Adam, from the *adamah* (Hebrew for "red clay" or dust). Although traditionally interpreted as male, *ha'adam* does not take a gender-specific form in Hebrew. Moreover, terms for male and female only appear after God fashions the woman out of the *ha'adam*.

That God creates humans out of preexisting creation points to our dependence on the earth and its natural processes and, through these, to our dependence on God. It suggests that God works through ordinary means to give and preserve life. This can ground an appreciation of secondary causes, such as genetics and evolution, as a means of God's creative work.

The Mind of the Maker

If creation is God's handiwork, an artifact of God's mind, it follows that it possesses a stable order, structure, and logic that are, at least in principle, discoverable by human reason. Sociologist and historian Toby Huff explains how convictions about creation's order and reasonableness contributed to the rise of early modern science. He says that once natural law theology taught that everyone could use reason to discover the moral order (the moral law), it was a short step to believing that one could use one's reason to discover the natural order (the laws of nature).[13]

11. Kass, *Beginning of Wisdom*, 28.
12. Stackhouse, "Godly Cooking."
13. Huff, *Rise of Early Modern Science*.

The idea that the natural order reveals God's mind has led some theologians to talk about creation as "the book of nature." By this, they mean that just as one can study the Bible to learn about God, one can study God's creation to discover God's majesty and intention. Sociologist Robert Merton claims that this idea spurred a number of English Puritans to engage in the scientific study of nature with the purpose of exploring God's mind and bringing honor to the Creator.[14] Properly understood, creation discourages the sort of credulity that shuns science, knowledge, and reason. The idea that reality reflects the rational mind of God has moderated a perennial human impulse to employ magic to influence the forces mysteriously governing the world. Nature is not irrational or capricious. Neither is it governed by petty, jealous forces that one must placate and manipulate. Sociologist Max Weber observed that this emphasis on the rational order of creation had the effect of "disenchanting" the world of gods, demons, and other spiritual agents.[15]

Theocentrism and Ownership

Since God created all things, it also follows that God owns all things. This qualifies human ownership and authority. We see this dynamic in a number of biblical passages. Psalm 24:1, for example, affirms, "The earth is the Lord's, and the fullness thereof."

The Levitical jubilee commands rest on the conviction that God owns everything. It directs the Israelites to redistribute the land every fifty years, limiting the possibility that, as wealth is passed down through the generations, it will become concentrated in the hands of a few and force the landless into slavery (Gen 47; Neh 5). Some scholars doubt that Israel ever followed this command. In fact, it seems to anticipate resistance, which may explain why it includes the emphatic assertion of God's ownership, "The land is mine!" (Lev 25:23).

Not only the land but all creatures belong to God. Psalm 50 claims that God owns the cattle on a thousand hills. While this might be news to the ranchers, it underwrites the idea that animal husbandry is a sacred trust. This trust is made explicit in the second creation story when God charges humans with caring for creation (Gen 2:15). This command addresses all humanity and provides a clear rationale for environmental stewardship. We

14. Merton, "Puritan Spur to Science."

15. Weber, *Science as a Vocation*, 148.

shall say more about this in the next chapter when we explore the idea that humans, as the bearers of the divine image, are called to mirror God's care for creation.

Eric Nelson claims that late Reformation convictions about divine ownership introduced the notion that the state should coercively seek an egalitarian distribution of property into Western political thought.[16] While it is debatable whether this idea is well rooted in the American political context, the notion that God owns all things provides metaphysical moral reasons to consider public purposes and goods that get ignored when private ownership is made absolute.

God's Pleasure

The doctrine of creation maintains that since God is the source of all things, God delights in all things. The church has interpreted God's repeated pronouncements that the creation is "good" as indicating that creation exists for God's good pleasure and glory. In the second creation account, the humans hear God walking through the garden in "the cool of the day," a time when the garden would be most enjoyable (Gen 3:8). Christian theologians frequently interpret Christ's incarnation, when the Word of God takes on created flesh, as a reaffirmation of God's assessment of creation's goodness. Ascriptions of divine pleasure appear throughout Scripture, suggesting that all things begin their existence as expressions of divine delight. These affirmations invite us to enjoy life's beauty and excellence. They promote gratitude, wonder, and a sense of responsibility for the welfare of God's good creatures.

Gratitude and wonder are types of happiness. They constitute the "set point" of emotional life to which we should return at some point, when disequilibrium generates fear, sadness, and rage. While each of these "negative emotions" is appropriate in the right context, they should not become the "set point" where we live most of our lives. Sadness can devolve into despair. Fear and rage can inspire violence. By contrast, gratitude can inspire generosity and wonder, leading us to a deep appreciation for life.

16. Nelson, *Hebrew Republic*, 57–87.

Two Moves

While we are called to mirror God's delight in creation, it is possible to love this world wrongly and allow it to replace God. When this happens, we get the sort of narrowing of attention and love associated with idolatry. Thinking this life is all there is, people stop trusting God and seek to secure their existence against every conceivable threat. They may build ever higher walls or strike out at every perceived provocation. They may hoard possessions to guard against poverty or prove themselves to their neighbors. They may find themselves on a treadmill, seeking ever bigger thrills and conquests to satisfy their emptiness and boredom. The consequences of this misplaced love and trust are hoarding, violence, and environmental destruction. The Christian tradition has viewed this behavior as expressing the apostle Paul's observation concerning the human propensity to worship creation instead of the Creator (Rom 1:25).

Theologian Diogenes Allen observes that "the magnitude of human aspirations, needs, and desires seems to be greater than the world can satisfy and suggests that this points to the possibility of God."[17] Whether or not one agrees with Allen, no one can deny that unless we learn to love the world rightly, we will destroy it.

To properly value this life, we need to make two moves. In the first move, we turn away from creation to God. In this move, we reject creation in favor of God's greater goodness and glory. This move does not deny the world's beauty and does not disparage the world's goodness but recognizes that it cannot satisfy our boundless desires. Good as the world is, it cannot secure our destiny, for our earthly destiny is to grow feeble and die.

Once we have made the first move, the love of God begins to reorient us. It prompts a second move, which turns us back to the world. Only now we no longer love the world so desperately, exploiting it for our neediness, expecting it to render something that it cannot possibly give. We are not indifferent to the world, but we no longer cling to the things of this life so tightly. Instead, we are prepared to love the world rightly, which is to love the world because God loves it, and in the way that God loves it in Christ. Loving the world rightly means honoring God's ownership and delight. In doing this, we participate in God's love for the world.[18]

17. Allen, "Witness of Nature," 31.

18. Mathewes, "On Using the World."

The practical implications of these two moves are many and substantial. Consider the difference it makes whether we view a forest as inanimate nature or as God's creation, as a possession or as our responsibility. The principle of creation may not dissuade a landowner from logging a forest, but it should shape how they go about it. Rather than simply extracting value as cheaply as possible to maximize their wealth, they should sense that they are stewards of God's creation and log it in a way that preserves water quality, biodiversity, and the claims of other stakeholders who depend on it

Creation provides a metaphysical moral rationale for public intervention to protect the environment from damage by short-sighted sinners who would, for a profit, destroy the earth and leave future generations to deal with the devastation. Notions of God's ownership expand the scope of resources that are available to promote human and creaturely flourishing.

God's Delight and Our Own

The credibility of God's appraisals of "good" and "very good" are challenged by creatures that annoy and threaten us, and by the reality of suffering and evil. In dealing with each of these, the church has held on to the divine affirmation of creation's goodness.

Threatening Creatures

Although we are to delight in creation, we should not presume that expressions of divine pleasure are identical to our own. God's thoughts are higher than ours, and God's purposes are more expansive than our own. Humans have the capacity to recognize creation's goodness, but it does not follow that everything is arranged to please us.

Mosquitos remind us that human beings are not the chief reason everything exists. Annoying and deadly as they can be to us, they play a role in the ecosystem as a food source and pollinators. Humans also play a role in the ecosystem. We have a worthy place in God's creation. This means that we have every right to resist feeding mosquitoes and protect ourselves from the diseases they spread. In the process, though, we should not kill all the bees and raptors or destroy the ecosystem.

Creation not only gives us a God-centered reason to value other creatures that annoy and threaten us, including other humans, God values our enemies, which is why Jesus directed us to love them and to pray for them

(Matt 5:44). God delights in the marginalized and oppressed. Everything exists for God's pleasure and glory. If we forget this, we will fail to honor God or God's creatures.

Suffering

The world contains enormous suffering and pain. As the church has sought to make sense of suffering, it has not relinquished its confidence that this is God's good creation. This differs from those who would explain suffering by saying that this world is badly made. Indeed, the early church's doctrines about Jesus' incarnation and the Trinity reinforce God's affirmation of the world's goodness. They deny that Jesus rescues us from a bad material world.

Confidence in God and creation's goodness has given believers in every time and place permission to honestly express grief, disappointment, despair, and their sense of God-forsakenness. The Psalms, the book of Job, and Jesus' cry of God's abandonment on the cross demonstrate and encourage full-throated expressions of grief and anger. The biblical book Lamentations exhaustively catalogues the range of conflicting emotions that accompanied the fall of Jerusalem in 586 BCE.[19] The Biblical tradition does not encourage people to mask their fear, grief, and rage in spiritual clichés.

Neither does the biblical tradition explain suffering. It knows that explanations will not restore the loss or ease the pain. They also tempt us to say things that are "too wonderful for us to know" (Job 42:3). Rather, it declares that somehow, through it all, we belong to God. It insists that because God is love, God is no stranger to suffering. Jesus endured suffering and death as an expression of solidarity with the godforsaken.[20] It believes that even when we feel most abandoned, nothing can separate us from the love of God in Christ. Finally, it trusts that suffering and death are not our destiny. God will redeem.

Evil

God's affirmation of creation's goodness has provided the foundation for the church's approach to evil. Some claim that evil and suffering point to the absurdity of a meaningless universe. Others claim that good and evil, death

19. Roberts, "Lamentations 3," 196–98.

20. Moltmann, *Crucified God.*

and life are just flip sides of the one coin called life. Recall how the "Enuma Elish" depicts killing and death as the source of life.

Still others subscribe to various dualisms. Dualisms take numerous forms. Some put the material world in opposition to the spiritual world. They identify everything that is wrong with a flawed or bad creation, viewing material life as bad. They posit a redeemer who will save us from this bad material world that is passing away.[21] By denying the goodness of creation, they devalue this life, our bodies, and the environment. Rather than loving the world rightly, they do not love it enough.

Cosmic dualism pits an evil, godlike principal in opposition to God. One thinks of Angra Mainyu, who opposes Ahura Mazda (the supreme deity) in Zoroastrianism. Some Christians imagine that Satan possesses a similar reality and power.

Prior to his conversion, Augustine, a third-century theologian, had been a member of a religious group called the Manicheans that subscribed to a kind of cosmic dualism. When he discusses the devil and the fall, he explicitly rejects Manichean dualism, insisting that the devil does not have "some sort of evil nature of his own, drawn, as it were, from some opposing principle." Indeed, he says, "it is implicit that the devil was once without sin."[22] The devil is one of the creatures God once declared good. Yet, because the devil possessed freedom, he rebelled against God. As an explanation of evil, this myth endorses the goodness of creation. Evil is not a separate principle from God—represented by a deity who opposes God with God-like powers—but merely a fallen creature. This means that evil lacks any independent basis for existence or power apart from the Creator. The worst anything can be is a corrupted good.

By rejecting dualisms, the doctrine of creation tempers the tendency that psychologists call "splitting," where people split people into extreme camps, imagining some to be good and others—enemies, outsiders, and members of scapegoated classes—as demonic. Throughout history, people have imagined that they could make a better world if they eliminated royalty, capitalists, communists, immigrants, liberals, conservatives, or some ethnic minority. Splitting frequently takes on religious overtones, with the in-groups projecting evil onto out-groups, while treating comembers as relative angels and excusing their foibles. Some observers suggest that growing political polarization in the US reflects splitting, as healthy

21. Ottati, *Theology for Twenty-First Century*, 90–96.

22. Augustine, *City of God*, 15.

political competition has devolved into what is sometimes called "affective polarization."[23] Because it is focused on othering, aversion, and moralization, it is less interested in the "triumphs of ideas than . . . dominating the abhorrent supporters of the opposing party."[24]

Against this tendency, the doctrine of creation insists that our enemies are God's good creatures. This is why Jesus enjoins us to pray for them. By praying for them, we attend to their humanity, hold out the possibility of their transformation, and train ourselves in wanting their good.

The fact that the worst anything can be is a "fallen good" explains why evil almost always presents itself as something good and necessary. This is why Samuel Johnson called patriotism "the last refuge of the scoundrel."[25] It is why philosopher Blaise Pascal observed, "People never do evil so completely and cheerfully as when they do it from religious conviction."[26] The Nazis did not sell the Holocaust to the German public by promising nightmare factories. They sold it as "the Final Solution." Putin justified the invasion of Ukraine as a means to rebuild the glorious Russian Empire and defend Christianity against a decadent West. In the American context, evil is pursued in the name of law and order, patriotism, and—I hate to say it—even Christianity. These deceptions explain why the Bible calls Satan "the Father of lies" (John 8:44).

The affirmation of creation's goodness and the rejection of dualism support a posture of "cosmic optimism." If the worst anything can be is a fallen creature, it follows that God, not the power of evil, holds our destiny. This warrants a tenacious hopefulness in the face of persistent suffering, systemic violence, and enduring oppression.[27]

When we say that God is Creator, we affirm that everything is God's good creation. This includes human beings. We now turn to a second affirmation of humanity, that they bear the divine image.

23. Iyengar et al., "Origins and Consequences."

24. Finkel et al., "Political Sectarianism in America."

25. Johnson, as cited in Boswell, *Life of Johnson*, 478.

26. Pascal, *Pensees*, 151.

27. MacComb, "Optimism of the Christian Religion."

Chapter Six

Imago Dei as Dignity and Calling

> God is every man's pedigree. He is either the Father of all men or of no man. The image of God is either in every man or in no man.
>
> —Abraham Joshua Heschel[1]

People in every culture and time have wondered about the place and worth of human beings in the cosmos. These questions have become more pressing over the course of this past century. Advances in cosmology dislodged humans from the central place many imagined they occupied in the universe. We now know that Earth is not the center of the universe. Neither is our star, which is one of over 100 to 400 billion stars in one of some two trillion galaxies in a universe of unimaginable immensity and extent.[2]

Deeper understandings of evolution and biology have challenged claims that humanity is the pinnacle of creation. We now know that it is incorrect to say that humans are more "highly evolved" than other creatures. It is more accurate to say that we evolved alongside other animals to fit our ecological niche. If you disagree, imagine how well humans evolved to survive underwater compared with jellyfish.

1. Heschel, *Insecurity of Freedom*, 95.
2. Gustafson, *Ethics from a Theocentric Perspective*, 88.

This realization has been accompanied by a rather late observation that other creatures are sentient. René Descartes, writing in the seventeenth century, thought that animal movements mimic human passions but that animals lack the passions themselves because they lack rational souls. Thinking that animals lack conscious thought, he claimed they were complex machines comparable to a clock, a fountain, or a mill.[3] Claims that human beings differ from all animals because they are rational, have the capacity for language, understand death, or possess a sense of justice no longer hold up. Other animals exercise reason, communicate, grieve, and demonstrate an understanding of fairness. Humans are distinguished from other animals not by the uniqueness of their capacities but by their magnitude.[4]

Technological changes, genetic engineering, the advent of artificial intelligence, and the gradual melding of human consciousness with digital technologies also raise questions about human significance. These developments coincide with the Anthropocene extinction and climate change, which suggest that humans have greatly overestimated nature's capacity to absorb and sustain unbound human consumption. Together, these cause us to question centuries-long assumptions about the place of human beings as the center and pinnacle of the natural order. Not only have humans destroyed much life on Earth, but our godlike powers make us capable of destroying civilization and ending human life. So we wonder, what is the place and value of humanity?

The Christian tradition has answered this question with the doctrine of *imago Dei*, which is Latin for "the image of God." This metaphor appears in the first creation account, which tells us that God created males and females in the divine image (Gen 1:26–27).

When we say that humans bear the image of God, we are saying that humans reflect something of the divine excellence. Theologians have wondered what this "something" is. Some have associated the divine image with a feature of human life or physical appearance, such as humanity's upright posture. Others have identified *imago Dei* with human reason or the capacity of the human imagination to transcend an immediate situation and see things "from above." Humans can even transcend their transcending, as it were, to reflect upon the significance of their capacity for transcendence. Still others identify the *imago Dei* with humanity's ability to engage in a

3. Descartes, *Descartes Selections*, 355.

4. Midgely, *Beast and Man*.

relationship with God. Yet, others wonder whether the divine image points to godlike capacities over the geo and biospheres.

Often, the traits that people associate with the divine image (intelligence, reason, morality, etc.) have been viewed as unique to the human species. James Gustafson notes the circularity of this tendency. On the one hand, traits associated with God were ascribed to humans. On the other hand, traits thought to be unique to humans were projected on God.[5] We have noted that many animals share capacities once thought to be exclusively human. Just because a fish cannot communicate to us does not mean that it is not experiencing something like anguish or dread upon being hooked in the mouth and pulled from the water. Furthermore, the biblical tradition's emphasis on creatures looking to God for their food and singing God's praise suggests that God-consciousness may not be uniquely human either. One does not need to relinquish the notion of humanity bearing the *imago Dei* to recognize that other creatures bear the Creator's imprint and possess sensibilities that we should respect.

Rather than engaging in ontological speculation about what in human nature reflects the divine nature, we should view it as an ethical category. This is how *imago Dei* is presented in Gen 9:6, after the flood, when God instructs humans not to kill other humans *because* they bear the divine image. As an ethical category, the image of God carries two primary meanings. First, everyone has an innate "dignity." Second, everyone has a calling to reflect the divine life by mirroring God's care for the world.

Image as Dignity

As a statement about human dignity, *imago Dei* has important practical implications. The first creation myth shows God creating both men and women in the divine image. This depiction should undermine patriarchal theologies, ideologies, and hierarchies. It is in tension with patriarchal interpretations of the second creation story that ignore the fact that the first human, *ha'adam,* is genderless and that claim that men bear a superior approximation of the divine image since they were made first. If both sexes bear God's image, it is ridiculous to claim that men should rule women or tolerate the fiction that women lack gifts to exercise authority, including ecclesiastical authority.

5. Gustafson, *Intersections*, 92.

Since both men and women bear the divine image, God must be beyond gender. It follows that the exclusive use of gendered theological language creates a malformed picture of God in the human imagination.

Since God is beyond gender, it also means that people who do not fit the gendered binary also bear the image of God. This conforms with a trajectory in the biblical witness that moves toward the full inclusion of non-binary eunuchs. Isaiah, for example, explicitly overturns a biblical command that excludes eunuchs (Deut 23:1), welcoming them into the worshipping community (Isa 54:4–7). Jesus acknowledges that some people who are non-binary were "born" (created) that way. He also affirms those who "have made themselves eunuchs," likely referring to castration, a gender-altering surgery (Matt 19:12).

In the book of Acts, the second gentile convert, Cornelius, is introduced by name (Acts 10). By contrast, the first gentile convert, an Ethiopian eunuch, is introduced by his gender and ethnicity (Acts 8:26–40). Lacking testosterone, the eunuch did not present as male. Just as Luke's first readers could see that the eunuch was Ethiopian; they could see the Ethiopian was a eunuch. Luke highlights the Ethiopian's ethnicity and gender to foreshadow the narrative arc of Acts, which tracks Jesus' instruction that his disciples be his witnesses to the "ends of the earth" (Acts 1:8).

In the story, Philip recognizes that the Ethiopian eunuch is reading from Isaiah and offers to explain it to him. In the process, Philip tells the story of Jesus' life, death, and resurrection. In response, the Ethiopian eunuch asks, "What prevents me from being baptized?" Philip baptized the eunuch, demonstrating the church's openness toward all who bears God's image.

The notion that everyone bears the image of God differs from ancient cultures, which claimed that the king alone bore the divine image or was a divine incarnation. It encourages expansive notions of equality and places it on a unique foundation. For example, *imago Dei* differs from approaches to dignity that recognize equal dignity within a closed community of people but deny it to outsiders. For example, ancient Greek society extended citizenship to men but excluded women, foreigners, and slaves. In a similar fashion, political scientist Daniel Philpot observes that the Treaty of Westphalia of 1648, which effectively ended the Thirty Years' War, recognized national sovereignty within the community of European nations but failed to extend this recognition to peoples and governments outside the community, notably to nations that would become colonies.[6] While we do

6. Philpot, *Revolutions in Sovereignty.*

have special obligations to others in families and nations, a point that we will explore in chapter 11, the principle of *imago Dei* does not allow us to dismiss the dignity of outsiders, aliens, or even enemies.

Imago Dei pushes us to recognize the fundamental equality and humanity of every person, even those our community deems inferior. The early church father Gregory of Nyssa drew on the "image of God" to discuss the evil of slavery in a sermon on Eccl 2. Commenting on the writer's boast, "I [bought] slaves and slave-girls," Nyssa says, "Tell me what sort of price you paid. What did you find in creation with a value corresponding to the nature of your purchase? What price did you put on rationality? For how many obols did you value the image of God? For how many coins did you sell this nature formed by God?"[7]

In the face of humankind's incredible diversity of status, gifts, and conditions, the belief that every human being bears the image of God undercuts elitist ideologies and ethnic prejudices. It authorizes a special concern for the poor, the weak, the vulnerable, the differently abled, the immigrant, and the enemy. It provides a point of solidarity that can bridge racial, national, linguistic, historical, tribal, and cultural differences.

Imago Dei has long been seen as having important moral and political implications. It grounds an ethic of reciprocity, to "love your neighbor as yourself" (Lev 19:18; Mark 12:31). It has also supplied a metaphysical-moral rationale to support classical liberal values, human rights, and equality before the law.[8] The decline of a shared theological vision has led some, such as Francis Fukuyama, to worry that "modern thought has arrived at an impasse, unable to come to a consensus on what constitutes man and his specific dignity, and consequently unable to define the rights of man."[9] Recovering *imago Dei* suggests a way forward.

Finally, the notion that everyone bears the image of God stands as judgment on societies that permit people to suffer from poverty, ignorance, malnutrition, and disease. It authorizes efforts to ensure that everyone has the nutrition, education, and healthcare they need to fully develop their God-given potential. This is reinforced by a twist Jesus puts on *imago Dei* and its identification of the divine with humanity. In the parable of the sheep and the goats, Jesus identifies with the least of these (Matt 25:31–46). He warns that

7. Gregory of Nyssa, "Gregory of Nyssa," para. 6.

8. Witte, *Christianity and Human Rights*.

9. Fukuyama, *End of History*, 337.

the "nations" will be judged by how they treat "the least of these," for in as much as they have cared for them, they cared for him.

Image as Calling

In addition to naming an inherent dignity, the image of God may be understood as a calling. This approach to *imago Dei* shifts our focus away from speculation about uniquely human capacities to consider how our abilities should be employed to mirror God's creative, self-giving rule. As a calling, the image of God suggests the possibility of a life that reflects God's wisdom, character, and love.

Viewing *imago Dei* as a calling helps us interpret what the first creation account means when it says that God granted humans "dominion" over the earth (Gen 1:26–28). In recent decades, the biblical concept of dominion has come under criticism for encouraging environmental annihilation.[10] This is understandable given how God's grant of dominion has been interpreted as mirroring human domination and, thus, authorizing human exploitation of God's other creatures. But if God owns the earth, as we discussed in the last chapter, then dominion cannot mean that we own the earth and can, therefore, do with it as we please. *Imago Dei* points in a different direction, inviting humans to mirror the life-giving authorship and authority of the One who creates and feeds the creatures.

This interpretation is supported by the biblical editors' decision to place the second creation account immediately following the first. In the second account, God charges the humans to "guard and protect" God's garden (Gen 2:15). If one reads these accounts together, as their juxtaposition encourages, God's instruction to care for creation naturally flows from notions of divine image and dominion.

This linkage is reinforced by numerous biblical passages that illustrate God exercising dominion by caring for and taking delight in creation. As Jesus observed, "Consider the birds of the air. They do not sow, reap, or gather into barns, yet your heavenly father feeds them" (Matt 6:26). This understanding of dominion as service is reinforced by Jesus' example (Phil 2). Christians claim that Jesus' life and teachings offer the purest reflection of the divine image, which is why Paul talks about Jesus as "the image of the invisible God" (Col 1:15).

10. White, "Historical Roots."

In summary, *imago Dei* may be understood as a calling to exercise God-like care for creation. This is illustrated by the Genesis flood story, which tells how Noah, a bearer of God's image, goes to extraordinary lengths to care for God's creatures. As we consider the flood of destruction brought on by the Anthropocene extinction, it suggests that humans should be using our God-like powers to care for and preserve creation. We who bear the divine image have the capacity and calling to engage in God-like, life-giving healing. If the image of God is a calling, it is because we share a moral capacity. It is to this topic that we now turn.

Chapter Seven

Natural Law as Human Capacity and Moral Order

> When Gentiles, who do not possess the law, do instinctively what the law requires, these, though not having the law, are a law to themselves. They show that what the law requires is written on their hearts, to which their own conscience also bears witness.
>
> —Romans 2:14–15

> Natural law rejects the notion that we must always defer to the law of the land, and it rejects the notion that we must always defer to the wisdom of the world. There is a higher law that trumps, and natural law theories provide an account of how to access that higher law. In short, it is accessed through nature; specifically through human nature.
>
> —Vincent W. Lloyd[1]

Is there a right or wrong? People wonder. Sometimes the complexity of a situation and the impossibility of honoring competing goods obscures our moral vision. Other times, though, the unfairness of an injustice may weigh upon us, as when we witness the suffering of a child. In moments of

1. Lloyd, *Black Natural Law*, 150.

despair, we may wonder whether the universe is indifferent. Does might make right? Does any of this matter? The possibility that it might not matter bothers us.

Some postmodernists doubt that we can know right and wrong since all moral judgments are socially constructed, culturally contingent, and tainted by interests. Nihilists go further and deny that right and wrong even exist. Richard Dawkins points to the indecent amount of suffering in the world and concludes, "The universe that we observe has precisely the properties we should expect if there is, at bottom, no design, no purpose, no evil, no good, nothing but pitiless indifference."[2] Yet, as we saw in chapter 5, Dawkins is better than his agnosticism, for he encourages us "human gene machines" to defy our selfish creators and cultivate altruism. This is not consistent with his claim that there is no good and evil. We make the distinction. Indeed, most moral agnostics have opinions about moral, social, and political issues that they think are more than mere personal opinion. They may despair whether anything matters in any ultimate sense, but if someone wrongs them or hurts someone they love, they will seek redress as if right and wrong actually exist. They will act as if their moral complaint is real. They will argue as if other people can see it.

Performance reveals more than theory. Nearly everyone acts as if there really is a right and a wrong.[3] Natural law, the idea that human beings can discern the moral order of things, explains why.

The Universal Moral Capacity

In the eleventh century, theologians married Greek notions of natural law and natural justice with the apostle Paul's observation that God has written the law on people's hearts (Rom 2:14–15), creating natural law theology. Natural law doctrine goes beyond positing that there is an objective right or wrong to propose that there is a universal capacity to know it. While God gives the Ten Commandments and other moral texts to provide a clear witness to God's law and guide believers in doing right, they did not think human beings require God's revealed law to know right from wrong.[4] God has given everyone a moral sense, a power sometimes attributed to the fact that humans bear the image of God. All people know, or should know, that

2. Dawkins, *River Out of Eden*, 133.

3. Lewis, *Mere Christianity*.

4. Puritan's Mind, *Westminster Larger Catechism*, q. 91.

murder, stealing, adultery, perjury, and covetousness are wrong and how the moral law applies in the ordinary circumstances of their lives.

The original natural law idea, the idea that people have a moral sense, has frequently been obscured by natural law advocates who too quickly equate natural law with conventional understandings of morality. However, the eleventh-century natural law theologians gave us something more radical. If everyone has a conscience, then everyone has a basis for questioning laws and customary morality. The fact that morality is up for debate does not reduce it to mere personal preference either. This is because God's moral order transcends and judges every understanding of it. Arguments can have traction, though not final resolution, in the real world of things.

The Impact of Natural Law

The medieval recovery and development of natural law had an enormous impact on Western civilization. It contributed to a growing appreciation for the rule of law, undermining absolutist claims that a sovereign's dictates were law and replacing it with the view that they served God's transcendent law.[5] This shift emboldened people to depose leaders who had, in their eyes, abandoned their moral responsibilities. Thus, Thomas Paine would later argue, "In free countries law ought to be king."[6]

The conviction that people are capable of reasoning and making moral judgments prepared the way for the Enlightenment. Immanuel Kant defined the Enlightenment as emerging from our "self-incurred immaturity" to claim the right and freedom to make public use of one's reason.[7] In chapter 5, we noted Toby Huff's observation that it was a short step from using reason to discern moral laws to using reason to discern the laws of nature.[8]

People who perceive God's moral order possess an inherent capacity for self-direction. It followed that they should have mastery over their personal choices. This affirmation was viewed as warranting natural rights, including freedom. It set in motion a trajectory that favored maximizing the sphere in which people are permitted to exercise their conscience, particularly when the choices impact their personal lives. At the same time, people understood

5. Johnson, *Sovereignty*.

6. Paine, *Common Sense*, 34.

7. Kant, *What is Enlightenment?*, 54.

8. Huff, *Rise of Early Modern Science*.

that the exercise of one's liberty was subject to natural law, including stipulations that one should not injure or infringe on another's freedoms.

In the seventeenth century, Hugo Grotius, a devout Christian, drew on natural law suppositions in articulating a secular basis for international law and government. Echoing the question Socrates first posed to Euthyphro—whether something is good because the gods command it, or whether the gods command it because it is good—Grotius claimed that the law of nature would still hold true "even if we should concede that which cannot be conceded without the utmost wickedness, that there is no God, or that the affairs of men are of no concern to Him."[9] In other words, the law need not reference divine commands to be valid. It is valid simply because human beings are capable of recognizing right and wrong. It is hard to imagine the US Constitution's prohibition of religious tests for office or public trust, its only explicit reference to religion, apart from natural law's insistence that everyone possesses a capacity for moral discernment.

People have repeatedly appealed to natural law's universalism to undercut classist, sexist, ethnic, racist, and religious prejudices that deny the moral capacities and agency of others. Jean Porter notes that the first natural law theologians used natural law arguments to combat the practice of arranged marriages. Even slave women, they insisted, were capable of deciding whom to marry. Furthermore, they claimed that since they were immersed in the circumstances and the most impacted, they were best situated to decide.[10]

Theologian Vincent Lloyd offers another insight into the importance of perspective. He reminds us, "Notoriously, natural law was once widely invoked to justify slavery. It was God's law that some were made black and others white, that some were made masters and others servants."[11] He notes that more "neutral" observers, distanced from the suffering, cannot appreciate the injustice and feel no urgency to solve the problem. By contrast, the oppressed are keenly aware of injustice. Their suffering gives them special knowledge of right and wrong. This, he says, is the source of the black natural law tradition in the United States that inspired resistance to slavery and segregation.[12]

9. Grotius, *War and Peace*, 169.

10. Porter, *Nature as Reason*, 352.

11. Lloyd, *Black Natural Law*, 149.

12. Lloyd, *Black Natural Law*, 150.

Natural Law and Pluralism

The universalism of natural law gives Christians a way to affirm pluralism. It explains why people of other religions or no religion so frequently manifest good will. It furnishes religious reasons to challenge exclusionary claims that would limit moral insight to religious texts, the interpreters of these texts, or the leaders or members of particular religious groups.

Natural law offers hope that, despite significant continuing religious and cultural disagreement, diverse people can reason together and find common purpose. It furnishes a theological rationale for welcoming people of other religions and cultures into public community, conversation, and decision-making. It grounds confidence that diverse individuals can transcend personal and group loyalties to pursue public goods and consider the goods and the rights of people who are not part of their group. In all these ways, it provides a foundation for solidarity and common moral purpose among dissimilar peoples, as evidenced by achievements such as the United Nations' Universal Declaration of Human Rights.

Natural law also implies that we can and should learn from one another. People are able to recognize truth. They are also able to sense moral excellence. While we may doubt that we will convince oppressors the errors of their ways, we trust that, in principle, it is possible. All people have a conscience, though it can be severely compromised.

The Limits of Natural Law

Some Enlightenment thinkers hoped that natural law's universal rationality would establish neutral ground where all reasonable persons could join in making purely rational, objective decisions that everyone would find obvious. Some dreamt that the elevation of reason would displace religion and the wars it inspired. This could not happen. "Reason alone" is not thick enough to displace human traditions, including religious traditions, that people require for wisdom and guidance.

Indeed, Enlightenment philosophers have been just as blinded by history, culture, interests, and social location as they've accused others of being. Thomas Jefferson penned that it is self-evident that all people are created equal, even as he enslaved people. His failure was not simply self-justification and a willingness to grant himself an exception. Like most people, he assumed that the prejudices and practices of his society reflected the natural order of things.

In addition to our inevitable historical, cultural, and social location, sin is always waiting to corrupt our reason and distort our sense of right and wrong. Theologically inclined supporters of natural law understood that all moral judgments are distorted by sin. This applied, at least in principle, to church councils—a conviction that made the Reformation possible.[13] Still, while natural law theologians allowed that the moral sense could become so damaged in some sociopaths that it is virtually obliterated, they did not think that sin destroyed the moral sense of most people. This led some Protestants to accuse advocates of natural law of downplaying the effects of the fall into sin and minimizing the need for grace to restore human moral capacities. More mainstream Protestants, however, brought natural law assumptions into their theological systems.[14]

Positive Law

The vagueness that is inherent with multiple subjective apprehensions of the moral law and the perversions of sin require nations to enact laws to order society and restrain evil. These human laws and statues are called "positive law." They testify to every society's need for rules to function and maintain justice. Every society must find a way to organize its life. No society can allow murder, theft, etc., to go unpunished. While positive laws vary across cultures and from nation to nation, their resemblances point to their common origin in natural law.

The relationship between natural law and positive law is complicated because the lines between religion, morality, and law are not clear. It is tempting, but misleading, to say flatly and finally that "government should not legislate morality." Yet, natural law always stands over positive law. This is true, as Abraham Lincoln pointed out in the Lincoln-Douglas debates, even when laws are passed with democratic support. Frederick Douglass argued that the people should decide whether they want slavery to be legal in their state or territory. Lincoln replied, "Any man can say that who does not see anything wrong in slavery, but no man can logically say it who does see a wrong in it."[15] Constitutional scholar Edward Corwin reminded us

13. United States Presbyterian Church, "Scots Confession," 20.

14. Graybill, *Rediscovering Natural Law.*

15. Belz, "Natural Law Tradition," para. 8.

that there is a long tradition of arguing for justice based on human law, and when human law will not support justice, to appeal to the higher laws of nature.[16]

Aristotle observed that the law is a teacher, and that one purpose of the law is to make people virtuous.[17] People rightly enact laws to achieve their visions of a moral life and a good society. This is true even though societies, being dynamic, never arrive at a final resolution concerning the moral values that are legislated and enforced by secular authority. Sometimes growing pluralism prompts people to decide that existing laws are relics of a bygone ethos. Other times, sectarian groups seek to impose their moral visions on the larger society. Every subgroup in society is constantly disappointed that its treasured values are not widely shared or recognized as universal. The majority of people currently in the United States do not think that cows are sacred, that commerce should cease on the Sabbath, or that a fertilized egg is a person.[18] This can leave groups feeling powerless and besieged, as if they are contributing to immorality or hindered in passing on their distinctive values to their children.

That said, compliance with the law depends on people generally thinking the law is moral and just. It is not enough for the law to tell people what is legal. Nor is it enough for laws to be vigorously enforced. Aristotle rightly observed the law's teaching function, but it does not follow that everyone will internalize its lessons and fall in line.[19] The law may train people's moral capacities, but it does not nullify them. People know that legal doesn't mean moral. When people think positive laws are immoral, lawbreaking becomes normalized. This is a problem because the good order of every society depends on public adherence to the law. Serious complications follow when we rely on secular law to enforce an excessive, intrusive morality.

It may seem counterintuitive, but there are moral reasons to permit people to make immoral choices, particularly when these choices impact their personal lives. Excessively restrictive laws negate the moral integrity and agency of individuals and encroach on freedom of conscience. Secular law is a blunt instrument that must apply in every case. When the government legislates too much, it inevitably fails to account for the circumstances

16. Corwin, "Higher Law Background," 149.

17. Aristotle, *Nicomachean Ethics*, 9.1180b23–25.

18. Jacobs, The Scientific Consensus.

19. Aristotle, *Nicomachean Ethics*, 9.1180b23–25.

of people's lives. In fact, excessive moral legislation can have the perverse consequence of constraining moral behavior.

Consider how, after the Supreme Court overturned Roe v. Wade, some states criminalized abortion in ways that discouraged doctors from aborting dead fetuses. Fearing that they could be charged with murder, doctors have forced women to carry dead fetuses to term, risking their lives and health. Even when laws allow exceptions to protect the life of the mother, it has been unclear who makes this determination (the doctor or the court) or whether such a determination can be made in a timely manner. Deadly consequences have followed.[20] Restrictive laws have prompted the migration of health professionals to more permissive states, undercutting prenatal healthcare in the states they departed.

A natural law perspective acknowledges that the status of the developing human life is morally and legally relevant. It also observes that most people doubt that a blastula is a "person" with legal rights and recoil at the idea of infanticide. While this agreement sets broad limits, the significance of emerging human life as it matures and the protections this demands of us is deeply contested. Most find attempts to enforce legal protections beginning at conception overreaching. These not only force potentially deadly medical complications on women; they impose long-lasting, life-altering burdens that many women are unprepared to shoulder. Because the law is such a blunt instrument, we should be cautious about excessive and intrusive moral legislation. Natural law reminds us that God gives women consciences and maintains that they are generally best positioned to make moral decisions that impact their lives.

Far from making people virtuous, excessive moral legislation can provoke cynicism and rebellion. Consider our nation's experiment with Prohibition. The passage of the Eighteenth Amendment, outlawing the manufacture, transportation, and sale of alcohol, was followed by a train of unintended, negative consequences, including widespread lawlessness. The public, recognizing the limits of secular law, revoked the amendment. Excessive moral regulation is "immoral" because it promotes contempt for the law. Furthermore, the harms associated with criminalizing behavior can be more damaging than the behavior itself. This seems to be the case with the criminalization of cannabis.

20. Johns Hopkins Bloomsburg School of Public Health, "Two New Studies."

The Limits of Positive Law

When people perceive that society is devolving into moral anarchy, they become anxious. Indeed, some people seem to have a posture toward the world that inclines them to moral hysteria. The media doesn't help when it fans the flames of moral panic.[21] People still do possess a moral sense. This is true even though, as we will see in the next chapter, this sense is severely compromised by sin. The morally anxious do well to recall the circumscribed parameters of John Calvin's second purpose of the law: the law's civil purpose is to "restrain evil."[22] Restraining evil is more limited than eliminating evil. Christians have good theological reasons to doubt that the state is capable of eliminating evil.

If we accept that the best the state can do is *restrain* evil, we may look for solutions to the problem of evil elsewhere. We might turn to Calvin's first purpose of the law, which is to convict us of sin and prepare us to receive God's mercy and regeneration. We might also remember Calvin's third use of the law, which is to lead the faithful into the way of righteousness. The belief that, at best, governments can restrain evil is reinforced by the principle of sin, which teaches us not to expect moral perfection before Christ's return. We explore this principle next.

21. Stanford, "Litter Boxes in Schools."

22. Calvin, *Institutes of the Christian Religion*, 348.

Chapter Eight

Sin and the Human Fault

For all have sinned and fallen short of the glory of God.

—Romans 3:23

Each of the principles we have examined asserts something positive about human nature. The doctrine of creation declares that human beings are God's good creatures. *Imago Dei* takes this further, teaching that human beings mirror the divine nature. The doctrine of natural law proposes that human beings have the capacity to know right from wrong. These positive declarations sharpen a set of perennial questions: Why do individuals and their communities continually fall into corruption? Why do brutality, injustice, and oppression persist? Why are humans so . . . well, inhumane?

The church has answered these questions with the doctrine of sin. The Calvinist version of this doctrine soberly states that human beings are totally depraved. Total depravity goes beyond alerting us to the fact that humans are capable of monstrous evil; it points to how sin infects the totality of human existence. It means that sin affects every aspect of human life, corrupts all faculties, and damages all interactions. Nothing is left untainted. Sin leads people to embrace evil and justify wrongdoing.

The doctrine of sin would seem to be in deep tension with the affirmations of human nature we've explored. How did people who were created "very good," who bear the image of God and have God's law written on their hearts, fall into such corruption? The church sought to answer these questions without relinquishing the positive affirmations. Instead of resolving the tensions, it leaned into the paradox. It maintained that people who do evil were not created evil; they were created "very good." It insisted that depraved sinners still bear the image of God. It claimed that although sin has spoiled every human faculty, it deforms but does not express created human nature.

Theologian Reinhold Niebuhr observed that the doctrine of sin provides a way to talk about the human fault without losing sight of human dignity. It holds that sin is not necessary, but it is inevitable.[1] This contrasts with understandings of human nature that lose sight of human dignity, either by claiming that human nature is evil (perhaps an expression of selfish genes), or by scapegoating others for society's problems.

People wonder how sin could enter the world. The myth of the fall says that sin came into the world because one of God's good creatures, a serpent, tempted the humans (Gen 3). Like every myth, it invites interpretation. Some read the story as Eve leading the man into temptation and, accordingly, blame women for sin and men's temptation. This reading has tended to sexualize sin and encourage female submissiveness.[2]

Others, following the story more closely, blame the serpent for coming up with the idea. This preserves the relative innocence of the humans, though some interpretations that follow this line place excessive influence on devilish temptation and ignore human agency. Still others interpret the advent of sin by talking about free will and the possibilities it allows. Humans, like the serpent, are given freedom to love God and do good, but we misuse it. The advantage of this reading is that it acknowledges human agency and responsibility.

Sin is not some latent, passive, hidden flaw that occasionally shows itself. It is on constant display. We are no strangers to the human fault. Christian thinkers, including Paul Tillich, Reinhold Niebuhr, and G. K. Chesterton claimed that the doctrine of sin is backed by significant empirical evidence. Many find the doctrine of sin compelling because it challenges easy optimism and names the chronic human tendency to estrangement and ruin. Reinhold Niebuhr's compelling retrieval of sin to describe human

1. Niebuhr, *Nature and Destiny*, 242.

2. Baard, *Sexism and Sin-Talk*.

dynamics led a group of Harvard professors to declare themselves "atheists for Niebuhr."[3]

The fact that sin is productive and ubiquitous prompted the church to develop a number of metaphors for sin. Jonathan Edwards has a gripping description of sin that is related to his definition of true virtue as benevolence to being in general (as it proceeds from God).

> Immediately upon the fall, the mind of man shrank from its primitive greatness and expandedness, to an exceeding smallness and contractedness. . . . Before, his soul was under the government of that noble principle of divine love, whereby it was enlarged to the comprehension of all his fellow creatures and their welfare. . . . But so soon as he had transgressed against God, these noble principles were immediately lost, and all this excellent enlargedness of man's soul was gone; and thenceforward he himself shrank, as it were, into a little space, circumscribed and closely shut up within itself to the exclusion of all things else. Sin, like some powerful astringent, contracted his soul to the very small dimensions of selfishness; and God was forsaken, and fellow creatures forsaken, and man retired within himself, and became totally governed by narrow and selfish principles and feelings.[4]

According to Edwards, sin contracts our attention and shrinks our love. Other metaphors for sin include alienation, bondage, brokenness, missing the mark, and being lost. The plentitude of metaphors testifies to sin's insidious and complex dynamics.

The Universal Fault

Sin is universal. This idea is expressed in the Psalms: "Everyone has turned away, all have become corrupt; there is no one who does good" (Ps 14:3); and it is reiterated by the apostle Paul, "All have sinned and fallen short of the glory of God" (Rom 3:23). Not even the saints escape sin's corruptions. Sin debases individuals, institutions, and movements that work for spiritual and moral improvement. The appalling, recurring failures of the church and its leaders are evidence that those who seek the cure of souls are themselves sin-sick.

3. Fackre, "Was Reinhold Niebuhr a Christian?"
4. Edwards, "Spirit of Charity."

The universality of sin is sometimes "explained" by concepts of "original sin," some versions of which speculate about how sin is passed down through the generations. Augustine, for example, theorized that original sin is passed on to children through their parents' lustful sexual intercourse. Such questionable theories do not obscure the doctrine's descriptive power. Original sin reminds us that sin is in many ways inherited. It is not simply something each generation invents out of its own perversions. While the first humans may have been free to choose not to sin, we, their descendants, are not. The corruptions of sin are imprinted upon us by sinful histories and sinful communities. Original sin names the way in which we are inevitably formed by, participate in, and perpetuate the continuing brokenness of the world.

The universality of sin not only points to the fact that everyone is a sinner but how sin infects every capacity of the human being. Sin even debases the supposedly "superior" aspects of human nature that some imagine will save us from sin's corruption. Sin degrades our reason, affections, moral sensibilities, and spiritual faculties.

Our view of sin can itself become sinfully corrupt. The reality of sin's universal corruption can also be used to argue that moral distinctions are impossible. Since all have sinned, who is to say that something is evil. Many others act as if their own guilt is theoretical. They lash out at anyone who challenges their pretensions to personal, group, or national innocence. Some single out "super sins," things so wicked and weird that they imagine that only really dissolute people would do it. People find super sins fascinating either because they find the sins alluring and an occasion for vicarious enjoyment or because they are entertained by the possibility that other people engage in things so repulsive, perverse, and unthinkable. In either case, the lurid details permit people to revel in the sin of pride, which some Christian traditions recognize as the source of many other sins. Some Christians identify sexual behavior and deviation as super sins. Others focus on sins associated with wealth, poverty, intellectual elitism, or the parochialism of the uneducated.

Notions of sin's universality should curb the tendency to externalize sin this way. It should also provoke humility, self-examination, and, when appropriate, confession and regret. When a sense of one's own sinfulness is coupled with a sense of forgiveness, we can surrender our defensiveness and efforts at self-justification.

Social Sin

Sin is universal not only because it infects every individual and debases every aspect of human nature. It is universal because its corruptions are entangled in the very fabric of our communities. Human beings are social creatures. Our lives are embedded in the sinful societies we inherit and pass on to others. Since these communities nurture us from birth, their injustice can seem natural, even beneficial.

The late-nineteenth-century social gospel leader Walter Rauschenbusch identified the concept of "social sin." By this, he meant that sin is not limited to individual acts but involves systemic injustice and corrupt structures in society.[5] He argued that these collective failures create widespread suffering and are just as damaging as personal sins.

Corporate or social sin identifies the perverse incentives that drive human behavior. Consider police misconduct. Some want to blame it on a few bad apples in the police force. Scapegoating a few officers is easy and saves us from asking why it is widespread. If we considered police misconduct not just as an individual fault (which, of course, it is) but as a social sin, it would force us to engage in the difficult work of examining and reforming models of policing, as well as departmental hiring practices, policies, and culture. It would prompt us to confront the abundance of guns in society and the fear this inspires in officers. It would lead us to address continuing racism and repair the legacy of residential segregation. In short, it would compel us to consider how we, as a society, have made police officers' jobs challenging and dangerous. Such an examination is difficult and provokes resistance from people invested in the status quo.

Commentators, recalling the concept of "original sin," talk about slavery as "America's original sin."[6] The term signals how racism predates any living person's participation or contribution to the problem. It points to how sin evolved as chattel slavery gave way to Jim Crow, redlining, and enduring alienation, leaving a world divided by residential segregation, a racial wealth gap, differences in opportunity, unconscious bias, and a host of other evils and estrangements. It suggests that these realities continue to shape how we all act, black and white. Discussion of original sin, either America's original sin or as a general concept, does not excuse the ways we contribute to the continued brokenness of the world. As with "original sin,"

5. Rauschenbusch, *Christianity and the Social Crisis.*

6. Ture and Hamilton, *Black Power.*

it acknowledges that while we did not invent sin's problems, we participate in them and have a responsibility for repairing wounds that we did not, ourselves, inflict.

Many sinful responses and choices are inspired by the way society structures the "rules of the game." Consider parents who are committed to education as a common good and, thus, available to every citizen, particularly for groups to whom it has been historically denied. Even with these convictions, they likely recognize that society treats education as a competitive good. They know that schools sort people in ways that determine educational attainment and life possibilities. This puts pressure on them to secure the best education they can for their own children. This may lead them to move to districts with better schools. As a result, they help preserve residential segregation and a lack of opportunity for the unlucky heirs of Jim Crow. Sin is universal, in part, because we can't *not* participate in a sinful society.[7]

Even when people know that the rules are rigged against others, they tend to fall in line and allow the "rules" to obscure their responsibility and guilt. Because the rules ensure privileges, beneficiaries tend to defend them. This is why American culture, which has been shaped in so many ways by the biblical imagination, hardly talks about societal sin.

The Hebrew prophets, however, did not limit their criticism to sinful individuals (corrupt kings, for instance) but pronounced God's judgment on the sins of the nation. They called the whole society to repent and interpreted the fall of Judah and Israel as God's judgment on the sinfulness of the whole nation. The fact that these events fell on the whole society prompted theological reflection about the nature of God's justice. The grief, dismay, guilt, betrayal, and anger associated with this grappling are recorded in the books of Job, Psalms, and Lamentations.

Jesus' ministry was also informed by notions of corporate sin. When he pronounced judgment on inauthentic displays of piety (Matt 23:1–36), he was not just criticizing hypocritical religious leaders but the way society institutionalized and encouraged this behavior. When Jesus condemned religious leaders for devouring widows' fortunes, he was not just criticizing particular religious leaders, but a system that refused to police this behavior.

The doctrine of corporate sin amplifies sensitivity to structural, systemic evil and its devastations. It exposes the ways we benefit from and justify evil, making it seem necessary, even "good." It forces us to recognize

7. Wallis, *America's Original Sin*.

the countless ways that society betrays its life-giving promise and falls short of God's glorious purpose. It unveils the suffering we tend to overlook and compels us to acknowledge that relatively moral people participate in immoral societies.[8] Reckoning with corporate sin should inspire us to engage in the exceedingly difficult work of reforming institutions and society.

Of course, no matter how just and fair the political-economic system, sinful individuals will exploit it. They will corrupt relatively fair systems and then seek to lock in their privileges. Consider how inequalities of wealth corrupt democracy, allowing the wealthy to spread propaganda and finance candidates who cater to their interests. America's founders foresaw this. They worried that an aristocracy would arise and destroy the republic and passed laws forbidding primogeniture (the eldest son inheriting everything in order to keep estates together).[9] Even landed gentry like Jefferson and Madison talked about breaking up large estates to ensure a middle class of yeomen farmers.[10]

Diluting Sin's Destruction

While preaching and moral exhortation are necessary, the doctrine of sin makes us skeptical that these, by themselves, are sufficient to change the hearts of the powerful, correct injustice, or protect the common good. "Good" leaders are not reliably better at resisting self-interest and responding to moral appeals than "bad" leaders. "Good" leaders feel pressured by the sinful institutions they lead. They know that if they address corporate sin and it negatively impacts stakeholders, they risk losing their jobs. If ethical instruction or the Christianization of our leaders could cure sin, there would never be a church scandal.

Rather than relying solely on moral exhortation and spiritual renewal, the doctrine of sin counsels us to address the problem of sin by diluting concentrations of power. Christian ethicists have suggested that this is best done by instituting and strengthening countervailing forces that limit, check, and balance power.

Consider the last chapter's discussion concerning the law's purpose in restraining evil. This sounds good until you realize that only sinners will do the restraining. Who restrains them? James Madison put the problem

8. Niebuhr, *Moral Man and Immoral Society.*

9. Ford, *Works of Thomas Jefferson.*

10. Boyd, *Papers of Thomas Jefferson.*

this way: "If men were angels, no government would be necessary. If angels were to govern men, neither external nor internal controls on government would be necessary."[11] This presents a conundrum, "You must first enable the government to control the governed; and in the next place, oblige it to control itself."[12] His solution for controlling the sinful, tyrannical tendencies of government officials entrusted with regulating the sinful passions of the people was to divide power in government and in society. He hoped to address sin's inevitable corruption and hold the powerful to account by setting faction against faction and ambition against ambition.

Concentrations of Power in Society

Sin opposes government becoming the totality of society. It prefers a society with a rich ecology of relatively independent "spheres": congregations, families, corporations, congregations, NGOs, the press, colleges and universities, and other institutions of civil society—so that power is divided and may be held to account. One purpose of First Amendment freedoms of religion, speech, association, and such is to ensure a plurality of institutions outside government. Sin signals alarm when state officials seek to control these institutions, anticipating that they will compel them to be subservient, eliminate any possibility of principled resistance, and prevent them from independently and efficiently fulfilling their distinct purposes.

In the same way, the principle of sin resists states taking over the means of production. It foresees that the state will play favorites, consolidate power, undermine more objective market forces, and create inefficiencies. It also knows that state ownership destroys the institutional independence required for it to enforce environmental laws, consumer protections, and worker safety standards. This is what happened in communist East Germany. They never enforced environmental laws because the government lacked independence to impose them on government-run businesses.[13]

The doctrine of sin also opposes subsuming religion under state authority. When the state "promotes" or "protects" religion, it always winds up using religion for its own purposes, blunting the prophetic impulse and persecuting minorities. Both religion and the state suffer.

11. Madison, *Writings*, 295.
12. Madison, *Writings*, 295.
13. Rink, *Environmental Policy*, 73–91.

Similarly, unchecked economic power will exploit and endanger workers, as well as jeopardize the environment, consumers, and public health. The doctrine of sin has sought to remedy these inevitabilities through governmental regulation. It has also encouraged labor to organize and companies to give workers a stake in company ownership. When a monopoly is inevitable in an industry (e.g., a power company), the doctrine of sin has established government oversight to prevent excessive profiteering and protect the public good.

In the same way, the principle of sin opposes monopolies that dominate selling and monopsonies that control buying, foreseeing that those who capture markets will manipulate them for their private benefit, to the detriment of others. In recent years, the media has become concentrated in the hands of a few giant corporations. Laws that once prevented a single company from dominating particular media markets have been abolished. Fairness doctrines have been rescinded. Limits on the number of radio or television stations a company may own have been relaxed. A few social media corporations control the algorithms that determine what users see. The result is that a handful of corporations and oligarchs control the media landscape and have outsized influence over public discourse.[14] The principle of sin would reverse this trend.

Concentrations of Power in Institutions

The principle of restraining sin by diluting power favors mechanisms of transparency and accountability to temper concentrations of power within institutions. This has special relevance for democratic government. The doctrine of sin supports reporting requirements, whistleblower protections, freedom of information laws, oversight boards, ethics watchdogs, inspector generals, the rule of law, the separation of powers, judicial review, congressional oversight committees, and a free press. It triggers pushback when leaders undermine the independence of the judicial and legislative branches, or when they wield regulatory, police, and prosecutorial powers for personal and political gain. It warns that where these are compromised, sinners will accumulate power, destroy republican government, and ravage the commonwealth.

The doctrine of sin gives us reasons to generally hold procedural goods superior to substantive goods. In other words, it maintains that the

14. Newman, "Overview and Key Findings."

democratic process (a procedural good) is more important than the particular decisions the process yields concerning things like roads, particular laws, etc. (substantive goods).

The doctrine of sin predicts that sinful people will follow democratic processes and make sinful choices. This is how fascists and other authoritarians get elected. However, it hopes that, if procedural goods remain intact, if power is divided, transparent, and responsive to the people, the people can later choose a better course. Consider how First Amendment freedoms and other democratic goods allowed the US to reverse policy in Vietnam. Given the superiority of procedural goods, we should continue to honor, uphold, and perfect them even when our candidates and issues are defeated. There are times when protecting democracy requires us to vote against our preferred political party and policy outcomes.

The democratic process can be frustrating, but we should not lose patience. Building political consensus is hard, long work. But we should trust that, over the long haul, democratic procedural goods are the best means to secure substantive goods and justice. Pursuing substantive goods at the expense of protecting procedural goods likely means that we get neither.

Finally, the doctrine of sin resists concentrations of unchecked power within religious institutions. It resists congregational structures that are incapable of holding charismatic congregational leaders accountable. It opposes episcopacies that do not answer to the people. In these ways, the doctrine of sin seeks to ameliorate the inevitable problems that accompany unchecked power by instituting countervailing powers and placing interest against interest.

Realism

The doctrine of sin inspires a sober realism that speaks to what is attainable and how it should be attained. Sin's realism questions overly idealistic ambitions. It recognizes, for example, that while eliminating all nuclear weapons would be highly desirable, it is unlikely to happen. Far from being a counsel to despair, sin's realism pushes us to build and maintain stable, transparent, and reliable systems of deterrence and détente (including inspection regimes, hotlines, more stabilizing delivery systems, de-targeting weapons, trust-building exercises, etc.). While sin's realism will be inclined to reduce nuclear arsenals, it also recognizes that if nuclear security guarantees lose their credibility, nations that depended on these guarantees may build their own nuclear weapons. This could, perversely, wind up being more destabilizing. Realism acknowledges the nobility of wanting to eliminate nuclear weapons and it knows that, until that day arrives, it is more important to ensure that they are never used.[15]

Sin's realism not only challenges dreams of resolving the problem of sin in human history, it also informs approaches to overcoming social sin. Reinhold Niebuhr observed, "The children of light have not been as wise as the children of darkness. . . . The children of light are foolish not merely because they underestimate the power of self-interest among the children of darkness. They underestimate this power among themselves."[16] Sin's realism questions narratives of out-group guilt and in-group innocence. It further teaches that if the human sinfulness of all parties is not anticipated, including the sinfulness of the reformers, reforms will fail. Again, this is not a counsel to despair. The forces of evil do not determine our ultimate destiny. It is to this possibility that we turn.

15. Roberts, "Keep the INF Treaty."

16. Niebuhr, *Children of Light*, 11.

Chapter Nine

Hope and the Possibilities of History

> Who hopes for what he already has?
>
> —Romans 8:24

Sin devastates personalities, communities, and creation. It fosters indifference to the humiliation and suffering of others and inflames hatreds that culminate in atrocities. It corrupts communities, leading to systematic dehumanization and methodical destruction. Its desolations are simultaneously monstrous and petty.

The persistence of sin's corruption is fatiguing. The inevitable and unending lies, malfeasance, and waste exhaust us. We tire of dysfunction, brokenness, and death. The powerless and oppressed are especially weary. This is why people in every time and place ask: Must it always be this way? Are sin, evil, alienation, and death our destiny? Are struggles for peace, justice, and flourishing losing battles? Is there any reason to hope things can change for the better?

Inevitable Eschatologies

These questions are universal and insistent. Not everyone hopes that things will improve, but everyone develops a sense of what is possible in history. In this chapter, we call this sense of history's possibilities an "eschatology." By this, we mean something broader and more universal than Christian theology's use of the term, which refers to teachings about last things and the end of the world. Although we will be surveying Christian teachings on these things, we first note that, in this general sense, eschatologies are inevitable. Everyone has a view of what is possible in history. Furthermore, their assessments reflect judgments of how the forces of goodness relate to the forces of evil.

Although everyone can transcend their moment in time to speculate on the meaning and direction of history, no one can grasp either the whole of history or wholly appreciate the ultimate significance of any event in history. This is why every hope, religious or otherwise, involves faith. When one trusts goodness to overcome evil, one is led to hope. When one doubts that the forces of goodness can bear the faith that has been placed in them, one becomes disillusioned. When one concludes that goodness cannot triumph over evil, the result is despair, cynicism, and, sometimes, nihilism.

Hope requires faith. This is because sin and evil are ever-present and the evidence for hope is always mixed. We may be encouraged by examples of moral courage and progress, only to be discouraged by revanchist movements and widespread apathy when hard-won achievements are dismantled. If sin is the most empirical doctrine, hope frequently seems counterfactual. As the apostle Paul observed, "Who hopes for what he has?" (Rom 8:24).

Religious Eschatologies

Many religious traditions hope for the triumph of goodness over evil. Schools of Judaic thought, for example, promote visions of a Messiah who will establish God's rule. Similarly, Muslims await the coming of the Mahdi, or "Guided One," expecting him to appear with Jesus, perhaps at a time of great turmoil. The Mahdi will establish the global kingdom of Islam and bring truth, righteousness, and justice to the world.

Buddhism, with its cycles of reincarnation and its view that the material world is not ultimately real, is almost ahistorical. Yet forms of

Buddhism await the appearance of the Maitreya (Sanskrit) or Metteyya (Pali). The Maitreya is the successor to the Buddha. He is a Bodhisattva (an "enlightened one" who, out of compassion, has postponed his ascension to Nirvana), who is waiting in heaven to be reborn. Some believe that the Maitreya's rebirth will occur after a period of general moral deterioration and that he will bring a new era of enlightenment and peace.

Although there are similarities, these religions are not calling the same messiah by a different name. Each vision is developed out of a distinct narrative and tradition. Indeed, there are divergent schools of thought within Judaism, Islam, and Buddhism concerning the meaning of these hopes. Each school holds a distinctive understanding of the nature of the human problem, what the faithful may expect, and the significance of religious hope for present life.

Not every religion has a linear view of history that ends well. Hinduism has a cyclical view of time wherein history moves through four consecutive cycles called "yugas." Together, these constitute a larger cosmic cycle called the *mahayuga*, which is thought to last some four million years. According to the Puranas, each age gets progressively worse, declining from Satya, the age of enlightenment, to the final age, the one we are in now, the Kali Yuga, an age of corruption and death. The Kali Yuga closes when Kalki appears. He is the final incarnation of Vishnu and will destroy the wicked. Kalki's purge and purification will commence a new Satya age, and the *mahayuga* will repeat.

Many Greek and Latin Stoics also shared a cyclical view of history. Like the Hindu version, it did not envision historical progress but decline. The Stoic view envisioned continued deterioration until the universe is destroyed in a conflagration called an *ekpyrosis*. Following this, the cosmos is reborn, and a new cycle ensues. This is the source of the Stoic concept of the "eternal return." Like more linear and hopeful views of history, these cyclical views of cosmic history locate people in a moral universe, though they present quite different possibilities for the near future and what it requires of us. The diversity of viewpoints suggest that everyone must locate themselves in the flux of time amidst the forces of good and evil. Eschatologies are inevitable.

Non-Religious Eschatologies

Eschatologies need not be overtly religious. Communism, for instance, purported to give a "scientific" account of history. It cast history as an evolving conflict between oppressor and oppressed classes, shaped by the means of production. With the advent of agriculture, hunter-gatherer communalism gave way to feudalism and conflict between lords and peasants. With industrialization, feudal conflicts gave way to capitalism and conflict between the bourgeoisie and the proletariat. Communists believe that the forces of historical materialism will culminate in an apocalyptic confrontation between workers and owners. The result will be the abolition of capitalist exploitation and the emergence of a utopian communist society. This society promises to be a classless workers' paradise, free from oppression. This hope gave Communism its power and functioned as a call to action.

For most of US history, Americans have interpreted the national purpose against a background of belief in human progress.[1] Bolstered by the scientific and technological conquest of nature, American optimism extended triumphs over despotism, ignorance, and illiberalism into the future. This hope has taken on religious, quasi-religious, and secular meanings. The US dollar bill, for example, bears the phrase *novum ordo seclorum*, "a new order for the ages." This phrase celebrates the establishment of the United States, with its principles of human and democratic rights, as introducing a new era of republican governance. At its best, this hope gave the nation a purpose larger than itself. It motivated the nation to get its own house in order so it could set an example for the world. It also inspired US leaders to work with other liberal democracies to spread democracy and human rights, pursue a "law-based" global order, and ameliorate poverty, ignorance, and disease.

Because nationalistic hopes so easily decay into idolatry, they tend to become demonic. That is, they become a spirit that possesses a people, inspiring them to do evil. Nationalistic hopes have fed an unwarranted sense of national innocence.[2] This has prevented an honest reckoning with the past and encouraged the demonization of geopolitical rivals and domestic political opponents. Blowback directed at those who question whitewashed versions of history testify to the investment people make in protecting the perceived virtue of the objects that bear their trust and hope.

1. Niebuhr, *Faith and History*, 1.
2. Niebuhr, *Irony of American History*.

Nationalistic hopes can also blind a nation to its limits. Following the attacks of 9/11, they were marshaled to justify "the Freedom Agenda" and fruitless wars to spread democracy in the Middle East. Misguided as those adventures were, the recent deterioration of nationalistic hope into cynicism and nihilism portends a willingness to abandon human and democratic rights at home, withdraw from humanitarian efforts, ignore international law, and engage in evil adventures abroad.

Eschatologies do not need to be well developed. Many adopt vague optimisms. Perhaps they dream of a future along the lines of Star Trek, hoping that human beings will overcome their differences and boldly explore new worlds. Others place their hope in genetic manipulation, fancying that we can improve human nature and hasten the evolution of a better society.[3] Artificial intelligence has prompted hopes of human progress as well as dread of authoritarian dystopia, human obsolescence, and extinction.

Still, others give up on history. Beleaguered people are always tempted to embrace despair. Faced with entrenched wickedness and a tsunami of lies, people surrender their dreams of a better world. They abandon the costly, risky work of seeking justice and resign themselves to iniquity, inequity, and dehumanization. Some philosophies embrace materialisms that deny the reality of anything beyond nature and reject the possibility of moral progress. Ignoring the dramas of history, many indulge in Epicurean pleasures.

Most just try to survive. They narrow their efforts to personal peace and advancement. Widespread capitulation and inertia discourage those who seek a better world, making their task more difficult. Still, the point remains: when it comes to eschatology, everybody's got one.

Varieties of Christian Millennialism

As is self-evident from the name—"Christ" coming from the Greek word for the Hebrew *messiah*—Christianity is a messianic religion. It has inspired a number of approaches to the possibility of hope in history, including various types of Christian millenarianism. Millennialism takes its name from a passage in Revelation where an angel locks up a dragon for one thousand years (a millennium) to prevent it from deceiving the nations, leading them to do evil (Rev 20:1–10). This is said to be the time of Christ's millennial

3. Wilson, *On Human Nature*, 208.

reign. We will survey types of Christian millennialism to introduce what has become the mainstream Christian approach.

Premillennialism

Premillennial Christianity, with its cherry-picked biblical proof texts, revolving candidates for antichrist, and ever-updated timelines, looks for Christ's return in history. In the near term. As in, this could happen at any moment. They do not interpret Christ's delayed appearance as making it less probable. Rather, they believe his delay signals that his *parousia* (literally "appearance" or "presence") is nearer than ever.

Premillennialists tend to get excited when things get worse. The advent of nuclear weapons made premillennialism plausible for many mid-twentieth-century Protestants. The possibility of global conflagration was greeted as a sign that Christ was coming soon. Some premillennialists believe that Christ will rapture and rescue believers before the coming tribulation. Others, doubting this, devote themselves to learning survival skills, building bunkers, and stockpiling resources to save their own from the coming social disintegration and violence.

As one might imagine, the conviction that this world is passing away cuts the nerve of human responsibility for environmental and social improvement. Premillennialists routinely ignore the explicit teachings of Christ and take a limited view of human responsibility. They have every incentive to allow things like climate change and nuclear tensions to deteriorate.

Postmillennialism

Whereas premillennialism fosters a passive, privatized approach to human responsibility, postmillennialists shoulder the burdens of history. Postmillennialists believe that God calls them to usher in Christ's millennial rule. During the Reformation, postmillennial hopes inspired a number of groups to take up the sword to inaugurate Christ's earthly kingdom. For example, in 1525, Thomas Müntzer led the German Peasants' War to establish earthly Christ's rule.

Other postmillennialists take a decidedly more peaceful, ethical approach. They believe that if believers are faithful, the world will become increasingly Christlike until Christ returns to reign. Postmillennial hopes inspired a number of American social gospelers in the late nineteenth century's progressive movement. Walter Rauschenbusch, for example, encouraged Christians to "Christianize the social order" by bringing the ethics of Jesus and the kingdom of God to bear on labor relations, government corruption, and other social ills.[4] Though his own views were more complex, the closing paragraph of his book *Christianity and the Social Crisis* rings with postmillennial confidence: "If at this juncture we can rally sufficient religious faith and moral strength to snap the bonds of evil and turn the present unparalleled economic and intellectual resources of humanity to the harmonious development of a true social life, the generations yet unborn will mark this as the great day of the Lord, for which the ages waited and counted us blessed for sharing in the apostolate that proclaimed it."[5]

Rauschenbusch was not alone. In 1900, the editors of *The Christian Oracle* changed the name of the magazine to *The Christian Century*, reflecting "the prevailing mood of early twentieth century US Protestantism—namely, one of triumphal optimism regarding Christianity's influence on society."[6] They hoped the twentieth century would be a Christian century.

Amillennialism

Mainstream Christian thought (Catholic or Protestant) has not taken the New Testament's millennial promises literally for two millennia. Rather, they have taken to heart Jesus' admonition that "nobody knows the day or the hour." They heeded Jesus' advice not to be distracted by political and geological upheaval, moral disintegration, the appearance of "abominations," or people who claim that the Messiah has come (Mark 13).

Resistance to literal interpretations of the millennial promises can be traced to the third-century theologian Augustine. In his influential take on Christianity, politics, and history, *The City of God*, he recommends interpreting the promises symbolically. With many examples, he notes the Bible's tendency to use "days" to mean "time" and a "thousand" to mean "beyond counting." He recommends that we interpret the millennia in Rev 20 as "a perfect number to designate the whole of time," similar to how 99 percent of people use 100 to represent a totality.[7]

4. Rauschenbusch, *Christianizing the Social Order*.
5. Rauschenbusch, *Christianity and the Social Crisis*, 422.
6. Christian Century, "About Us."
7. Augustine, *City of God*, 400.

Augustine's approach discourages the premillennialist impulse to view the present moment as resting precariously on the cusp of Christ's return and the temptation to read too much into momentous events like the sack of Rome, which inspired him to write *The City of God*. He discouraged speculation, insisting that "the experience of the actual events will teach us then far more fully than any human intelligence can grasp them now."[8] Instead, he invited people to view the present time, between Christ's coming and the end of history, as a *seclorum* or "age." Augustine also discourages premillennialist tendencies to narrow and privatize their moral concerns by urging his readers to seek the welfare of the earthly city. His emphasis on the last judgment has countered tendencies to ignore Jesus' teachings.

At the same time, Augustine's approach discourages postmillennial utopianism. He insisted that the earthly city can never achieve the justice promised in eternal life. Referencing Jesus' parable of the wheat and the tares (or weeds), he says that good and evil must grow together for now (not just coexist), but that they will be separated at the harvest or last judgment (Matt 13:24–30). While possibilities for goodness abound, the tares cannot be all removed.[9] This realism about sin makes postmillennial hopes of ushering in Christ's reign fanciful.

Perhaps it is inevitable that many Christians throw Augustine's counsel to the wind and enthusiastically speculate about the future. Like everyone else, they spin hope out of their sense of how the forces of good relate to the forces of evil. Yet, Augustine's views, sometimes called "amillennialism" (meaning, literally, "no millennia"), remain immensely influential on Catholic and Protestant thought.

Christ as the Meaning of History

The experience of the risen Christ framed the New Testament writers' presentation of Jesus and continues to shape the church's perception of how God relates to the forces of evil. Among other meanings, the confession that Jesus is "the Christ," or Messiah, suggests that his life is the event in history that discloses the pattern of the whole. As the Christ, Jesus is viewed as pointing to the "now" of God's redeeming kingdom and to the "not yet" of redemption's fulfillment at the end of time.

8. Augustine, *City of God*, 445.

9. Augustine, *City of God*, 394.

Redemption refers to God's work of delivering creation from sin, evil, and its effects. The most literal meaning of redemption is regaining possession of something or someone in exchange for a payment. In addition to this image, the broad theological tradition has assembled numerous other metaphors to describe how God amends sin and its consequences. Redemption means reconciliation where there is alienation, liberation where there is bondage, salvation where there is peril, forgiveness where there is condemnation, healing where there is brokenness, reorientation where people are lost, justification where people are out of line, an enlargement of concern where sin's astringent has contracted it, and new life where there is death.[10] These metaphors describe God's loving response to the plight of God's creation and inspire hope in the face of persistent sin and evil. They invite and guide participation in the redeeming work of God.

The "Now" of God's Redeeming Rule

Christians do not believe that God's redeeming is limited to Jesus, but they do believe that God's redeeming work has a Christ-shaped character. Jesus did not proclaim himself but declared, "The kingdom of God is at hand, repent and believe the good news" (Mark 1:15). Consistent with the biblical prophets, Jesus characterized God's action in history as an all-encompassing government through which God rules, judges, and redeems the world. This theocentric perspective reframes how one views the relative power, goodness, and possibilities of the other actors in history, on whom and through whom God is working. Jesus paired this announcement with an invitation to align one's life with God's reign. With this summons, Jesus indicated that God is the decisive actor to whom they must answer, not the Roman occupation, the religious leaders, or any other power in their lives.

This was Jesus' central message, and he returned to this theme repeatedly throughout his ministry, illustrating God's rule with parables and other teachings. He demonstrated God's rule in his ministry of healing, exorcism, teaching, feeding the hungry, eating with sinners, welcoming outcasts, challenging the powerful, and forgiving his enemies. The teachings and example of Jesus guide his followers in seeking first the kingdom

10. Author credits Douglas Ottati for observing the relationship between metaphors for sin and metaphors for redemption in a private conversation. The depiction here reflects the author's flawed memory.

of God in the present. They also foreshadow the consummation of God's rule at the end of history.

A full exploration of what Jesus' life and ministry reveal about the character of Christian hope is beyond the scope of this chapter. That said, Jesus' identification with the lowly and the outcast is so central to the gospels and so frequently ignored that we should not pass over it. The gospel of Luke puts special emphasis on this point. Luke's birth narrative introduces Jesus by featuring Mary's Magnificat, a revolutionary song about God bringing down the mighty and lifting up the humble (Luke 1:46–55). Immediately after this, Luke shows God lifting up humble, low-caste shepherds by sending angels to invite them to witness the "Lord's birth" at the manger. Luke reinforces this by telling us that Jesus began his ministry by quoting Isaiah: "The Spirit of the Lord has anointed me to preach good news to the poor, liberty to the prisoners, recovery of sight for the blind, to set the oppressed free, and to declare the year of Jubilee" (a year when debts are forgiven) (Luke 4:18–19). Later, Luke tells us that Jesus "went down" to a level place to deliver a sermon in which he pronounced blessings on the poor and woe to the rich (Luke 6:17–26). Jesus tells the parable of a rich man, who, for decades, ignored the suffering of a destitute man named Lazarus (which means "God is my helper") and how their roles were reversed in the afterlife (Luke 16:19–31). Luke carried the theme of radical redistribution into his account of the early church, where he tells us that the early church "held all things in common and none had any need" (Acts 2:44–45).

Jesus' concern for the lowly is portrayed in every gospel and echoes throughout the New Testament. His concern is consistent with God's concern for the Hebrew slaves in Egypt and the biblical prophets who decried inequality and the way the powerful "grind the face of the poor" (Isa 3:15). Authentic Christian hope cannot ignore God's intention to deliver us from evil by overturning dehumanizing oppression and poverty. This should not lead us to idealize or romanticize poverty but should encourage a preference for lifting the poor into the middle classes.

The cross may be the clearest expression of Jesus' identification with "the least of these" (Matt 25). The world is full of literal crosses like the Roman instrument of torturous death. The world is also full of metaphorical crosses on which innocents suffer for the sins of the guilty. Ambitious political leaders send soldiers to die in battle.[11] Rapacious pharmaceutical companies addict people to opioids. Greedy polluters cause cancer. Parents abuse their children.

11. Niebuhr, "War as Judgment of God," 63–70.

Factory farms treat animals as if they were insensate automatons. The Gospels depict Jesus as sharing the victims' experience of betrayal, violence, suffering, and death. Mark's and Matthew's Gospels recount Jesus' crying, "My God, my God, why have you forsaken me," suggesting that Jesus' agony not only involved physical pain but emotional anguish. Since this cry was uttered by God's own son, Christians have interpreted it as indicating that no one is God-forsaken. The suffering of the innocents reveals the meaning of Jesus' suffering, showing us, that God has freely and purposefully joined them in their agony. Similarly, Jesus' suffering lends meaning to the suffering of the innocents, showing us that they are not God-forsaken, and that the God of resurrection holds their destiny, not the guilty who crucify them.

We are so familiar with the cross that it is hard to imagine how astonishing it was to the ancients. The Greeks had little trouble believing that God took human form. Their gods did that all the time. Rather, the ancients found it incredible that the Son of God would become a servant and voluntarily die on a Roman cross.[12] This is why Paul tells us, "The cross is foolishness to the Greeks" (1 Cor 1:23). The centrality of the cross in every Gospel narrative suggests that the writers leaned into this absurdity.

At the same time, because they believed Christ had been raised, they did not depict Jesus as a hapless victim. Instead, his life and death is portrayed as somehow redeeming. The church developed the New Testament's nascent ideas into "theories" for how this might work. As the term "theories" suggests, these set forth avenues for understanding the mystery of God's justice and mercy in the cross and resurrection, and what it does for believers. While an exploration of these theories is beyond the scope of this chapter, one can intuit how the incarnation and resurrection support the hope that God acts in history to redeem. They signal that God does not abandon the persecuted, suffering, and dying. If sin, evil, and death did not determine Jesus' destiny, they do not determine ours.

The "Not Yet" of Redemption's Consummation

The New Testament's emphasis on the "now" of Jesus' summons to seek first the dominion of God is balanced by the anticipation of the consummation of God's rule at the end of time. The New Testament depicts this "not yet" dimension of hope with numerous symbols. Theologian Wolfhart Pannenberg advises that, whatever one thinks of their literal meaning, one

12. Holland, *Dominion*.

should not "infer the unreality of the matter from the metaphorical form of statement."[13] In a similar vein, theologian Reinhold Niebuhr observes that while many modern people find these symbols embarrassing, they are necessary for a Christian interpretation of history.[14] For example, the New Testament's extravagant description of the New Jerusalem, replete with images of pearly gates, jasper walls, jewel-encrusted foundations, streets paved with gold, and eternal light, symbolizes the discontinuity between temporal and eternal life. The prospect of a shining city filled with the divine presence, devoid of poverty, and overflowing with compassion and abundance was intended to encourage the faithful.

By contrast, the "resurrection of the body" signals continuity between this life and the next. It differs from views that minimize aspects of human existence, perhaps by limiting eternal significance to that part of human existence called an "immortal soul." In contrast to this, the resurrection points to the transfiguration and consummation of bodily life.[15] It signals that temporal life matters and is, somehow, redeemed.

"Eternal life" symbolizes life's significance in a world where death not only annihilates the *intrinsic* meaning of temporal life but also the meaning *derived* in reference to some other aspect of life. For example, when a soldier marches off to battle, they and their loved ones may derive significance from the nation and its cause. However, death soon consigns nations and their causes to the ash heap of history as well.[16] Every person, movement, cause, nation, culture, species, and even life on this planet faces extinction.[17] Death threatens to annul every life and render every achievement absurd. In the face of this, the promise of eternal life signals that there is meaning untouched by death.[18] It lends significance to the present by pointing to life's ultimate fulfillment in God's goodness, justice, and glory. This is why the Gospel of John describes eternal life not as infinite time but as abundant life (John 10:10).

The New Testament anticipates Christ's triumphal return at the end of history to judge the living and the dead. This image expresses confidence in God's victory over sin, evil, and death, as well as God's sovereignty over the

13. Pannenberg, *Systematic Theology*, 621.

14. Niebuhr, *Faith and History*, 214.

15. Niebuhr, *Faith and History*, 237

16. Neibuhr, *Faith and History*, 87.

17. Niebuhr, *Theology, History, and Culture*, 84.

18. Tillich, *Interpretation of History*, 278.

historical process.[19] The "antichrist" symbolizes any actor or movement with messianic pretensions that defies God's redeeming purpose. It can also be read as a caution against a common form of syncretism (blending the sacred and profane). Specifically, it warns against advancing national, ecclesial, and egoistic purposes in the name of Christ. The concept of the antichrist names this insidious, deceptive form of idolatry as explicitly evil.[20]

The "last judgment" carries multiple meanings. It depicts judgment being passed on everyone, not just those we deem evil, fosters humility. Even moral victories must pass through the judgment. As the *last* judgment, it alerts us to the fact that all our judgments concerning history are provisional. It also reminds us that history's executors of judgment are incapable of banishing evil.[21] Believers welcome the prospect of judgment because they trust that Christ, who judges, is also our gracious Redeemer. As such, they expect God's judgment to be an event of purification, liberation, and reconciliation with God and others.

The vision of a "new heavens and a new earth" signifies the broad scope of God's redemption. It reinforces apostle Paul's view that God was in Christ reconciling "all things" (Col 1:20) or reconciling the "cosmos" (2 Cor 5:19). It indicates that believers should not cherish hope solely for themselves but should hope in the cause of God that embraces all of life.[22]

Together, these images of God's "not yet" consummated kingdom protest evil's dehumanization and destruction. Even though the fullness of God's triumph is pushed out to the close of the age, it is thought to disclose the general pattern of history. God's vindication of history's meaning at the end of time provides a framework for interpreting the significance of the present moment, including its victories and defeats. These images lift us out of the present and provide critical distance for viewing the causes and leaders who bear our hopes. They help us resist utopian illusions and save us from the hubris of thinking that salvation from evil finally depends on us. Although they reject the idea that we will live to see the ultimate triumph of God, they promise that we *will* see it, saving us from the despair of thinking that sin, evil, and death hold our destiny. This hope fosters patient endurance and a defiant refusal to concede to evil. It empowers believers to take the risks and make the sacrifices that love requires.

19. Niebuhr, *Nature and Destiny*, 290.

20. Niebuhr, *Faith and History*, 235.

21. Niebuhr, *Faith and History*, 215.

22. Pannenberg, *Systematic Theology*, 179.

Hopeful Realism

Karl Marx famously observed that when religious hope is pushed entirely off to the afterlife, it becomes otherworldly. It is drained of its transforming power and is reduced to a psychic compensation for present humiliation and hardship. It becomes, he said, "the sigh of the oppressed creature" and "the opiate of the people."[23] Of course, the powerful prefer that people place their hope in the next life. They do not want their subjects dreaming that change is possible, lest it inspire them to challenge current social, political, and economic arrangements. As we will touch on in chapter 12, throughout history, the powerful have invested in state religion, insisted on appointing religious leaders, and persecuted religious dissenters. King James I of England, for example, suppressed the printing and distribution of the Geneva Bible because it suggested that the people had a right to depose tyrants and threatened the divine right of kings. In every civilization, the powerful require religion to supply the metaphysical and moral justification for their authority.

In light of Marx's criticism, it is worth asking what Christians can hope for now, in the near term, where our agency matters. What does Christian hope believe is possible and lead us to attempt? Theologian Douglas Ottati outlines a position he calls "hopeful realism." He describes this as "an orienting posture or practical stance that refuses both easy optimisms and cynical pessimisms."[24] He says that hopeful realism is shaped by the interweaving of four theological convictions: creation, sin, judgment, and redemption. Reviewing these can provide a more granular understanding of the possibilities that lie before us.

Creation and Redemption

As we saw in chapter 5, creation affirms the world's goodness. It holds that the origin of evil does not lie in nature but is a historical development made possible by creaturely freedom. Rather than a divine principle opposed to God, evil is merely a corrupted creature. This metaphysical difference reinforces a sense of God's potency relative to the historical process. Redemption echoes creation's optimism with its depiction of God's promise

23. Marx and Engels, *Basic Writings*, 263.

24. Ottati, *Theology for the Twenty-First Century*, 636.

to deliver creation from sin, evil, and its effects. Together, these lead us out of and away from "cynical pessimism."

Convictions about the power of God relative to evil provide a powerful antidote to the fatalism, helplessness, and despair people inevitably feel when they face entrenched sin. When nineteenth-century pastor and abolitionist Theodore Parker faced the evil of slavery and the seemingly insurmountable obstacles to overturning it, he drew on this hope, saying, "I do not pretend to understand the moral universe; the arc is a long one, my eye reaches but little ways. I cannot calculate the curve and complete the figure by the experience of sight; I can divine it by conscience. But from what I see I am sure it bends towards justice."[25] This was reiterated by Martin Luther King Jr. when he said, "The arc of the moral universe is long, but it bends toward justice,"[26] as he faced a majority white population in the Southern states that supported, or was indifferent to, the evils of Jim Crow. The counsel that the moral arc is long moderates hopes of immediate success. It prepares people for the protracted, difficult work of social justice. At the same time, hope that the moral arc bends to justice means that the toil and sacrifice are not futile. If God really is a power and presence governing history, judging sin, and redeeming the world from evil, then evil does not stand a chance. God is bending the moral arc of the universe at every moment. Without such hope, it is hard to imagine that movements for social change would ever get off the ground.

Sin and Redemption

In chapter 8, we noted that sin contributes realism about people, movements, and institutions. The principle of sin imparts a pragmatism regarding the self, one's leaders, communities, and causes. It resists giving unchecked power to those who bear our hopes. It insists that programs for social, political, and economic improvement reflect the reality of the chronic human tendency to corruption. Realism about sin pairs with the "not yet" aspect of redemption to reject "easy optimisms." It resists perfectionist rhetoric and utopian agendas, and the correlating temptation to demonize one's political opponents and rivals.

While the moral arc of the universe may bend toward justice, the doctrine of sin and the "not yet" of redemption's fulfillment tell us that no

25. Parker, *Ten Sermons*, 84.

26. King, "Remaining Awake," para. 21.

moral victory is permanent. In this age, sinners will always be working to bend the moral arc to injustice. Progress is not inevitable. It will not be achieved without conflict. Although God is bending the moral arc of the universe, the moral arc will not fully conform to God's justice until redemption's consummation at the end of history. Even then, every moral victory must pass through the last judgment.

Judgment and Redemption

Redemption is predicated on God's judgment of sin, evil, and death, for if God judged everything "fine," God would not need to redeem. In the popular imagination, when the idea of God's judgment is not ignored entirely, it is viewed as God meting out punishment—if not in this life, then in the life to come. We assume the guilty will get what's coming to them. We imagine that God's judgment mirrors the crosses of the thieves who were crucified with Jesus. The thought of divine retribution has inspired generations of artists to paint lurid portraits of hell where God inflicts punishment on the guilty.

While the Bible sometimes depicts judgment as the just punishment of sinners, there are good theological reasons for thinking that notions of divine vengeance are inadequate. For one thing, it is hard to square vindictiveness with the notion that God is love. For another, if we understand that God is the ordering power of the universe who works through the structures of creation, God's judgment is the impersonal consequence on those who stray from the divine order of things. There are penalties for ignoring justice and abusing the environment. When parents abuse their children, they will likely bear consequences. Their children and society certainly will.

This brings us to another reason for thinking that vengeance inadequately encapsulates God's judgment: the consequences of sin usually fall upon the innocent.[27] Consider the crucifixions mentioned earlier, when war's pains fall upon the innocent, pharmaceutical companies addict people to opioids, or polluters cause cancer. The innocent suffer most, not the guilty.

Believers can only begin to make sense of this because they believe that Christ is the Innocent One who suffered for the sins of the guilty. They believe that his cross, not the crosses of the thieves, is the decisive judgment for humankind. Theologian H. Richard Niebuhr explained that Christ's cross

27. Niebuhr, *War in the Twentieth Century*, 47.

> is the final, convincing demonstration of the fact that the order of the universe is not one of retribution in which goodness is rewarded and evil punished, but rather an order of graciousness wherein, as Jesus had observed, the sun is made to shine on evil and on good and the rain to descend on the just and the unjust.[28]

This gracious order reframes our understanding of God's judgment and redemption. Because Jesus did not call down the armies of heaven to vanquish his enemies but asked God to forgive those who crucified him, Christians view the cross as disarming violence, draining the poison of retribution, and disclosing the suffering love of God. God turns his cross from an instrument of torture and death into an instrument of life.

Believing that Christ bears our judgment, we sense our forgiveness. We've been justified. This relieves us of the compulsion to be self-defensive, as if we must or can justify ourselves to the universe or to others. As we face our guilt and accept our forgiveness, we find it harder to excuse the temptation to execute judgment on our sinful enemies. We, too, have fallen short of God's glory. When we discover that the deep order of the universe is grace, we can begin to leave vindictiveness behind. In the same way that God did not abandon the thieves on the crosses, we hope that the guilty can be redeemed. When we must use force to maintain a just and peaceable societal order, it should be free of retribution. We are not instruments of God's vengeance (Rom 12:19).

Christians believe that the resurrection also discloses God's judgment. By raising Jesus, God passed judgment on a miscarriage of justice and overturned an irreversible sentence: death. God affirmed Jesus' ministry and teaching, including his solidarity with those who suffer.

Christians believe that the cross and resurrection demonstrate that the universe is not indifferent. Because God is love, God suffers.[29] Jesus is present wherever "the least of these" appears God-forsaken (Matt 25:31–46). His presence confirms that the suffering of the innocent represents God's judgment on the sins of the guilty. His companionship in suffering is the source of the believer's hope. He enables us to persevere despite our inability to see around history's bend and perceive the curvature of history's moral arc. If one imagines that the suffering innocent bear witness to God's judgment, there is only one possible response: Repent and participate in God's work of redeeming the world from sin and evil. It is to this vocation that we now turn.

28. Niebuhr, *War in the Twentieth Century*, 68.

29. Moltmann, *Crucified God*.

Chapter Ten

Vocation and Human Purpose

> Whatever task you must do, work as if your soul depends on it, as for the Lord and not for people.
>
> —COLOSSIANS 3:23

IN THE BEGINNING WAS the work.

According to Genesis, work is woven into the very fabric of life. The first creation myth depicts God working six days to create the world. The second creation myth has God forming the humans from the earth, planting a garden, and entrusting humans with the task of caring for God's garden (Gen 2:15). Work is depicted as both the means of creation and a gift of God's good creation.

Work can be a blessing. The fruits of one's labor can be sweet. Maybe you have experienced the good tired that can follow a day of hard labor, enjoyed the camaraderie of coworkers, felt success and accomplishment at a job well-done, or discovered meaning and purpose when you contribute and play a role in society.

Despite its initial positivity, the Bible quickly acknowledges that people experience work as a curse. After Adam and Eve eat from the tree of knowledge of good and evil, God outlines a number of consequences. In addition to painful labor during childbirth, God says, "Cursed is the ground because of you; in toil you shall eat of it all the days of your life;

thorns and thistles it shall bring forth for you . . . By the sweat of your face you shall eat bread until you return to the ground, for out of it you were taken; you are dust, and to dust you shall return" (Gen 3:17–19). The toil is bad enough; the futility makes it worse.

Work can be difficult; other people can make it harder. Worse than the challenging employee, colleague, or customer are those who exploit the labor of others. Looming over the whole Bible and shaping its imagination at every turn is the experience of slavery in Egypt. When the Hebrews were slaves in Egypt, most of their work consisted of the toil Pharaoh didn't want to do. Slavery negatively impacted work in other ways. It limited the agency of the enslaved. If Pharaoh said they must make bricks and did not provide straw to bind the mud, they were forced to gather their own straw (Exod 5). If Pharaoh said they could not take time to worship God, they worked every day without rest (Exod 7). Pharaoh's wish was their directive.

As the principle of sin would predict, the inequality inherent in the institution of slavery, then and now, encourages cruelty and dehumanization. Many slaves are treated as little more than beasts. They are abused until they display learned helplessness. To justify their dominant position over time, owners concoct myths of supremacy, including scientific racism and racialized religion. These myths become institutionalized in caste systems and enslaving institutions. They are reinforced by the dehumanization associated with poverty, malnutrition, disease, a lack of education, and economic and social insecurity that prevent people from developing the full potential of their God-given gifts. The enslaved's diminished lives and spirit reinforces the enslavers bogus sense of superiority.

Finally, there is the fact that the enslaved don't own or fully benefit from what they produce. They do not own the work of their hands. As Marx said of low-paid factory workers, slaves are "alienated from their labor."[1] Country singer Merle Travis captured this idea in a song about coal miners in debt bondage: "You load sixteen tons and what do you get? Another day older and deeper in debt."[2] Little wonder that the Israelite slaves cried out to God for relief (Exod 3). Work was a curse.

The Bible has yet another thread that addresses bad work. It comes from a surprisingly different social location, not slavery but from a place of immense privilege. Ecclesiastes is written by someone who enjoyed abundance. The writer has seen it all, done it all, and concludes that everything is

1. Marx, *Economic and Philosophic Manuscripts*, 69–84.

2. Travis, "Sixteen Tons."

vanity. He's accumulated great wealth and lots of servants. He's built, or his servants have built, houses, vineyards, and gardens. Despite this, he's found no lasting joy or meaning. In fact, he finds all his work is vanity, a chasing after wind. He's watched good people die in their youth and evil people thrive into old age. He's seen people work hard, scrimp, and save, only to have their idiot children squander their inheritance. He's jaded and cynical. At one point, he concludes,

> Enjoy life with the wife whom you love, all the days of your *vain* life that are given you under the sun, because that is your portion in life and in your *toil* at which you *toil* under the sun. Whatever your hand finds to do, do with your might; *for there is no work or thought or knowledge or wisdom in Sheol, where you are going.* (Eccl 9:9–10, emphasis mine)

His counsel: enjoy life and endure the toil because you are headed for oblivion.

The futility brought on by ceaseless toil, exploitation, and fleeting satisfaction raises perennial human questions about work and human purpose. What am I? What am I doing? What am I supposed to be doing? What are we, collectively, supposed to be doing? The church has answered these questions with the principle of vocation.

Origins of Vocation

The word "vocation" comes from the Latin word *vocare*, which also gives us our word "voice." Although in secular usage, vocation sometimes means paid work or public service, it originated in the church's notion of religious vocations.[3] People were thought to enter religious service because they sensed a calling from God. This idea comes from the Bible. God called Abram and Sarai to be a great nation. God called Moses from the burning bush to tell Pharaoh to let his people go. God called prophets, such as Samuel, Isaiah, and Jeremiah, to speak God's Word (1 Sam 3, Isa 6, Jer 1). Jesus called the first disciples to leave their nets and fish for people (Mark 1:17). God called humans to a work that gave them purpose and a cause greater than the self. That said, the examples of Jesus and the prophets demonstrate that we should not think that good work is necessarily easy or even psychologically rewarding.

3. Schuurman, *Vocation*, 1.

During the Protestant Reformation, reformers, like Martin Luther, developed a theology that affirmed the dignity of ordinary life. In the process, they broadened the concept of vocation to include secular or non-religious work. Vocation was used to describe the responsibilities a spouse or member to a household or a citizen to a political body. Some insisted that God is just as pleased and just as well served by humble work, such as dish washing and changing diapers, as by preaching. As they considered the concept of vocation, they distinguished God's universal call to follow Christ from the particular callings that God extended to particular people for particular tasks. They taught that everyone had a particular calling in a world of callings.

What almost mattered more than the job itself was the attitude of the person doing the work. This led sixteenth-century Puritan Joseph Hall to say, "God loveth adverbs; and cares not how good, but how well."[4] The apostle Paul offered similar encouragement, saying, "Whatever task you must do, work as if your soul depends on it, as for the Lord and not for humans" (Col 3:23). Since the principle of vocation views work as service to God, it calls forth attitudes of attentiveness, diligence, kindness, and care. Work done for God shuns idleness, sloppiness, and sloth. It understands that while a lot of work may not seem very creative or satisfactory, one should take advantage of moments when one can be of genuine help and advance a good cause.

Theologian Doug Ottati wisely notes that vocation's elevation of lowly work and its emphasis on internal attitudes of humility and service has been misused to impose submission and quietism on women and the poor, who are usually saddled with menial labor.[5] When I was a child, my teacher warned the class that if we did not apply ourselves, we would suffer the curse of ditch digging. We would work hard and go home monetarily and bodily broken. But if ditch digging is a calling that society needs doing, it should not be despised or exploited. If God has called people to particular vocations, no matter how lowly, that work serves God's creative and redemptive purposes. Such work should be honored and properly remunerated. The indignity we force on people who do hard, dirty work is an affront to God.

4. Quoted by Taylor, *Sources of the Self*, 224.

5. Ottati, *Theology for the Twenty-First Century*, 623.

Vocation, Work, and World

Vocation has a unique way of locating work in the larger world. Consider how it differs from other common words for work. The word "career," for example, comes from the proto-Indo-European root that gives us the words car, cart, cargo, and carriage, meaning "to run" or "to move." A career describes work in terms of advancement. Thus, we say someone went far in their career or that their career was derailed. A career, however, does not carry (another morpheme) many people. Careerists generally calculate the paths of their careers privately, without regard to the service of others or larger purpose.[6] Again, occupation and employment define work as an engagement of time and attention. Tasks and chores point to the particular work at hand. Labor and toil reference the physical and mental effort involved in work. A job is employment for pay. Like service, which means work done on someone else's behalf, vocation has a larger vision of work's purpose and impact. In a theological context, this vision is theocentric and inclusive.

Vocation situates work in the world by asking, what needs doing? What is God calling you to contribute? How can you be useful in God's economy? Seventeenth-century English Puritan William Perkins said that a calling is "a certain kind of life, ordained and imposed on man [*sic*] by God for the common good."[7] By this, Perkins lifts up the public dimension of God's general calling to follow Christ as well as the public dimension of particular callings.

Vocation's vision of individuals and their institutions serving God by serving the neighbor brings to mind Marley's response to Ebenezer Scrooge in *A Christmas Carol*. When Scrooge observes that Marley was a good man of business, Marley retorts, "Mankind was my business. The common welfare was my business; charity, mercy, forbearance, benevolence, were all my business. The dealings of my trade were but a drop of water in the comprehensive ocean of my business!"[8] Marley echoes vocation's insight that human work is best rendered as service to one's neighbor.

Vocation points to the larger world in yet another way. Theological treatments of vocation generally encourage people to discern their particular callings by taking inventory of their gifts and opportunities.[9] Vocation

6. May, *Beleaguered Rules*, 16.

7. Morgan, "William Perkins on Callings," 36.

8. Dickens, *Christmas Carol*, para. 127.

9. Cotton, "Christian Calling," 319.

asks, what has God equipped, inspired, and prepared you to do? Perhaps you don't have the qualifications yet, and your intermediate calling is to pursue these qualifications. One's internal passions and ambition should be counted among one's gifts, and there is much to be gained in appreciating the origins of one's passions.

A comprehensive inventory of our gifts will remind us of the gifts we have received from family, teachers, mentors, and schools. This should put to mind our obligations to those who make our work possible. It should also draw us out of the mindset that views gifts as given for our private benefit and prompt us to view them as a trust from God the Giver. As a child, I once attended a friend's birthday party. When we got in the car to go, my mother asked if I had my gift. The gift was not mine to keep, of course, but to give. A comprehensive inventory of our gifts will lead us to appreciate the One who is the inexhaustible fountain of giving. This can embolden liberality in giving and service. By casting work as service, inquiring about one's gifts and providential preparation, and asking about the world's need, vocation locates work and human purpose in God's world.

God's Work of Creation and Redemption

Vocation builds on the insight we discussed in the principle of *imago Dei*, that humans are called to mirror God's work. God's work is generally understood as falling into two main categories: creation and redemption. God's work of creation is not a one-time event but continues through the ongoing generation and continuance of life. Human beings are called to participate in God's work of creation in countless ways: by producing and caring for children, feeding people and creatures, and ensuring the conditions for human and creaturely flourishing.

In our analysis of the principle of creation, we noted that the creation myths depict God as feeding the humans. This thought is extended to all creatures in Ps 104. When people thank God for their daily bread, they recognize God is the source of life. They should also consider how God works in and through the work of countless others to provide the food on their table. There are the farmers who grow the food, farm workers who harvest it, truck drivers who deliver it, clerks who stock the shelves, cashiers at the registers, and the hands that prepare it. There are also agri-businesses that provide fertilizer and seed, state extension agencies that educate farmers, equipment and truck manufacturers, food companies, and supermarket chains. We also depend on the natural world, weather systems, geological and microbial life that produces the soil, and the cosmological saga that forged the elements in the stars. When we give thanks to God for our daily bread, we are giving thanks for the ways God works in and through all of this to create and sustain life.

Human beings participate in God's creative work in countless ways. Consider how children are born unfinished. Before they become adults, they require people to care for them and teach them skills. They need parents and other family, uncles and grandmothers, childcare workers, teachers and mentors, and people who make schools run. Each of these participates in God's creative work of forming adults.[10] Participation in God's work of creation extends beyond the generation and development of human life. People who improve crops and livestock participate in God's creative work. So do people who manage forests and wildlife and conserve the environment.

Similarly, human beings are also called to participate in God's work, redeeming creation from sin, evil, and death. In Scripture, God's work includes liberating the children of Israel out of slavery, giving the law, calling prophets, and sending apostles. God's work of redemption is most clearly revealed in Jesus Christ, who healed the sick, found the lost, challenged injustice, helped people find their true purpose, and, on the cross, brought reconciliation and peace. When we think about participating in God's work of redemption, we think of medical professionals, diplomats negotiating a peace treaty, or a community organizer pulling people together to address a problem. We think of courts that pursue justice and hospitals that promote healing.

When we talk about how we are called to participate in God's work, we are not saying that human beings are co-creators or co-redeemers as if God works over here and humans over there. We are claiming that God works through us to accomplish the divine purpose. Consider God's call for Israel to be a nation of priests that mediates between God and the world (Exod 19:6). Consider Martin Luther's claim, "[God] will be working all things through you; He will milk the cow through you and perform the most servile duties through you, and all the greatest and least duties alike will be pleasing to Him."[11] Consider also, the apostle Paul, who wrote his Epistle to the Colossians from prison and told them not to grieve his imprisonment: "I rejoice in my suffering because, in my flesh I am completing

10. Roberts, "Renewing Public School Teaching," 9.

11. Luther, *Lectures on Genesis*, 10.

what is lacking in Christ's afflictions" (Col 1:24). The possibility that God was using his affliction to accomplish some positive good gave him joy. In a similar manner, we can discuss how a parent or a teacher's care mediates God's love and care. Returning to the image of God, when we are faithful in our vocations, we mirror God's image. It reflects well on God, who is the source of life and healing.

It may be easy for a farmer to identify their work as participating in God's work of creation, or for a mediator to identify their work as participating in God's work of reconciliation, but a lot of work does not neatly fit the creation/redemption binary. A food service worker in a hospital, for example, participates in God's work of both creation and healing. Ultimately, it does not matter whether we are able to clearly identify our work with creation or redemption. Just as the monotheism of the Trinity reminds us that the Creator is also the Redeemer, so all good work serves the purpose of the one God. One God works through us all (1 Cor 12:4–6).

Unfortunately, a lot of work can seem abstracted from any creative, redeeming, or even useful purpose.[12] Some work is bureaucratic and administrative. Other work lacks fiduciary, social, and psychic rewards. Still other work is mind-numbingly repetitive, back-breaking, and soul-draining. The concept of vocation prompts us to improve the quality of life for people stuck in such jobs.

The notion of good work—work that participates in God's work—implicitly suggests the existence of bad work that does not serve God's purpose. This would include work *intended* to hurt, harm, exploit, enslave, or destroy. God does not call people to criminal activity, addicting people to dangerous drugs, pimping, murdering, blackmailing, misleading people, exacerbating animosity, or engaging in efforts to overthrow the good order of a relatively just and peaceful society. Such work may be profitable. One may even feel great internal motivation to do it, but it does not qualify as a vocation because it does not participate in God's work. Indeed, God's redeeming seeks to limit the destruction associated with such work.

This leaves numerous questions about work that involves coercion and violence, such as policing, soldiering, political leadership, and anything involving the criminal justice system. The church has frequently found these occupations vexing. In the Gospel of Luke, soldiers ask John the Baptist how they should prepare for the coming of Christ. Rather than telling the soldiers to leave soldiering, John tells them to be good soldiers, to shun brutality

12. Graeber, "Bullshit Jobs"; Heller, "Bullshit-Job Boom."

and not misuse their power (Luke 3:14). Other passages, such as Matthew's sermon on the mount and Jesus' example on the cross, point to an ethic of non-violence. Many early church leaders did not believe that Christians could serve as soldiers of the Roman Empire, particularly since it required them to participate in the pagan Caesar cult. Similarly, monastic communities were seen as following the "counsels of perfection" in Jesus' teaching that encourage a higher level of spiritual and moral practice. Mennonites, Amish, and others in the Anabaptist tradition carried this ethic into ordinary life, forbidding Christians to engage in coercion and violence.

Mainstream Christian thought considered restraining evil essential for maintaining the tranquility of order, necessary for human and creaturely flourishing, and, hence, as serving God's purpose. With that in mind, they thought Christians could engage in soldiering, policing, criminal justice, and political leadership, but that it must be conducted in a manner that follows the sorts of principles outlined in this book.[13] It must serve a larger, theocentric purpose, respect and enhance creation, respect the image of God, follow the moral law, consider the reality of human sin, seek to heal the world, and honor our obligations to others.

A Roman general named Boniface once asked St. Augustine whether he should give up soldiering and join him in the monastery. Augustine replied that he should not think that everyone can live the monastic life during this present age before Christ's return. He advised him that, as he put on his armor, he should remember that his goal in waging war was peace and adopt the spirit of a peacemaker.[14]

There are all sorts of questions one may ask about how and whether one adopts the spirit of a peacemaker as one prepares to defeat an enemy in battle (likely by killing them). Many Christians find Augustine's advice contradictory. Yet, as a matter of principle, it recognizes that war and violence represent the disorder of sin and evil and that we should work for a day when God and all creatures—even enemies—embrace. It also acknowledges that, under certain circumstances, violence may be tragically necessary to restrain evil and maintain a relatively just and orderly society in which people can thrive. This means that soldiers must seek to minimize harm to innocents and have the redeeming goal of restoring peace and maintaining justice.

These sorts of emphases have distinguished Christian soldiering (and, until recently, US military training) from a pagan warrior ethos that glories

13. Cook, "Soldiering."

14. Augustine, "Letter to Boniface," 553.

in bloodlust, vengeance, and domination.[15] When paired with the principle of sin (which invites a person to question the innocence of their own actions and aims), it provides reasons to resist casting one's cause as a righteous crusade, to avoid demonizing one's enemies, and to observe the sorts of limits on violence that are outlined in just war theory. Christian ethicist Tobias Winright observes that these sorts of considerations not only apply to soldiering but also policing, where one is called to ameliorate the effects of sin and evil, not to escalate violence or deepen alienation.[16]

Finally, studies of soldiers suggest the laws of armed conflict that limit the use of force and shield civilians also protect them from the form of post-traumatic syndrome known as "moral harm." Moral harm involves the sense that one has participated in and done something very, very wrong. Soldiers who ignore these restraints, whether by following orders or joining their comrades in bloodletting, wind up doing real and lasting damage to themselves. They not only remind us of society's responsibility to encourage lawful combat toward just ends, but they prompt us to consider how the twin goals of God's creative and redeeming purposes set important moral limits and guidance for all work.

Institutional Vocation

Not only do individuals have particular callings, so do institutions and groups. Police are empowered to protect and to serve. Courts and legal systems exist to pursue justice, hospitals to promote health. Journalism exists to inform and empower a democratic citizenry. States exist to order the common life, promote the general welfare, uphold justice, defend against enemies, and secure the blessings of liberty. Families exist to support the friendship and partnership of spouses, nurture children, and direct our sexual urges into building up community.

The idea of institutional vocation, like an individual calling, means that in God's economy, every institution, organization, and community serves causes greater than itself. The purposes of the family, for example, are not limited to private goods. The blessings of healthy family life redound to the common good and serve God's creative and redeeming purposes. Again, nations don't exist merely to promote the welfare of their citizens; they are called to seek peace and justice among the nations and the flourishing of

15. Cohen, "U.S. Needs Soldiers."

16. Winright, *Serve and Protect.*

creation. The church's purpose encompasses more than merely satisfying members' needs. H. Richard Niebuhr summarized it as increasing the love of God and neighbor in the world.[17]

The idea of institutional vocation can offset an overemphasis on profit in business. In this connection, recall that sociologist Max Weber differentiated profit from greed, noting that greed is endemic in every society and not unique to capitalism. "Profit," by contrast, is a term associated with double-entry accounting. The ability to track credits and debits, profits and losses contributed to the rise of capitalism by enabling the rational ordering of business, hence the association. Because business leaders manage the wealth and assets of others, maximizing profits and other measures of shareholder value has become the *sine qua non* for business managers. Yet companies have obligations to other constituencies: workers, customers, communities, and the ecosystem. These obligations point to a businesses' larger institutional vocation. While a focus on profit is necessary, since unprofitable businesses generally do not serve investors or other constituencies, it is not enough.

George W. Merck, CEO of Merck Pharmaceuticals, a man of faith, once declared, "We try never to forget that medicine is for the people. It is not for the profits."[18] At its best, this led Merck to scrupulously research the products it sold. It also led it to research the prevention and cure of diseases such as Ebola, river blindness, Chagas, and sleeping sickness, for which there was no profit.

Clarifying an institution's vocation can also be helpful in setting priorities. I remember working with a wonderful music director of a church in Philadelphia. She started a concert series with musicians from the Philadelphia Symphony and the Curtis School of Music. Despite the good effort she put into it, attendance was poor. After thinking about the purpose of the church, we decided to cancel the series. Mission creep is inevitable with institutions.

Identifying an institutional vocation may be helpful at this point in American life, when so many institutions of American society are dysfunctional and beset by inefficiencies. Higher education, for example, has become burdened by distractions, such as sports and services that do not advance its central educational purpose. US healthcare produces worse aggregate outcomes while costing much more per person than peer nations.

17. Niebuhr, *Purpose of the Church*.

18. New York Community Trust, "Donor Biography," para. 37.

Mainstream Protestants would benefit from renewed focus on reaching people with their ideas as a means of increasing the love of God and neighbor.

As a sense of responsibility for public goods has eroded, corporations have entered sectors of society that used to be run by non-profits and government, such as hospitals, schools, prisons, policing, the military, etc. The argument for handing government and other services over to private corporations is that it is easier for corporations to raise capital for construction than governments, which can require public referendums to go in debt. Also, it is argued that the search for profits will motivate business leaders to find other efficiencies. Unfortunately, the need to cream a profit introduces a significant inefficiency and creates perverse incentives. Also, without functioning markets, there is no competition to spur innovation or improve value for the public. It soon devolves into rent-seeking.

Studies of for-profit prisons show that they are more dangerous for prisoners and employees, despite housing fewer violent offenders than state-run prisons.[19] They also provide lower-quality services, such as drug rehabilitation, compared with state-run institutions.[20] Many for-profit prison contracts demand that communities guarantee to keep the prison full.[21] For-profit prison companies have lobbied legislatures to change the criminal code with an eye toward self-enrichment and have bribed judges to render unjust and harsher sentences, as in the "kids-for-cash" scandal.[22] Institutional vocation asks whether public purposes and private business interests align and whether "market solutions" really exist.

Vocation and Human Purpose

Vocation is a way of talking about work because it is a way to talk about human purpose. This is why, since Martin Luther, people have talked about marriage, parenting, and caring for older adults as callings. Just as a calling transcends remuneration, it encompasses more than employment. Vocation reminds us that good work finds its chief, lasting meaning not in the position it confers, in its remuneration, or even in the monuments it may

19. Lopez, "For-Profit Prisons More Dangerous."

20. Vedantam, "How Private Prisons Affect Sentencing"; Galinato and Rohla, "Privately-Owned Prisons Increase Incarceration?"

21. Blakely and Bumphus, "Private and Public Sector Prisons."

22. Associated Press, "Judges Ordered to Pay $200m."

leave for a time but in how it participates in God's glorious work of creation and redemption.

We live in a world of callings. Vocation not only informs how we think about our own work and purpose, but it summons us to consider others. People have vocations and responsibilities beyond their employment, to families, their synagogue, the PTA. They are responsible to God for this "work." While a job is not a charity, employers should recognize this reality. Employers cannot expect employees to be on call all the time 24/7, seven days a week, fifty-two weeks a year.

The biblical Sabbath not only demands that the faithful rest one day a week, but it directs them to give servants, children, foreigners, and other creatures a day of rest. Sabbath keeping is not just about finding spiritual balance in one's own personal life. It is designed to protect workers' rights so they may be true to their callings to God and others. Sabbath reminds us that people do not live to work—they work to live.

Chapter Eleven

Covenant and the Social Dimension of Humanity

> No one seriously immersed in the Jewish and Christian traditions has escaped the theological impact of the covenant idea. Covenant was once the subject of so many theological treatises. . . . On the other hand, covenant is less a theological concept than a theo-political one. . . . Even so, far too little has been written about covenant as a factor in political affairs.
>
> —Daniel Elazar[1]

When Star Trek made its television debut in 1966, its depiction of diverse nations, races, and worlds engaged in a common mission and relating to one another in egalitarian fashion presented a stark contrast to Cold War rivalries and the indignities of Jim Crow. To explain how such an internationally and intergalactically diverse crew lived and worked together, Gene Roddenberry drew on an old political idea: the federation.

Star Trek notwithstanding, the meaning and relevance of federalism and other related covenantal concepts have largely receded from public consciousness. Although covenant has long been a central theme in Protestant theology, few modern Christians are acquainted with the rich

1. Elazar, *Covenant and Polity*, 1.

covenantal theological and political tradition or recognize federalism's roots in the Bible. Some, understandably, associate covenant with racist real estate covenants that prevented people of color from owning property in white neighborhoods. Between the amnesia and negative associations, the covenant principle needs reintroduction and rehabilitation.

Covenant is one of the several English words used to translate the Hebrew word *brit*, which primarily means "to bind." As a principle, covenant answers perennial human questions. Why do I sense ties and obligations to others? How do we form and sustain communities of mutual regard, responsibility, and support?[2]

While we may not be acquainted with covenant as a principle, we are familiar with the reality it points to. We sense covenantal ties when we appreciate our dependence on families, congregations, cities, nations, the environment, and the great chain of being emanating from God. These bonds inspire gratitude. They also produce a sense that we owe something to others.

English is saturated with covenantal language, though the depth of its meaning no longer resonates the way it once did. The English word "covenant" comes from the old French *convenant*, signifying an agreement, pact, or promise. We refer to the covenantal dimension of human existence when we say that a couple "tied the knot" in a marriage ceremony, when a congregation sings, "blest be the tie that binds," or when a political leader talks about the "sinews of peace" that bind nations in the pursuit of a harmonious world.[3]

A number of Latin words that were used to translate the Hebrew *brit* have entered the English language, including *pactum*, *compactum*, *foedus*, and *testamentum*. "Pacts" and "compacts" are binding promissory agreements. Federations and confederations (from the Latin *foedus*) are political covenants. A person's last will and testament binds the executor of their estate after they have died. Christians refer to Old and New Testaments to distinguish the books associated with the original covenant from those associated with the new covenant in Christ.

English also includes numerous words containing morphemes of the word "ligament" that carry covenantal overtones. When people are bound by their word, we say that they are "re*li*able." When people talk about "ob*lig*ations," they refer to moral duties they are bound to perform. When people say that they are "much ob*lig*ed," they mean that they are "bound"

2. Stackhouse, *Public Theology and Political Economy*, 26.

3. Churchill, "Sinews of Peace."

to return a favor. "Re*lig*ion" refers to obligations placed on us by the gods. All these point to the covenantal reality; our lives are bound to others. The sheer number of these linguistic artifacts suggests a time when covenantal themes were more culturally prominent, before they were displaced by America's rugged individualism and a libertarian creed that scorns communal ties and obligations.

Notwithstanding the achievements of individualism, a culture that celebrates autonomy to the detriment of community has lost its balance. As much as we desire to be free, our lives are inevitably constrained by communal "bands" or "ligaments." An examination of these bonds would prevent us from reducing freedom to license to do as we please. It would help us appreciate that the ties that constrain are also the lifelines that make our lives possible. Recovering the principle of covenant promises to give us language to name and navigate the social dimension of human existence. It has the potential to challenge fantasies of atomized, self-made, selfish individuals spontaneously producing a virtuous society out of their vice. It should also help us appreciate that "the pursuit of happiness" cannot be reduced to an entirely individual quest but must include the pursuit of a happy society that supports flourishing. Covenant reminds us that we are all in this together.

Biblical Roots

Daniel Elazar, a Jewish political philosopher, reminds us that following the Protestant Reformation, federal theologians elaborated on the theological, social, and political implications of covenantal concepts found in the Bible. In the process, they developed practical wisdom for the ordering of the communities we inhabit, including marriage, politics, and the economy. Heinrich Bullinger and, somewhat independently, John Calvin did the initial theological work. Later thinkers, such as Johannes Althusius, Johannes Cocceius, Hugo Grotius, and others, frequently called "federal theologians," expanded on this initial work.[4]

Covenant, as a concept, comes from ancient Mesopotamian political agreements in which sovereigns made promises to vassals in exchange for assurances. The Biblical writers employed these agreements as a metaphor for the divine-human-creaturely relationship.[5] The Bible depicts God

4. Elazar and Kincaid, *Covenant Connection*, 352.

5. Mendenhall, "Covenant Forms in Israelite Tradition," 25.

making a series of pacts with humans and creatures. Covenantal themes run throughout Scripture. Covenant promises and the divine-human relationship they represent are assumed in every narrative. This is even true of the book of Job, which interrogates God's covenant faithfulness in light of Job's undeserved suffering.

The prominence of these covenants requires interpreters of the Bible to organize them to make sense of the whole. Some (called dispensationalists) saw the covenants as distinct and discontinuous, viewing later covenants as replacing earlier agreements. Christians in the Reformed tradition, the federal theologians, tended to view them as expressions of a single covenant of grace running through both testaments.[6] This view holds that the biblical covenants are reaffirmations, clarifications, and fulfillments of God's primal covenant with all people through Adam and Eve.[7] According to this interpretation, God's promise that Eve's offspring will "crush the head of the serpent" (Gen 3:15) is a promise to defeat evil. God's purpose is reiterated in the seemingly more exclusive covenants God makes with Israel, as when God promises that all people will find a blessing through Abram and Sarai (Gen 12:1–3), and when God promises that Israel will be a kingdom of priests for the nations (Exod 19:3–6). God never loses sight of his covenant with all people and creatures.

Following this rubric, reformed theologians concluded that far from replacing God's covenant with the Jews, the new covenant in Christ continues the biblical pattern of later covenants illuminating and accomplishing God's initial promise. This aligns with New Testament portrayals of God's redeeming purpose in Christ as embracing not just the church but "all nations" (Matt 25), "the world" (John 3:16; 2 Cor 5:19), "all people" (1 Tim 4:10), and "all things" (Col 1:19–20). When Jesus calls his disciples the "salt of the earth" and the "light of the world," he invites his followers to join Israel in their vocation to bless the nations (Matt 5:13–16).

Features of Covenant Life

Covenantal thinkers identified a number of features of covenant that describe and govern social life.

6. Presbyterian Church USA, "Scots Confession," 12.

7. Calvin, *Institutes of the Christian Religion*, 2.9.10.

The Promissory Nature of Social Relationships

The covenant principle understands that human relationships have a promissory aspect. That is, they rest on implicit and explicit promises that bind the parties in relationship. Covenantal promises can be formal, as when a couple enters marriage, an immigrant becomes a naturalized citizen, or a person joins a religious community. Theologian Joseph Allen observes that when people make promises and enter covenants, they generate expectations. Promise makers invite other partners in the covenant to entrust themselves to them.[8]

While some promises are publicly formalized, many are not. Over time, a couple that lives together signals to the other partner something about their future intentions; namely, that they may be counted on to be faithful to the relationship. Though promises are never made, at some point it would be wrong to abandon a partner when sickness, poverty, or other struggle arises. This is why it can feel like a divorce when couples who have been living together break up. Admittedly, it is difficult to say exactly when covenant obligations have been undertaken or what promises are being telegraphed. One value of publicly formalized marriage covenants is that they clarify expectations for the couple and the community.

Social ethicist William F. May claims that covenants respond to an incipient relationship. Thus, it is more accurate to say that covenantal promises formalize an existing relationship than to say they create a new relationship.[9] Thus, God's covenant in the Ten Commandments begins with a recitation of the gift of liberation: "I am the Lord your God who brought you out of Egypt, out of the land of slavery" (Exod 20:2; Deut 5:6). Similarly, in the Western tradition, when couples take the vows of marriage, they are not inventing a relationship out of nothing. They are responding to the gifts of courtship and formalizing their association before witnesses.[10]

Covenantal obligations and expectations of performance can exist even though nobody has taken vows. No living American was present at the American founding to sign the Declaration of Independence, which is a classic covenantal political document. Yet, by virtue of living in the United States, citizens enjoy the privileges and thereby incur the duties of the national covenant. They never pledged "[their] Lives, [their] Fortunes

8. Allen, *Love and Conflict*.

9. May, *Testing the National Covenant*, 15.

10. May, *Testing the National Covenant*, 93.

and [their] sacred Honor,"[11] but they are still bound to defend the country, pay taxes, and follow its laws.

The same is true of the primal covenants that bind creation and humankind. We are obliged to care for creation, though we never agreed to do it. Similarly, we are bound to help people who are not part of our covenant communities. Consider how the Bible repeatedly commands people to welcome foreigners and treat them well (Exod 23:9; Lev 19:33; Deut 27:19; Jer 7:6). These remind us that covenantal obligations extend to people outside our communities.

In this connection, we should note that a society that has benefitted from immigrants who have paid taxes, contributed to society, or served in the military has consented to incipient relationships. Nations commonly honor certain forms of immigrant service with citizenship. People of good will can debate how and at what point this should happen. They can also debate how to minimize perverse incentives and unrealistic expectations such recognition may create for would-be immigrants. It remains that nations that receive benefits incur obligations.

Covenant and Constitution

Covenantal political theory teaches that once a relationship is established, there needs to be agreement on how the relationship will be *constituted*. A constitution provides a framework by which the community organizes its life, pursues substantive goods, and protects the rights of its members. Daniel Elazar suggests that Deuteronomy (which means "second law") served as an updated constitution for ancient Israel in a new political context. The new context may explain why Deuteronomy more directly portrays the Sabbath command as a labor law and why the periodic redistribution of wealth is focused on debt forgiveness rather than land redistribution.

The constitution of a marriage following the taking of wedding vows is the informal work of the couple. It involves negotiating responsibilities, navigating ways of resolving conflict, and developing a pattern of life together. For good and ill, much of this is informed by culture and families of origin.

In larger groups, the work of constituting life together requires a more formal process. The Articles of Confederation sought to structure the relationship formed by the Declaration of Independence. This was replaced

11. National Archives, "Declaration of Independence," para. 32.

by the US Constitution, which secured a better balance between freedom and order, enabling the continual renegotiation of rights, obligations, and duties of life together. The last point is particularly important because, like every human document, the original Constitution required amending to outlaw slavery and to extend civil and voting rights to all. Arguably, other flaws remain, and some features have become archaic.

Covenants and Contracts

Although both covenantal and contractual relationships involve voluntary agreements between the parties; they should be distinguished. Contractual relationships are transactional. Parties enter a contract to get something out of it. They seek to maximize their advantages and limit their obligations. By contrast, when parties enter covenantal relationships, they bind their lives together. This is why the traditional promises of marriage are so comprehensive, explicitly naming poverty, sickness, and hardship.

Unlike contractual relationships, where seemingly everything is up for negotiation, covenants recognize a "givenness" to the structure and duties of human relationships. This is why the language of the old *1662 Book of Common Prayer* talked about couples entering an "estate" of marriage.[12] Although every marriage is as idiosyncratic as the couple, some features and expectations are common to every marriage. This coheres with the principle of natural law as well as with Leo Tolstoy's observation that all happy families are alike, but every unhappy family is unhappy in its own way.[13]

Inner and Outer Covenants

Covenant theologians distinguished between inner and outer covenants. By the outer covenant, they meant the duties of life together. In a nation, these duties include voting, paying taxes, and ensuring that every member of society can reach their God-given potential. In a family, these include the duties of ordinary life together, household chores, attending to family members and assisting them where we can.

Duties can come to feel like lifeless legalisms, empty husks, shells of a relationship that used to be alive. While one frequently must carry out the duties of the outer covenant even when they may feel onerous, it is much

12. Bray and Keane, *1662 Book of Common Prayer.*

13. Tolstoy, *Anna Karenina.*

easier when our actions are motivated by gratitude, solidarity, wonder, and love. These emotional attachments, what the Hebrew Bible calls *hesed*, constitute the inner covenant. They look beyond the letter of the law to the spirit of the law.

Some observe that the United States is fracturing along numerous lines.[14] A sense of fellow-feeling has been lost. People treat their political opponents like the enemy, forgetting that, for better or for worse, we are all in this together. They have become cold to the greatness of the American experiment and what it requires to succeed. This fraying of the inner covenant (loss of love for fellow citizens, for country, and for the genius of democracy) is expressed in the fraying of the outer covenant (a disregard for the law and democratic norms and contempt for political opponents).

Covenantal thinkers taught that the inner covenant—with God, religious communities, marriages, friendships, even political communities—requires a devotional life. Devotional lives take numerous forms, though they generally involve rituals that guide us in patterned, focused attention. These can be anniversaries, the singing of national anthems, or Memorial Day speeches and parades. They frequently involve a meal, such as a seder, Communion, the annual Thanksgiving dinner, or a regular date night. These rituals reconnect us with other covenant partners and align us with a project that is bigger than ourselves. They give us an occasion to recognize our dependence on the community and give thanks for the good we have received. They recall the community's highest ideals and purposes and remind us of the things that communal life requires of us. They celebrate the promise of a relationship and invite us to rededicate ourselves to repairing what is broken. In these ways, rituals intensify affections and shape a way of life. When we ignore our devotional lives, we create conditions for our hearts to wander.

Important as public rituals are, it is also true that the public cannot force observance of a ritual without compelling hypocrisy. The public needs to allow room for respectful expressions of grievance. Without such freedom, rituals are reduced to empty performances and risk becoming meaningless. Worse, they can generate sullen resentment.

Inner and outer covenants are mutually reinforcing. Attending to the inner covenant helps us discharge the duties of the outer covenant with joy. Similarly, faithful performance of the duties of the outer covenant can carry us through difficult seasons in a relationship. Theologian Dietrich

14. Hunter, *Democracy and Solidarity*.

Bonhoeffer pointed to how the outer covenant reinforces the inner covenant in a wedding sermon, observing, "It is not your love that sustains the marriage, but from now on, the marriage sustains your love."[15]

Covenants Broken and Renewed

The doctrine of sin predicts that people will break covenant with one another. As the foregoing suggests, broken covenants are rooted in broken promises. Sometimes, especially when the covenant is implicit, people seek to be "free riders." They adopt an extractive approach, taking the good things a community offers, roads, hospitals, arts, schools, while they avoid contributing what the community or the relationship requires to remain healthy and functional.

People rationalize their neglect. They downplay the gifts they have received and minimize their responsibilities. This has been encouraged by cultural developments, the waning of covenantal ideas, the rise of political philosophies that celebrate a transactional approach to responsibilities, and psychologies that aim to liberate individuals from obligations to family and community. While some emphasis on freedom has been necessary to release people from unhealthy relationships, many arguments for autonomy and personal fulfillment have amplified resentment over the ordinary demands of life together.

The resentments of the powerless are sometimes expressed in nihilistic and anarchic fantasies. These frequently fail to appreciate how human flourishing rests on the good order of society. The resentments of the wealthy and powerful, by contrast, tend to reflect libertarian fantasies of unfettered people magically creating a functioning community by pursuing their selfish desires. The resentments of the marginalized may be misguided, but they are understandable. The resentments of the wealthy are ironic because they arguably benefit most from a healthy society. They begrudge carrying the tax burden for infrastructure, defense, law enforcement, justice, research, and education, which make wealth creation possible. Because it takes time for the neglect of public institutions to culminate in disorder, the public may not immediately appreciate the impact when they are abandoned. Yet, when public institutions starve for resources, they become dysfunctional. This creates an unvirtuous cycle, wherein dysfunction breeds distrust and further erodes support.

15. Bonhoeffer, *Letters and Papers from Prison*, 46.

Just as covenants can be broken, they can be renewed. Reconciliation involves truth-telling, forgiveness, reparations, and trust-building. Such work is extremely difficult. It is frequently difficult to get people to even acknowledge that the covenant has been broken. The search for justice can take generations.

Covenant renewal frequently occurs after the community encounters a crisis or some new circumstance. One thinks of Joshua inviting Israel to renew the covenant as they prepared to settle in the promised land (Josh 24). One also thinks of a couple renegotiating their relationships after a job loss or following the birth of a child. Similarly, a foreign attack can cause people to set aside previously insurmountable differences and renew a sense of common destiny. This is why economic and social leveling, such as universal health care and expansions of civil rights, usually only happen after a war or other social disruption.[16]

Covenant Equality

Daniel Elazar says that Hebraic society was distinguished by covenant equality. This idea held that partners to human covenants stand as equals before the God who witnesses their promises.[17] Covenant equality reinforced *imago Dei's* stress on equal human dignity as well as theocentrism's emphasis on equality of people before their Creator. Rabbi Joshua Berman echoes this, noting that in other Late Bronze Age literature, the gods converse with the kings, not the masses. "By contrast, the theology of the covenant in the Pentateuch strips earthly hierarchies of their sacred legitimation. Every Israelite man is endowed with equal status, that of a King."[18]

In similar fashion, theocentrism and *imago Dei* interrogate essentialist visions of the sexes that are used to subordinate and oppress women. The understanding that the marriage covenant is a partnership of equals reflects these egalitarian impulses. It resists patriarchalism, demarcating marriage as an equal-regard institution that requires mutual submission.

Covenant equality is related to a distinctly Hebraic theory of property that was shaped by the experience of slavery in Egypt. The faith community remembered how Joseph built granaries for Pharaoh. Then, when famine

16. Picketty, *Capital in the Twenty-First.*
17. Elazar, *Covenant and Polity*, 70.
18. Berman, *Created Equal*, 20.

hit, Joseph used the grain to buy all the land and enslave the people (Gen 47:20–26). Landlessness led to slavery.

This experience inspired biblical laws that dictated regular land redistribution and the forgiveness of debts (Lev 25; Deut 15). These were designed to prevent inequalities of wealth from undermining equality and freedom. Soon after the Babylonian exile, while rebuilding Jerusalem, a famine forced poor Israelites to sell their land for food. The newly landless complained to Nehemiah that the wealthy were forcing them into slavery and their daughters into sex work. Nehemiah condemned the profiteering as a violation of their covenant obligations and demanded that they make restitution (Neh 5). The close connection between ownership, covenant equality, and freedom explain Isaiah's pronouncement, "Woe to you who add house to house and join field to field" (Isa 5:8). It also informed prophetic visions of a day when every Israelite would sit under their own vine and fig tree (Isa 36:16; Mic 4:4).

The equality of covenant partners before God explains the centrality of the Bible's concern, even preference, for weaker members of the community, such as the poor and oppressed. It animates prophetic declarations, from Samuel's resistance to the people's desire for a king (1 Sam 8), to Amos's denunciation of the wealthy for "selling the needy for a pair of sandals and trampling the head of the poor in the dust" (Amos 2:6–7). It informs Mary's revolutionary song about filling the poor with good things and sending the rich empty away (Luke 1:46–55) and Luke's description of the early church as holding all things in common (Acts 2:44). Cultural historian Eric Nelson notes that covenant equality together with the Hebraic theory of property contributed to republican views of freedom as "non-domination," which he claims differs from liberal views of freedom as "noninterference."[19] It is not hard to see how great inequalities of wealth injure republican governance.

Covenant and Political Order

Covenant's social portrait of human nature speaks to politics. Daniel Elazar claims that our understanding of modern democratic political theory is incomplete if we fail to include the contributions of the federal/covenant tradition. When we reviewed the promissory nature of human relationships, we noted covenant's observation that our lives are bound to others. When we discussed covenant and contracts, we saw that covenant differs

19. Nelson, *Hebrew Republic*, 57.

from approaches to common life that seek only to extract value for ourselves without contributing to the good of the whole. The analysis of inner and outer covenants highlighted the importance of rituals for political life.

Covenantal ideas shaped America's founding. The Puritans and others who migrated to the shores of North America brought federal covenantal concepts with them. We see them expressed in John Winthrop's sermon "Model of Christian Charity," delivered aboard the *Arabella* before the community disembarked on the shores of North America. We see them in the Mayflower Compact, in colonial and early state constitutions, and in other political documents from the founding period. Covenantal political theory also inspired the social contract political theories of Hobbes and Locke that influenced America's founders.[20]

The Declaration of Independence follows classic covenantal form. It dissolved "the political bands" that tied the colonies to Britain. The signers, as representatives of the colonies, bound the country together, pledging their "lives, fortunes, and sacred honor" to engage in "Acts and Things which Independent States may of right do."[21] Furthermore, in good covenant fashion, they called on "the Supreme Judge of the world" and "divine Providence" to witness the promises.[22] Though the Declaration of Independence has no legal authority, it serves as the basis of national life and generates obligations and expectations of the community and its citizens. These have not always been kept. In his "I Have a Dream" speech, Martin Luther King Jr. described the Declaration as a promissory note, a bad check that has come back marked "insufficient funds."[23]

Elazar observes that communities created by covenantal agreement exhibit fundamental differences from communities formed in other ways. Political communities founded by conquest, colonization, and domination find it difficult to recognize the rights and equality of the subjugated. Communities formed by the emergence of an authoritarian leader who establishes a center of power and imposes his will on others struggle to recognize political equality.[24] Ethno-nationalists rise to power by denying the rights of racial, religious, or ethnic out-groups. By contrast, the openness of federal political

20. Greenberg, "Between Covenant and Contract."

21. National Archives, "Declaration of Independence," para. 32.

22. National Archives, "Declaration of Independence," para. 32.

23. King, *Testament of Hope*, 217.

24. Elazar, *Covenant and Polity*, 35–52.

compacts to people of diverse identities suggests that social solidarity and political community can be grounded in mutual agreement.

Elazar notes that covenantal ideas have parallels in other cultures. Similarities between covenant and medieval Icelandic society and the Iroquois Confederacy, for example, suggest that covenant reflects something irrepressible in human nature.[25] This gives it a basis in natural law, apart from its biblical origins, making it suitable for pluralistic societies. At its best, the United States has demonstrated how a remarkably diverse people may bind their lives in common cause.

Covenant grasps that our lives and destinies really are bound together. By establishing a relationship of equality between peoples who are genuinely different, it lays a foundation for the difficult work of politics. This recognition of our common plight pushes us to find common purpose in a life that must be lived together.

Covenant and Economics

Covenant's attentiveness to the social dimensions of human nature also speaks to economic life. When we discussed the promissory nature of human relationships, we noted that covenantal perspectives know that individuals are not self-made. They have been raised, taught, and given opportunities by the people and communities that nurtured them and incur obligations to others. In the section on covenant and contracts, we distinguished between covenantal bonds and contractual agreements, noting that covenant views partners as more than competitors for scarce goods. In the section on covenant equality, we reviewed how creation and covenant equality contribute to Hebraic understandings of ownership. In this section, we extend these insights by briefly surveying other covenantal insights on the economy.

Covenant's appreciation for the social dimensions of human nature suggests a broader range of human impulses than perspectives that reduce economic motivation to rational self-interest and utility maximization. Covenant observes that human lives are bound and sustained by many relationships. It follows that humans are motivated by multiple loves, including family, friends, work, one's country, community, company, coworkers, peers, customers, school, religious institution, self, and God. Any of these can inspire hard work, frugality, investment, entrepreneurship, and

25. Elazar, *Covenant and Commonwealth*, 179.

sacrificial giving. Love's attachments will drive people to do things that make no economic sense from a purely selfish perspective. Covenant's portrait of humans as social creatures provides a truer picture of economic incentives and agency than many alternative understandings of human nature.

Because it attends to the social dimension of human being, covenant recognizes better than libertarian alternatives that individuals create wealth in concert with others. Entrepreneurs depend on the gifts of human culture, knowledge, institutions, and technology. They rely on trading partners and people with whom they divide labor. In developed countries, individuals benefit from well-defended, ordered, healthy, and educated societies, with functioning markets, law enforcement, and research. Hard work is important but never enough. We see dysfunctional societies around the globe where people toil endlessly and have nothing to show for it. The lesson we should take from this is that government governs best not when it governs least but when it governs well. Failed states produce chaos. Chaos produces poverty.

Covenant appreciates that, apart from society, the only wealth you would possess is what you produce with your own hands. If you did not live in society, your shoes, if you had any, would be the clogs you carved from wood or the moccasins you fashioned from the skins of animals that you killed and tanned. Wealthy people may work, but they do not produce wealth on their own any more than the pharaohs built the pyramids by themselves.

Thomas Paine employed this truth to justify taxation: "All accumulation . . . of personal property, beyond what a man's own hands produce, is derived to him by living in society; and he owes on every principle of justice, of gratitude, and of civilization, a part of that accumulation back again to society from whence the whole came."[26] This is why calling taxation "theft" is neither truthful nor helpful. It obscures the source of our wealth and the obligations we incur to the larger community and each other. The commonwealth is a collective benefit and responsibility.

Covenant and the Ideologies

Covenant's attention to the social dimension of human beings differs from libertarian ideologies that downplay our reliance on others, minimize our obligations, and teach that life is fundamentally competitive. Covenant does not valorize selfishness as a virtue. Neither does it look kindly on usury, greed, ostentation, great inequalities of wealth, nor the exploitation

26. Paine, "Agrarian Justice," 18.

of others. While other perspectives teach that if we all pursue self-interest, "the invisible hand" of economics will magically produce the greatest social good, covenant foresees that unchecked avarice will produce impoverished and enslaved covenant partners. It denies that "the invisible hand" justifies extreme inequality, poverty, and suffering. While covenant appreciates that the economy holds potential for immense good, it recognizes that its inequitable possibilities call for the sorts of checks on power that we discussed under the principle of sin.

Despite covenant's robust appreciation of the social dimension of human nature, it also differs from communist ideologies. Because the covenantal perspective celebrates multiple covenants, it resists making any covenantal community the totality of society. It cast a critical eye when government encroaches on independent sectors of society, universities, law firms, political parties, businesses, religious institutions, etc. Similarly, it opposes religious efforts to cut people off from other communities. Federalism forms community and builds alliances; it does not absorb partners into a larger collective. It does not assimilate people into sameness but values diversity.

Libertarians regularly accuse social portraits of human nature of encouraging laziness, discouraging economic activity, and stifling freedom. Whatever may be said about other views, covenantal perspectives are associated with the Protestant work ethic and the rise of early capitalism (which should be differentiated from the monopolies, cronyism, and and rent-seeking we see today). Federal theologians valued hard work, frugality, the rational ordering of business (for profit), and communal health. In this way, covenant paves a middle way between atomistic individualism and tight collectivism by putting the impetus for personal autonomy in creative tension with the fundamental need for an orderly, just, and predictable communal life.[27]

Daniel Elazar notes that federalism presumes the free engagement of the parties to the covenant.[28] Even our relationship with God, he says, is not characterized by unquestioning domination and submission but by freedom and responsiveness. This is captured in the Hebrew word *shema,* or "hear." Humans hear God's voice. Covenant partners "obey," not in involuntary obedience but in the sense of its Latin root *obedire,* which means to listen to God's call. That is, covenant partners hear, consider, agree, and

27. Adams, *Voluntary Associations*, 243.

28. Elazar, "Recovenanting the American Polity," para. 22.

then act.[29] Religious people and others have struggled to create social space to allow people to freely respond to God's call. It is to this struggle that we now turn.

29. Elazar, *Covenant and Polity*, 70.

Chapter Twelve

Freedom of Church and Conscience

Why should my liberty be subject to the judgment of someone else's conscience?

—1 CORINTHIANS 10:29[1]

For just as the body is one and has many members, and all the members of the body, though many, are one body, so it is with Christ.

—1 CORINTHIANS 12:12

EVERY SOCIETY MUST MAKE sense of its life in relationship to its deepest metaphysical-moral convictions; that is, to its religious beliefs. In tribal societies, the responsibility of mediating the unseen vitalities and mysteries of life on which community life depends may fall on a single individual. In larger, more complex societies with ethnic and religious diversity, the question of responsibility becomes more challenging and contentious. Whether people live in a small clan or a complex civilization, they face a perennial human question: How should we institutionalize our religious traditions?

People miss that this is a universal question because it is asked for strikingly different reasons. Members of religious communities wonder how they

1. Translated by David Little in Witte and Alexander, *Christianity and Law*, 266.

can appropriately relate to God or the gods, maintain a life of integrity, carry out their mission, shape society according to their values, and transmit a way of life to their children. Members of pluralistic societies wonder how we can all get along or how they can be left alone. The politically and economically powerful ask how they can use religion to consolidate power.

The relationship between religion and temporal power, like religion itself, has taken many forms. Because our deepest metaphysical and moral beliefs always get embedded in the institutions and practices of ordinary life, the form this relationship takes always has economic, political, social, and, of course, religious implications. The way we answer this question impacts how the majority and the minority live. Will women have independent authority and rights? Will there be days of enforced community religious observance? Will things our group finds morally abhorrent be legal? Can money lenders charge interest? Will intoxicating substances be lawful? Can people eat animals considered sacred or unclean? Can minority groups fully participate in society? What glue will bind society together and help it find common purpose? Will there be a transcendent narrative that political figures draw on to make sense of great events, as Abraham Lincoln did in his second inaugural address or Reagan did after the *Challenger* disaster? These questions return us to the fundamental, perennial question, how shall we institutionalize religious tradition(s)?

Mainstream American Protestantism's answer to this question is the separation of church and state. This answer is shorthand for a cluster of ideas, including freedom of conscience and its pubic manifestations: freedom of speech, freedom of association, and freedom of assembly. When we talk about the separation of church and state, we are saying that religion should be organized and its mission should be conducted in a social space, a body distinct from the state, called a "church."

Of course, not every religion has a "church." Hinduism has mandirs, Islam has mosques, Judaism has synagogues, and Buddhists have temples. Although we commonly refer to the "separation of church and state," the idea assumes that other groups—Hindu, Muslim, Jewish, Buddhist, and nonbelievers—share the same rights and freedoms to explore, express, and extend their views. No matter how their faith developed relative to temporal power or what privileges they enjoyed or burdens they bore in their country of origin, these groups may operate here like a "church."

A host of other influences contributed to the development of religious liberty in the United States. In addition to the bloody history of European persecution and wars of religion, Enlightenment ideas of toleration, and the religious pluralism of the original colonies that prevented the formation of a national church, there were also religious contributions to religious liberty. These are appreciated by historians, but they are not well appreciated by the public.[2] As a result, rules protecting religious liberty are frequently credited or blamed, depending on one's standpoint, on a process frequently referred to as "secularization," which is frequently characterized as an erosion of belief.[3]

Many claim that liberalism and religious liberty are not religiously neutral but give advantages to an a-religious or anti-religious viewpoint. These people may be helped if they understood the religious contributions to religious freedom. Rather than perceiving the separation of church and state solely as a limit, they might welcome it as a gift. It is an invitation to follow one's conscience, to congregate, worship, and organize to accomplish one's mission. When we forget the religious struggle for freedom of church and conscience, its achievements are jeopardized.

Church as Corporation

The corporation, as a social form, comes from the church. It originates in Paul's first letter to the Corinthians, where he says the church is the *corpus* (body) of Christ (1 Cor 12). Of course, there are always predecessor ideas. Theological ethicist Max Stackhouse notes that "the deepest roots of the corporation are in the synagogue and burial or mystery cults" of the ancient Greco-Roman world that Christians modified into the church.[4] Paul used the image of the church as Christ's body to criticize affluent members ("member" meaning not someone with "club privileges" but "part of a body") who indulged in meals at the expense of poor members. The corporate image of the church not only grounded an ethic of equality within the church; it distinguished the nascent Christian community from the rest of society.

The body of Christ was not a "natural" society in the way people are born into a family or nation. Individuals join the body of Christ by baptism, which Paul pointed out unites diverse people, "whether Jew or Greek, slave or free" (1 Cor 12:13). The body of Christ differentiated itself from family,

2. Siedentop, *Inventing the Individual*, 349.

3. Lilla, *Stillborn God*, 4.

4. Stackhouse, "Moral Roots of the Corporation," 31.

ethnicity, and government. This helped them reject "civic religion, the rule of Caesar, and territoriality in the spheres of religious commitment and faith."[5]

Several early church fathers mounted defenses of religious freedom. Tertullian, writing around 217 CE to the proconsul of Carthage, argued, "It is a fundamental human right, a privilege of nature, that every man should worship according to his own convictions: one man's religion neither harms nor helps another man. It is assuredly no part of religion to compel religion, to which free-will and not force should lead us."[6] Some observe that this sounds like something Thomas Jefferson could have been written.[7]

A century later, Lactantius, a rhetorician, sent the newly converted Emperor Constantine a treatise on Christianity. Among other things, his treatise accused pagans of using violence to coerce conversions, whereas Christians sought to persuade with arguments. "Religion," he said, "cannot be imposed by force; the matter must be carried on by words rather than by blows, that the will may be affected." This is because "nothing is so much a matter of free-will as religion."[8] The arguments of Tertullian, Lactantius, and other early church leaders rested on theological claims about the church, the nature of faith, and human dignity. While this thought did not endure long after Constantine's conversion, it would be retrieved as the church sought to ground arguments for religious freedom in the deeper theological tradition.

The Merger

With the conversion of Constantine in 312 CE, the church moved from the fringes to the center of culture. This movement was accompanied by a fusing of religious and civic identity and authority. Early popes tried to assert authority over temporal power. For example, in the fifth century, Pope Gelasius wrote Emperor Anastasius,

> There are two, august Emperor, by which this world is chiefly ruled, namely, the sacred authority of the priests and the royal power. Of these, that of the priests is weightier, since they have to render an account for even the kings of men in the divine judgment. You are

5. Adams, *Voluntary Associations*, 175.
6. Roberts and Donaldson, *Tertullian*, 105.
7. Wilkin, *Liberty in Things of God.*
8. Lactantius in Roberts and Donaldson, *Ante-Nicene Fathers*, vol. 7, 156.

> also aware, most clement son, that while you are permitted honorably to rule over humankind, yet in divine matters you bend your neck devotedly to the bishops and await from them the means of your salvation. In the reception and proper disposition of the heavenly sacraments you recognize that you should be subordinate rather than superior to the religious order.[9]

Gelasius's vision met with limited success. The emperor, not ecclesial authorities, owned church property, called church councils to resolve disputes, and appointed bishops and other leaders. In the Byzantine East, the "empire was transformed into a spiritual dignity, gathering up into itself the religious purpose of the church; in return, however, it made the church a department of the state."[10]

Following the schism of Eastern Orthodoxy from Western Christianity in 1054, the Western Church developed the idea of a territorial church. "Its fundamental idea was that the rights of property and of possession enjoyed by the sovereign Princes extended over whatever Church might happen to be under their jurisdiction."[11] Kings and dukes owned all church property and appointed people (frequently close relatives) to bishoprics and other offices. Bishoprics could be lucrative because they were sometimes attached to large estates, which the bishops managed and from which they were required to render revenue. The result was a type of ecclesiastical vassalage which made clergy "the real officials of the Empire and the main supporters of royal power."[12] This entanglement resulted in considerable corruption and spiritual drift.

The notion of the church as a distinct corporation was retrieved and developed during the eleventh and twelfth centuries. Pope Gregory VII challenged imperial, royal, and local lay lordship over the church. Drawing on the image of the church as the body of Christ, he asserted that the universal church was a corporation or body distinct from the state. He also insisted that he, as pope, was the head of the church. Since the pope possessed supreme legal authority over all Christians, he, not the secular rulers, appointed the bishops.[13] Temporal rulers resisted this challenge, creating what became known as "the investiture crisis." It lasted for half a century

9. Robinson, *Readings in European History*, 72–73.

10. Troeltsch, *Social Teachings*, 213.

11. Troeltsch, *Social Teachings*, 216.

12. Troeltsch, *Social Teachings*, 222.

13. Berman, *Law and Revolution*, 94.

and ended with a compromise whereby the pope picked the bishops, and the bishop would then swear an oath to the king.

Soon after the church distinguished itself as a separate corporation, guilds, towns, universities, and other charitable organizations incorporated as a way to assert independence from imperial authority. This turned out to be an important step on the way to the development of the modern corporation. As the church asserted its independence as a separate body, canon lawyers in the church developed a new system of church corporate law to address practical legal conflicts between the church and secular power. Legal historian Harold J. Berman says that this development became the foundation for modern law and was the basis for a new institution of learning: the law school.[14]

Although the reforms instituted by Gregory VII achieved a degree of independence, they did not fully separate the body of Christ from political authority. Indeed, Gregory did not intend to dismantle territorial Christendom but to set it on a different foundation. His goal was to give the church a stronger basis from which it could exercise authority through its monopoly on the means of grace via the sacraments. The pope's attempt to exercise spiritual authority, not only over the church but over kings, too, is sometimes described as a papal theocracy. The church hierarchy was to operate as a body distinct from the state while also incorporating the whole of society in the body of Christ. In this way, spiritual values were supposed to penetrate the temporal realms of ordinary life.

While the Reformation would eventually challenge this model, early Protestant reformers sought support from state authorities. This is not surprising since, with the lone exception of Scotland, the Reformation was only possible because secular rulers supported it. Early reformers maintained that magistrates were responsible for the spiritual life of the people. John Calvin, for example, claimed that while the authority of the magistrate is "completely distinct" from Christ's spiritual kingdom, magistrates are charged with preventing "idolatry, sacrilege against God's name, blasphemies against his truth, and other public offenses against religion."[15] Of course, rulers had their own agendas. In exchange for protecting the church, they expected the church to enhance the bonds of internal cohesion and strengthen their temporal authority.

14. Berman, *Law and Revolution*, 217.

15. Calvin, *Institutes of the Christian Religion*, 1488.

Competition between Catholic and Protestant states led to wars of religion, which were only brought under control with the Treaty of Westphalia in 1648. This treaty mandated that signatory nations recognize the sovereignty of other signatories. Sovereignty included the right of each state to determine its national religion and how it would deal with minority faiths, even allowing for persecution. Despite such inauspicious beginnings, the Reformation managed to launch trajectories that led to greater religious toleration.

The Rise of Dutch Toleration

The Union of Utrecht in 1579 unified northern Dutch provinces against Catholic Spain's allies in the Southern provinces. It established the Reformed faith as the official faith in Holland but mandated freedom of conscience in most provinces, even for Catholics. This freedom was revoked two years later, when many Dutch Catholics remained loyal to the Catholic regime in the South.

The Synods of Dort in 1618 ended Calvinist toleration of Protestant Arminian theology, which emphasized the necessity of human choice in salvation. Remonstrant (or objecting) theologians, inspired by Arminianism, such as Simon Episcopius and Philip van Limbroch, became advocates of religious freedom. They were concerned that a decision for Christ was meaningless if the state did not allow people freedom to reject the faith. It is thought that Locke's anonymous dedication in "A Letter Concerning Toleration" is directed to van Limbroch.

Historian Eric Nelson notes that a number of Dutch thinkers, such as Baruch Spinoza and Menno Simons, were early advocates of toleration.[16] None, however, made the practical impact of the reformed theologians he calls "Hebraists." The Hebraists included many of the same figures that Daniel Elazar calls "federal theologians," people like Hugo Grotius and Peter Cunaeus. They studied the Hebrew Bible, the Talmud and other midrash, and later rabbinic commentaries and determined that while the ancient Israelite theocracies passed religious laws, they did not attempt to establish uniformity of belief and permitted considerable religious freedom in the Hebrew commonwealths. The Hebraists concluded that while religion must be under civil authority, laws concerning religion must advance the peace and good order of society. In this connection, they observed that

16. Nelson, *Hebrew Republic.*

laws suppressing belief did not really serve a civil purpose. Based on this analysis, Nelson says that "the set of religious matters deemed worthy of civil legislation grew steadily smaller—until at last it was virtually empty. . . . [This] proceeded under the fervent belief that God himself required the emptying."[17] Drawing on this history, Eric Nelson concludes that "the turn toward toleration in Western Europe . . . was primarily inspired by the religious conviction of the Biblical Century, not by creeping secularization."[18]

Reformation in the British Isles

The reformation of the English church commenced when Henry VIII failed to persuade Pope Clement VII to annul his marriage to Catherine of Aragon. Following this, Parliament passed the Supremacy Act of 1534, making Henry VIII the head of the Church of England, formally breaking ties with Rome. Henry VIII disbanded all Catholic monasteries, priories, convents, and friaries, seizing their wealth and assets. Thomas Cranmer, archbishop of Canterbury, who had made the legal case for Henry's annulment, compiled the *Book of Common Prayer* and revised church worship and practice according to his Lutheran convictions.

Some years later, at age nine, Edward VI was crowned king and continued Protestant reforms. As he neared the end of his short life (he died at age sixteen), Edward sought to pass the English crown to the learned and Protestant Lady Jane Grey, bypassing his half-sisters Mary and Elizabeth. Nine days after Lady Jane Grey assumed the throne, Mary I usurped. She later had Lady Jane Grey beheaded for treason. Mary I restored Catholicism as the official religion and brutally persecuted the Protestants, burning Cranmer at the stake. Many Protestants fled to Geneva, where they came under the influence of John Calvin. This brought them in contact with other European Calvinists, including the Dutch Hebraists.

Fortunes reversed when Elizabeth assumed the throne and reasserted royal supremacy over the Church of England. She sought a middle ground between the more extreme Protestant reforms of Edward VI and Catholic Mary I, restoring elements of Catholicism to worship to promote civil unity. This drew the ire of more zealous Protestants.

The Reformation of the church followed a different path in Scotland, where it was initiated in opposition to Catholic Mary Queen of Scots. This

17. Nelson, *Hebrew Republic*, 91.

18. Nelson, *Hebrew Republic*, 89.

had a significant impact on the church's self-understanding. To this day, the Church of Scotland recognizes Jesus Christ alone as "King and Head of the Church." This contrasts with the Catholic church's papal supremacy and the Church of England, where the monarch remains the "supreme governor." When the General Assembly of the Church of Scotland is in session, the lord high commissioner, who represents the crown, is not allowed to address the assembly from the pulpit but must sit and speak from a separate area known as "the throne gallery" that overlooks the General Assembly. It is even accessed by a different stairway, symbolizing the church's independence from the Crown.

In 1560, Catholic Mary Queen of Scots was deposed in favor of her Protestant infant son, James VI. Though initially supportive of the Puritan movement, when he ascended to the throne of England (becoming James I), he began to view Puritan efforts to reform the episcopacy as a threat to the monarchy. At the Hampton Court Conference of 1604, which he called to address Puritan concerns, he gave voice to the stakes, as he saw them, "No Bishops, no king!"

During the reign of James I, England began settling colonies in North America. Unsurprisingly, settlers in New England and in the southern colonies sought to recreate Christian commonwealths. Although church governments in the New England colonies differed from the episcopacy of the Church of England, they sought to maintain ties and a common identity. Neither the northern nor the southern colonies allowed much toleration.

In 1637, King Charles I tried to introduce a Scottish version of *The Book of Common Prayer* to St. Giles's Cathedral. *The Book of Common Prayer* was "common" because Acts of Uniformity passed by the English Parliament mandated its use to unify religious practice and suppress dissent in England. The idea that the king would impose a book of common prayer on Scotland provoked the worshippers to riot. Subsequently, civil unrest spread throughout Edinburgh. This event inspired the signing of the National Covenant of February 1638, which declared, among other things, that innovations like the prayer book must first be approved by the Scottish Parliament and the General Assembly of the church. In November that year, bishops were formally expelled from the Church of Scotland, and the church was established on a full Presbyterian basis. While independent of political authority and the Church of England, it was still a state church.

Beyond Toleration

Dissenters and sectarians had long advocated for the separation of church and state. Menno Simons left the Catholic priesthood in 1536 and joined a Dutch community that would later become known as the Mennonites. He wrote *The Foundation of Christian Doctrine* in 1538, which made a biblical case for toleration in religion.[19] Although he failed to persuade magistrates in the Netherlands and Northern Germany, in Rhode Island, dissenters got their chance.

Roger Williams

Roger Williams became a Puritan at Cambridge University while studying for ordination in the Church of England. Disillusioned with the church's resistance to reform and its suppression of Puritanism, he became a separatist. Historian David L. Mueller says that "Williams regarded the alliance of Church and state as the greatest disaster which had ever befallen the Body of Christ."[20]

Williams migrated to Massachusetts in 1631 only to be banished four years later for voicing a number of offending views. Williams called for the complete separation of church and state and for breaking ties with the Church of England. He also attacked the colony's charter on the grounds that the King of England had no right to grant it because the land belonged to the Native Americans.

Following his banishment, Williams founded the settlement of Providence, Rhode Island, purchasing the land from the Narragansett tribe in 1638. He attracted followers, including dissenters from other colonies who were drawn by the possibility of liberty of conscience in matters of religion.

In the colony's first religious freedom case, they disenfranchised Joshua Verin for beating his wife, Jane, to prevent her from exercising her right to religious freedom. Historian Margaret Manchester says, "This incident appears to be the first time that a wife's liberty of conscience, independent of her husband's, was upheld in the English colonies." Verin left Rhode Island for Massachusetts, forcing his wife to come with him. It appears that Verin later abandoned his family and migrated to Barbados and remarried. Around this

19. Simons, "Foundation of Christian Doctrine."

20. Mueller, "On the Church and Ministry," 169.

time, the Puritans in Massachusetts enacted the first laws anywhere in the world against the "domestic tyranny" of spousal and child abuse.[21]

In 1647, while in England seeking a royal charter to strengthen the Rhode Island colony's claim, Williams wrote *The Bloudy Tenent of Persecution for Cause of Conscience*. In this treatise, he presented a number of arguments for religious freedom. He recalled the bloody history of persecution and observed that "the proud" are always calling others "Schismaticks and Hereticks." He insisted that unless worship and ministry are offered to God with faith and true persuasion, they are sinful. This is because believers are aiming to please humans rather than God. Furthermore, faith and true persuasion are only possible if believers seek the truth, which requires freedom to follow one's conscience.[22] Although Parliament ordered the common hangman to burn the tract, it became an influential document throughout the English-speaking world.

John Cotton, a learned Boston pastor, replied to Williams. He maintained that political authorities have a responsibility to curb impiety because it can disturb civil peace. He distinguished a rightly informed conscience from an erroneous conscience and claimed that persecution was justifiable only in the latter case. Williams retorted that history showed that magistrates are unable to recognize a rightly informed conscience and that the civil weapons they wield are unable to bring the desired effect upon the soul. At best, they compel hypocrisy, which, he insisted, amounted to "soul rape."[23]

Williams was a classical, even fervent Calvinist. Historian and theologian James Calvin Davis says that this better prepared him to deal with "hard cases of conscientious social deviance" than "Enlightenment thinkers whose proposals characteristically were based on thinner conceptions of religion."[24] Like other Puritans, Williams believed that human beings are endowed with a moral sense, similar to what we discussed in connection with natural law. This gave him confidence in the possibilities of religious freedom and reinforced his idea that the government does not receive its authority immediately from God but from the people. Notably, it helped him appreciate the moral capacities of the native Narragansetts, whom he sometimes reckoned as ethically superior to the Christian English. The fundamental respect he had for them helped him establish a good relationship.

21. Manchester, "Much Afflicted with Conscience," 211–35.

22. Williams, *On Religious Liberty*, 85.

23. Miller and Johnson, *Puritans*, 214.

24. Davis, *Moral Theology*, 3.

Others, recognizing this, frequently asked him to negotiate when relationships between native Americans and other colonists became strained.[25]

Even as Williams lifted up the human capacity for moral discernment, he had a Calvinist's sense of the dire state of human depravity. He was not theologically tolerant. Political philosopher and historian Gary Wills thinks that, contrary to what one might expect, Williams's intolerance inspired his dedication to religious freedom. He admitted Catholics to Rhode Island; but why not, since he accused nearly every other group—Quaker and Puritan—of being dupes of the pope? He was lax in punishing witches, but why single them out when he accused nearly everyone else of being in league with the devil? How else could one explain why Quakers were quaking and running around naked? He supported a government accountable to the will of the people, but he knew that the people were just as sinful as their rulers. Such sinfulness was why the state should never speak for God, for it would only "pull God and Christ, and Spirit out of heaven and subject them unto natural, sinful, inconstant men."[26] Gary Wills concludes that Williams presents in microcosm the process by which religious freedom was realized in North America: "The secular state came from the zeal of religion itself."[27]

William Penn

In 1681, William Penn, a Quaker, was granted a royal charter for his "holy experiment" in religious freedom. Like many dissenters, Penn interpreted the apostle Paul as teaching that the church was a body separate from the state. Noting that the church is honorably called "the body and bride of Christ," he insisted, "only Christ can be head."[28] Writing three years before England's Act of Toleration in 1689 gave religious freedom to religious nonconformists such as himself, he penned, "That there is such a thing as conscience, and the liberty of it, in reference to faith and worship toward God, must not be denied, even by those most scandalized at the ill use some seem to have made of such pretenses."[29]

Pennsylvania quickly became a haven for a variety of dissenting religious groups from all over Europe, as Mennonites, Schwenkfelders,

25. Davis, *Moral Theology*, 50.

26. Roger Williams quoted by Wills, *Under God*, 352

27. Wills, *Under God*, 352.

28. Penn, *Select Works*, 106.

29. Gaustad, *Documentary History*, 119.

Dunkers, and Amish groups migrated there. Philadelphia was where the Protestant Episcopal Church, the Philadelphia Association of Baptists, and the first American Presbytery were organized. It was the site where the African Methodist Episcopal Church and the American Philosophical Society were formed. American church historian Sydney Ahlstrom observed, "Within the borders of no other state was so much American church history anticipated or enacted."[30]

Witherspoon and the Presbyterians

Although Presbyterians were the second largest religious group in many colonies, they received no state support. In several colonies, they had to obtain a license to preach, which was not always granted.[31] They were a somewhat diverse group. Some preferred more formal worship, others less formal. Presbyterians who immigrated from Ireland and Scotland had a stricter take on how the church should be organized than Presbyterians born in congregationalist New England. The First Great Awakening (1740–1776) further divided them into groups that supported revival and those that did not. Still, like other settlers in the middle colonies, they supported the disestablishment of religion.[32]

Presbyterian John Witherspoon was the only clergyman and college president to sign the Declaration of Independence. He thought that religion was essential for good public order and preached political sermons from the pulpit, even claiming God's support for independence. He strongly opposed an established church.

Witherspoon's antipathy to state-supported religion developed when he was a young clergyman and a leader of the Popular Party in the Church of Scotland. The Popular Party supported the right of congregations to choose their own ministers, believing that this would ensure better preaching and teaching. They were opposed by the Moderate Party that defended landowners' patronage rights to pick the clergy (since they were paying the bills).[33] The battle soured Witherspoon on the state church. "As his sense of estrangement grew, the Church of Scotland—and therefore also Scotland—became increasingly a 'diseased, bad, faulty, or unfavourable place,' a 'failed

30. Ahlstrom, *Religious History*, 213.

31. Bluford, *On the Borders of Eternity*.

32. Adams, *Voluntary Associations*, 180.

33. McIntosh, *Popular Party in Scotland*.

utopia.'"[34] His discouragement contributed to his taking the call to become president of Princeton College in New Jersey in 1768.

As president of Princeton College, Witherspoon taught a large number of clergy and exercised considerable influence on the budding American Presbyterian movement. He was appointed chair of the committee that wrote *The Form of Government* when Presbyterians organized a national church in 1787.[35] *The Form of Government* began by articulating a number of principles. The first was a strong statement on liberty of conscience that began with a quote lifted from the *Westminster Confession of Faith* of 1647 (in itallics below). It supported liberty of conscience not only in society but in the church (clergy were held to a stricter standard). It stated that freedom was not for freedom's sake but to allow obedience to the One who alone is Lord of the conscience. It went on to clarify how the church must be separate from the state.

> *God alone is Lord of the conscience, and hath left it free from the doctrines and commandments of men which are in anything contrary to his Word, or beside it, in matters of faith or worship.* Therefore we consider the rights of private judgment, in all matters that respect religion, as universal and unalienable: We do not even wish to see any religious constitution aided by the civil power, further than may be necessary for protection and security, and at the same time, be equal and common to all others (emphasis mine).[36]

The second principle built on the first and asserted the "common right" of every religious society to organize its life according to its own lights, and even to make "great errors," so long as they do not "infringe upon the liberty or the rights of others."[37] As Presbyterians adopted *The Form of Government*, they also adopted the "Westminster Confession of Faith" to guide the church.[38] Witherspoon encouraged a revision of its chapter on the civil magistrate, removing a statement that gave magistrates authority to suppress blasphemy and heresy.

One of Witherspoon's students was the very able James Madison. He became a leader in the cause of religious freedom. His *Memorial and Remonstrance* successfully derailed a bill that would have broken with the

34. Gorie, "Failed Utopia," para. 62.

35. Dreisbach et al., *Founders on God and Government*, 131.

36. Presbyterian Church USA, "Historic Principles of Church Order," 11.

37. Presbyterian Church USA, "Historic Principles of Church Order," 11.

38. Presbyterian Church USA, "Westminster Confession of Faith."

Church of England, established general Christianity as Virginia's state religion, and levied a tax to support it.[39] He worked with Thomas Jefferson to pass the Virginia Statute for Religious Freedom (1786). He also drafted the First Amendment of the Constitution (1791), which prohibits government from establishing religion or limiting its free exercise, from limiting free speech, or forbidding people the right to peaceably assemble.

George Washington, in his 1790 letter to the Hebrew Congregation in Newport, Rhode Island, summarized the new freedoms.

> All possess alike liberty of conscience and immunities of citizenship It is now no more that toleration is spoken of, as if it was by the indulgence of one class of people, that another enjoyed the exercise of their inherent natural rights. For happily the Government of the United States, which gives to bigotry no sanction, to persecution no assistance requires only that they who live under its protection should demean themselves as good citizens, in giving it on all occasions their effectual support.[40]

Washington's letter recognizes progress beyond tolerance to embrace "liberty of conscience."

In 1816, John Adams reaffirmed his commitment to religious freedom in a letter to Thomas Jefferson. He wrote, "I do not like that Jesuits are coming to our country. . . . Shall we not have Swarms of them here? as many Shapes and disguises as ever a King of the Gypsies . . . in the shape of Printers, Editors, Writers, School masters &c. . . . If ever any Congregation of Men could merit, eternal Perdition on Earth and in Hell . . . it is this Company of Loyola." But then Adams transcends his prejudice to say, "Our System however of Religious Liberty must afford them an Assylum."[41] Adams recognized that everyone had a right to religious liberty.

The Problem with Forgetting

Religion played a significant role in untangling itself from state church and government control and securing freedom to pursue authentic faith. Roger Williams wrote his influential *Bloudy Tenent* forty-two years before John Locke's persuasive *A Letter Concerning Toleration* and one hundred forty

39. Madison, "Memorial and Remonstrance."

40. Washington, "Washington to the Hebrew Congregation," para. 3.

41. Adams, "Letter to Thomas Jefferson," para. 8.

years before the Virginia General Assembly passed Madison and Jefferson's Virginia Statute for Religious Freedom. Historian David Little summarizes, "The decisive historical locus of the idea of a right to religious liberty generally consonant with a human rights understanding was not the Enlightenment, however, but mid-seventeenth-century England and America. . . . Locke's ideas, and by extension Jefferson and Madison's, derived from Williams and from the supporting figures of the period."[42]

It is important to remember the religious roots of religious freedom because those who forget exaggerate the role of emerging secularism. Such amnesia is epidemic among Protestant Christian nationalist and Catholic integralist writers. Both define liberalism not as religiously neutral but as a hostile ideology.

Liberal "Totalitarianism"

In chapter 2, we noted that Protestant Christian nationalist Stephen Wolfe attacks the separation of church and state, claiming that we are living under "liberal totalitarianism."[43] In a similar manner, we observed that Patrick Deneen, an integralist, attacks the "so-called separation of church and state," calling liberalism a "totalitarian" ideology.[44] Deneen calls liberalism "totalitarian" because it "denies that there can be any objective good for humans that is not simply the aggregation of individual opinion." Although he does not make as much of it as others, this is apiece with the inspiration integralists take from the medieval church and Gregory VII. According to them, when the medieval church ran things, it established an "objective good." People "naïvely" (as philosopher Charles Taylor says) shared a faith that located them in the cosmos and in society.[45] When the spiritual ruled the temporal, elites were led to care for the people instead of pursuing their private happiness the way liberalism allows. Brother Anthony Maria Akerman claims, "Integralism . . . is not only a rejection of the liberal notion of the separation of Church and State, but is also a positive vision of what God has ordained, that the State ought to be united to the Church in harmonious concord."[46]

42. Little, "Religious Liberty," 263.
43. Wolfe, "Interview with Stephen Wolfe."
44. Deneen, *Regime Change*, 228.
45. Taylor, *Secular Age*, 21.
46. Akerman, "Against Christian Nationalism," para. 6.

There are several things one needs to say in reply. First, it is no accident that integralists ignore the counterevidence—inquisitions, despotism, crusades, depravity, persecutions, pogroms, and expulsions—that challenge their descriptions of a bucolic past. Their romantic portraits of the medieval church confuse repression with social unity. Historian Mark Lilla rejects these idealized portraits, saying that if they are right and medieval society truly reflected the values of Jesus, then the painter "Hieronymus Bosch must have been high."[47]

The second thing to say is that when Christian nationalists and integralists call liberalism and its commitment to religious freedom "totalitarian," they completely misrepresent liberalism. Liberalism is a bulwark against totalitarian ideologies. As we reviewed in chapter 2, historian James Simpson confirms that while liberalism (including religious freedom) is derived from Protestant religion, it did not evolve as a straightforward development. Rather, it emerged as a revolt against illiberal forms of Protestantism.[48]

Simpson agrees with Deneen's assessment that liberalism cannot produce a thick account of the good beyond aggregate public opinion. He admits that liberalism is "hollow," or as Michael Walzer might put it, "thin." But this, he insists, is not a fault; it's a feature. Liberalism, with its insistence on religious freedom, is a *second-order belief system*, not a *first-order belief system*. It is a tool for managing first-order belief systems because "the clash of first-order belief systems leads to violence."[49] Because it is a second-order belief system, it is not trying to impose a vision of the good beyond managing the violence that first-order belief systems frequently inflict. Ironically, when Wolfe and Deneen complain about liberalism's failure to provide an "objective" good for society, they highlight why it is nonsense to call it totalitarian. For all their caterwauling about liberal totalitarianism, Wolfe and Deneen are free to criticize liberalism all they want. No government official is censoring them or forcing liberalism's ideology upon them. Deneen can call for regime change and nobody comes knocking at his door.

Simpson observes that liberalism will always look "weak so long as liberals claim that it is a worldview rather than a tool for governing worldviews."[50] "S/he is free to adopt any first-order belief system" so long as they sign on to the mediating mechanisms of liberalism, which include the

47. Lilla, "Blame it on the Reformation," para. 20.

48. Simpson, *Permanent Revolution*, 347.

49. Simpson, *Permanent Revolution*, 349.

50. Simpson, *Permanent Revolution*, 349.

division of powers, the separation of church and state, equality before the law, toleration of minorities, freedom of association, respect for liberty and privacy of conscience, etc.[51]

Political philosopher Larry Siedentop makes a similar argument, though he takes a much longer historical view. By his telling, secularism's insistence that there should be a sphere in which people are free to make their own decisions originates in Christianity's belief in the moral capacity and the universal dignity and equality of human beings. Far from viewing secular liberalism as a form of nonbelief or indifference, he argues, "Properly understood . . . secularism is Christianity's gift to the world."[52] Rather than opposing religion, secularism grants people the right to exercise conscience and liberates religion to contend for hearts and minds.

The argument of this book is that liberalism is a second-order worldview. Because it is "thin," it works best when it is supported by thicker accounts of its freedoms and mechanisms for upholding a liberal order. As Jonathan Rauch observed, "Liberalism floats on a substrate of things it cannot create."[53] Versions of Protestantism, such as the one offered in this book, as well as Catholicism, Islam, Hinduism, and other thicker philosophies, are required to support the mechanisms of liberal order, including its commitment to religious freedom.

Internal *and* External

Stephen Wolfe talks about freedom of conscience by distinguishing between internal and external religion. He maintains that internal religion lies beyond a magistrate's responsibility, for only God can see what is in a person's heart. He defines external religion expansively to "include professions of faith . . . ceremonies of worship, teaching, etc." Since "these are outward and visible and can affect others," he says, "external religion belongs to the kind of things that external authorities can regulate."[54]

Wolfe's distinction between internal and external religion is nearly identical to the distinction drawn by Cotton Mather in opposition to Roger

51. Simpson, *Permanent Revolution*, 350.

52. Siedentop, *Inventing the Individual*, 360.

53. Quote from Jonathan Rauch from the Liberalism for the Twenty-First Century Conference in August 2025 in Washington. Any variance with what Rauch said or intended is entirely the author's fault.

54. Wolfe, *Case for Christian Nationalism*, 358.

Williams. Mather feared that if people are allowed to freely express their beliefs, they will disturb the civil peace. "If there be power given to speak great things, then look for great blasphemies, look for a licentious abuse of it. It is counted a matter of danger to the State to limit Prerogatives; it is a further danger, not to have them limited: They will be like a Tempest, if they be not limited."[55] Mather is not wrong to anticipate that free public expression invites great blasphemies. If one's ideal of civil peace requires unanimity of belief, then blasphemies are disruptive. Yet, as the Dutch Christian Hebraists observed, suppressing blasphemy also has a way of sabotaging civil peace.

A distinction between internal and external religion also informed Thomas Jefferson's more expansive idea of freedom. We see this in his professed indifference to religion: "It does me no injury for my neighbor to say there are twenty gods, or no God. It neither picks my pocket nor breaks my leg."[56] If only religious freedom were so simple as regulating stealing and assault. But as Williams knew religious freedom requires liberty to engage in public acts, such as gathering and associating with coreligionists, spreading one's ideas, petitioning the government, and other practices that are not purely private but impinge on the public.

The Religious Freedom Restoration Act of 1993 followed the Dutch Hebraists' trajectory, further limiting state interference in religion and expanding the scope of allowable practices. It demanded that government show a compelling interest before it regulated behavior. It extended religious freedom to include the right to grow facial hair and wear some religious garb while in military uniform. It also granted the right to engage in ceremonial illegal drug use. These had previously been viewed as disruptive to civil peace. Religious freedom will continue to be revisited as the public seeks to determine how it may justly honor freedom of conscience and pursue the public good together.

The Challenge of the Present Moment

We live in a challenging time. Our shared cultural resources have worn thin. Democracy is in crisis. Polarization is deep. Mainstream Protestants have not made a compelling witness that is able to attract, form, and sustain members. We face the long, difficult task of rebuilding a church capable of forming and supporting a thick faith and joining with others in the shared

55. Miller and Johnson, *Puritans*, 213.

56. Jefferson, *Life and Selected Writings*, 275.

task of rebuilding republican institutions. We now consider how mainstream Protestants might recover a thick and faithful witness.

Chapter Thirteen

Toward a Thicker Christianity

Every time a society finds itself in crisis it instinctively turns its eyes toward its origins and looks there for a sign.

—Octavio Paz[1]

I write this on the eve of the 250th anniversary of the American Revolution and its subsequent founding. While the founders were convinced that a government responsive to the people was superior to a monarchy, they also knew that previous republics had not survived for very long. Republics were fragile. To counter this, they built safeguards into the government, instituting things like the rule of law, the separation of powers, and freedom of the press. These were designed to prevent a demagogue from taking power and ensure that the government would remain responsive to the public.

Important as these devices were, the founders understood that these fail-safe mechanisms did not run themselves. They were run by people. They required courageous leaders who approached public life with a purpose larger than what they hoped to extract from holding political office. They depended on citizens who are vigilant in defending democratic ideals, institutions, and norms. This is why, when Elizabeth Willing Powel asked

1. Paz, "Reflections," 138.

whether the founders had settled on a monarchy or a republic, Benjamin Franklin said, "A republic . . . if you can keep it."[2]

Keeping it was never a foregone conclusion.

If You Can Keep It

Today, the United States faces serious threats to constitutional governance. The Trump administration has assumed congressional powers and ignored court orders. Trump has directed the FBI and the Justice Department to prosecute critics and political opponents. He has attacked journalists, employed the power of his office to punish coverage he does not like, and interfered in the governance of media companies. He has politicized the military, deploying it in American cities. He has subjugated sectors of society, universities, law firms, the media, and corporations that could potentially resist his administration's policies. He has issued executive orders to surveil anyone his administration deems as advancing "anti-Americanism, anti-capitalism, and anti-Christianity . . . extremism on migration, race, and gender; and hostility towards those who hold traditional American views on family, religion, and morality."[3] These efforts are assisted by the erosion of democratic culture and a digital media landscape built on outrage merchants and misinformation.

The erosion of democratic norms has accompanied a weakening cohesion among citizens and declining compassion for strangers. James Davison Hunter describes a loss of solidarity between citizens.[4] We see this exhibited in the coarsening rhetoric and the antipathy that people express toward members of opposing political parties. John Compton reports a loss of empathy.[5] We see this in the abandonment of human and democratic rights at home and abroad, the toleration of brutal treatment of immigrants, and the general indifference at ending aid programs that have saved nearly one hundred million lives.[6]

Many search the past for lessons that can guide us out of the current morass. Some look to the Civil War, others to the McCarthyism of the 1950s; still others recall the political polarization of the late 1960s. Legal

2. Franklin, *Records of the Federal Convention*, 85.
3. Patel, "Trump's Orders Targeting," para. 11.
4. Hunter, *Democracy and Solidarity*.
5. Compton, *End of Empathy*.
6. Feldscher, "USAID Shutdown."

scholar and historian John Fabian Witt suggests that the 1920s provide a more apt and hopeful parallel to our own time. He reminds us,

> At the outset of the 1920s, a wave of attempted assassinations and political violence crested alongside new barriers to immigration, a campaign of deportations and a government crackdown on dissenting speech. America was fresh off a pandemic in which divisive public health measures yielded widespread anger and distrust. Staggering levels of economic inequality underlaid a fast-changing industrial landscape and rapidly evolving racial demographics. Influential voices in the press warned that a crisis of misinformation in the media had wrecked the most basic democratic processes.[7]

Many doubted whether republican government was working for the people and entertained anarchical and authoritarian alternatives.

The cultural crisis of the 1920s was not confined to the economic and political spheres. Protestantism was also adrift. The "Protestant Century" in American life had ended. Protestants reacted to the advent of Darwin and biblical criticism by splitting into fundamentalist and modernists factions. The fundamentalist wing alienated many intellectuals.[8] Immigration changed the religious flavor of the nation. New media and the emerging urban jazz and flapper culture challenged familiar moral standards. Protestants succeeded in passing Prohibition, but it was proving to be deeply unpopular. Sabbath observance slipped, challenged by industrialization's endless cycle of production, the automobile, and the rise of the secular weekend. Sinclair Lewis became the first American to receive the Nobel Prize for, among other works, *Elmer Gantry*, a lurid tale of a predatory evangelist. In 1925, H. L. Mencken remarked, "Protestantism is down with a wasting disease."[9]

Yet, Protestantism did not fade into obscurity but entered a period of intellectual renaissance and renewed cultural influence. This was led by neo-orthodox thinkers, including Reinhold Niebuhr, his brother H. Richard Niebuhr, Paul Tillich, John C. Bennett, and others. Moving beyond the rigidities of fundamentalism, they recast traditional Christian doctrines, demonstrating their continuing relevance to the challenges of modern life. While they worked within existing ecclesial and academic institutions, they also launched publications and founded ministries to spread their ideas

7. Witt, "How to Save the American," para. 2.
8. Sloan, *Faith and Knowledge*, 1–15.
9. Ahlstrom, *Religious History*, 915.

to the church, the academy, and the public. They joined hands with allies to spread democratic ideas.[10] Reinhold Niebuhr and other neo-orthodox thinkers forged a theology of international engagement that informed the public rationale for entering World War II and stimulated American leadership in constructing international organizations to promote a peaceful postwar global order.[11] They shaped an ecclesiastical ethos that would later support efforts to expand civil rights and address poverty.[12]

The broad effort that began in the 1920s renewed liberal democracy and enabled it to survive the upheavals of the Great Depression and World War II. As evidenced by democracies that descended into fascism, this outcome was not foreordained. Witt concludes that we need "to craft new modes of [democratic] renewal adequate to the landscape of the world in which we find ourselves . . . perhaps fueled by the generative civil society engine of the new vast nonprofit world."[13]

Although many actors will need to collaborate to revitalize our culture, mainstream churches have a particular responsibility to contribute to this renewal. They are stewards of a theological tradition that has left an imprint on our political ideas and institutions. Many of these ideas have linguistic currency outside theological contexts. They continue to possess power to ground public moral commitment. If their meaning was deepened and were given a more prominent place in the moral imagination of the church, they could help the public find common cause in building a free and flourishing society.

Civics and Beyond

Many may conclude that I think the church merely needs a theologically informed civics textbook, however, my concerns about the church go deeper. While the presenting problem is that mainstream Protestants have failed to form responsible citizens, this is symptomatic of a more troubling problem: the failure of mainstream Protestants to fashion responsible Christians. If the church were effectively passing the faith on to its children, communicating its ideas, and inviting Christian commitment, it would not need to worry about citizenship.

10. Witt, *Radical Fund.*
11. Warren, *Theologians of a New World.*
12. Zubovich, *Before the Religious Right.*
13. Witt, "How to Save the American," para. 45.

Indeed, if the church too narrowly limits its focus to Christian citizenship, it will fall into the trap of utilitarian Christianity that we discussed in the introduction. Worse, it may aggravate a significant source of mainstream Protestant weakness; namely, that many members have concluded that being a Christian simply means being a good American, and that being a good American is enough for them and their children.

Toward a Thicker Christianity

Jonathan Rauch, author of *Cross Purposes: Christianity's Broken Bargain with Democracy*, observes that mainstream Christianity has become thin. By "thin," Rauch means something similar to Walzer's distinction between "thick" and "thin." He means that the church is unable "to provide meaning and morals to the culture and thus reliably support democratic society."[14] Rauch contrasts "thin" Christianity with the "sharp" Christianity of illiberal Christians. He also differentiates "thin" Christianity from what he calls "thick Christianity." Thick Christianity can demand deeper commitment. Because of this, it is able to transmit its values to its members.

Jonathan Rauch has asked, "Where's the mainline church? You have a heritage and theology to strengthen democracy. Why aren't you leading the way in addressing this problem?"[15] Chapter 1 attempted to answer this question by noting the church's neglect of educational institutions and organs of communication. Yet these failures reflect a deeper cultural and spiritual problem in the church. The deeper problem is that too many leaders and members are unable to articulate the difference Christianity makes in people's lives. This has led to a loss of urgency and focus. While the public principles we have outlined should infuse the church with new purpose and clarity, the recovery of a thick, mainstream Protestantism will require a deeper, richer theological renewal.

This renewal begins with the church reclaiming its theological voice. For example, it would help if, as churches advocated for their preferred policies, they showed how these policies are supported by their deeper, thicker theological convictions. When I was new in ministry, I was involved in an ecumenical advocacy group whose leader never tired of reminding us, "Doctrine divides, action unites!" I have heard this phrase

14. Rauch, *Cross Purposes*, 33.

15. My paraphrase of a private conversation with Rauch. Any variance with what Rauch said or intended are the fault of the author.

echoed throughout my ministry. It is certainly true that doctrine can be approached in a divisive way. But it is also true that when church advocacy is never explained theologically, it teaches that theology is irrelevant. When theological rationale is never rehearsed, the church's capacity for moral reasoning becomes thin. Advocacy cut off from theology looks like, and is frequently dismissed as, raw partisanship.

Theological reasoning should not be esoteric, but it should clearly link broad theological themes with preferred moral action. For example, it could connect creation as God's good and beloved possession with environmental stewardship, *imago Dei* as human dignity with human rights, sin with support for institutions that hold the powerful to account, and so on.

If mainstream Protestants want to form thick faith, they will need to do more than recover their theological vocabulary. They will need to revive existing organizations and build new institutions capable of transmitting their values. For this to happen, they will need to tell a better, more hopeful story; reimagine their educational institutions; establish clear, practicable spiritual exercises; and develop a responsible media presence for sharing their ideas with members and the world. Since these efforts require a larger, more energized movement than they currently have, they need to intentionally work to revitalize the faith of their members.

A Better Story

David Bonnema interviewed a large number of mid-level church executives in the PC(USA) and concluded that "a lack of any hopeful vision plagues presbyteries across the PC(USA)."[16] Mid-level church executives report that instead of giving birth to new congregations, they spend all their energy running a hospice for dying congregations. Bonnema found that the pessimism is self-fulfilling and presbyteries that voice hopelessness are not forming new worshipping communities to replace the ones they are losing. Bonnema concludes that mainstream Protestants need to start telling another, more hopeful story to overcome a widespread sense of defeatism.

A better story would be rooted in the deepest elements of faith and reflect the church's core mission to make disciples (learners and followers) of Jesus Christ. It would not only appreciate the responsibility but the *opportunity* that lies before the church. It would acknowledge the disquiet that possesses so many people in our culture. It would recognize that people's

16. Bonnema, "What May Be?," para. 35.

spiritual longings are not satisfied just because they are momentarily misdirected. It would grant that Augustine is still right; people's hearts are restless until they find their rest in God. In addition to acknowledging the rampant hunger in our society for significance and meaning, it would be moved by the epidemic of loneliness that correlates with a decline in mental health and contributes to "deaths of despair."[17] In short, a better story would recognize that "the fields are white for harvest" (John 4:35).

A better story would be chastened by the realization that as the mainstream Protestant voice has diminished, responsible voices have not stepped up to fill the vacuum. It would recognize that just because diverse people *can* share moral values and purpose does not mean they *do*. It would become familiar enough with its own values that it is able to make an honest theological and moral argument while exhibiting a generous spirit. It would relearn how to speak the truth in love.

In this connection, the church should not be satisfied with issuing prophetic statements that disappear into a file on the denominational website. The adoption of denominational policy statements needs to be coupled with strategies to build support for the policy. As previously mentioned, church policy statements should not neglect thick theological justifications. Finally, the church must become more intentional and strategic about forming a prophetic community capable of making a common witness to the public implications of its democratic and republican faith.

On issues of great importance, ecumenical partners should initiate a public conversation, similar to the Catholic bishops' discussion of nuclear war in *The Challenge of Peace: God's Promise Our Response.* Such conversation should engage experts from inside and outside the church and should involve the church's core beliefs. Now would be a good time to hold public hearings on the future of republican government.

Finally, a better story would be encouraged by faith that God is redeeming the world. Without relinquishing academic integrity and engagement, it would recover the life of the Spirit, which has the power to attract and change lives. It would find encouragement in gatherings that celebrate God's goodness, glory, and power as a transforming presence. Members who have experienced the difference faith makes and have found purpose in working to heal the world will want to share that experience with others.

A better story would reframe lay and professional ministry. It would acknowledge that while ministry can be extraordinarily challenging, it can

17. Case and Deaton, *Deaths of Despair.*

be about the most interesting, creative, and meaningful vocation there is. Rather than expecting pastors to work as lone rangers in isolated congregations, it would nurture cross-congregational ministry partnerships. It would shift mid-level bodies away from the formal work of governance toward structures that equip, encourage, and hold clergy and lay leaders accountable for ministry. These partnerships would avoid duplication of effort and create a shared strategy for their communities. They would encourage congregations to combine their resources for ministries that none could do by themselves.

Educating the Laity

Mainstream Protestants need to reimagine and build educational institutions capable of calling and forming the faith of members, lay leaders, and pastors. This reimagining needs to include existing institutions, Sunday school, youth ministry, confirmation, camps, campus ministries, denominational colleges, and seminaries. It also needs to include new approaches that digital technology makes possible. Denominations and seminaries should lead this effort. It should not be done in silos. There should be coordination between seminaries and even between mainstream denominations to deploy resources effectively.

The church must rethink its strategy for junior and senior high ministry, making it more substantive and formative. In some communities, it may be connected to efforts to promote literacy. In other communities, it may take the form of after-school or summer enrichment programs. Recovering a substantive curriculum will require support from parents and the teens themselves, many of whom are currently choosing sports over Sunday school.

Denominational leaders, middle judicatories, ecumenical bodies, and churches near institutions of higher learning need to organize a new major effort at campus ministry, recognizing that college students are making decisions about their vocations, identity, and place in God's world. A vibrant campus ministry would have trained leaders, constitute a visible presence on campuses, and have the goal of inviting and forming disciples of Jesus Christ. It would help students and faculty appreciate the intersections between theology and fields of study. Toward this end, it would be helpful for a seminary to create a campus ministry program along the lines of Austin Seminary's master of arts in youth ministry. In addition, the church should consider reinstituting the mid-twentieth-century model of sending compelling theologians and speakers to campuses around the country to speak at events that reach beyond the local community.

There was once a time when denominationally related colleges required Bible courses and religious course offerings. Mainline Protestants relied on these to train lay leaders and to equip members to carry Christian values into their vocations. It would be worth endowing professorships, programs, and speakerships that revitalize religious course offerings, especially given recent cuts to the humanities.

A New Golden Age

Given how digital technology makes it possible to extend the reach of particularly excellent teachers, the church should plan on entering a golden age of adult Christian education. There is no reason that individuals and groups cannot enter into conversation with the best thinkers and teachers of the church on the Bible, church history, theology, and ethics.

But that is not all.

Many colleges have abandoned the humanities. Many students never take classes in a core liberal arts curriculum. Too few are acquainted with the larger conversation about humanity and life. As a result, the public is losing historical depth, a broader vision of life, and the capacity for thoughtful reflection. A republic needs educated people who possess intellectually coherent, grounded views of the world. How can the public exercise responsible oversight of its military unless some portion of the public appreciates the history of just war thinking, the development of Westphalian nation states, and international law? How can the public have an intelligent conversation about, say, US policy in the Middle East unless some portion of the public understands the geography, the legacy of colonialism, the diversity of Islamic groups, and current-day power dynamics? One imagines that the public conversation following the 9/11 terrorist attacks might have led to a different outcome had a larger portion of the public grasped the centuries-long struggle between Sunni and Shiite Islam and anticipated the chaos that would be unleashed by toppling Saddam Hussein.

The church has an opportunity to help members and others explore the relationship between faith and the humanities, history, political science, economics, literature, philosophy, religion, the arts, etc. These topics are not reducible to confessional thinking, but they intersect with Christian intellectual and ethical commitments. Such a curriculum should not be dumbed down and it should introduce people to a broad range of experts who hold diverse views. Denominations, seminaries, and church-related colleges have a responsibility to lead in this endeavor, recruiting the best teachers and experts from across the church and academia, curating the curriculum, organizing programs, maintaining standards of quality, managing credentialing, and upholding systems of accountability. Many adults are curious and interested in substantive conversations. This could provide a potent venue for the church to share its ideas and values with the world.

Educating Teacher-Leaders

If the church wants to have a public influence, it will need to consider how to best educate clergy to be teacher-leaders. For most of American history, the clergy in certain denominations have been among the most highly educated persons in society. Their education positioned them to serve as leaders, not just in their congregations but their communities. It gave them a depth and range of knowledge to equip their members to bring Christian values to bear on work and civic life.

As we think about clergy leadership, it helps to remember that there are three primary sources of pastoral authority. Pastoral authority can be rooted in the authority of the church, bestowed on clergy in ordination. Pastoral authority can also be based on charisma, the perception among peers and congregants that the pastor manifests spiritual gifts that give them insight and persuasiveness. Finally, pastoral authority can rest on a pastor's special training and knowledge. This equips pastors to lead by teaching.

Of course, teacher-leaders must know the predictable "churchy" stuff. They need to master the Bible and internalize theology so they can articulate the theological dimensions of life. They also need to know how to communicate, organize people, and offer pastoral care. They need to possess emotional intelligence, social competence, a rooted spirituality, and a sense of mission. This is the bare minimum for successful church leadership.

But if seminaries want clergy who can credibly lead in the broader culture, as least some of them will need to know something about the world. This requires a curriculum that goes beyond the core subjects and gives clergy intellectual breadth and depth to connect the values of Christ to a wide range of issues. Historically, mainline seminary education built on a liberal arts curriculum that acquainted students with history, philosophy, political science, etc. Today's younger seminary students, as a cohort, are not well socialized in the faith, church culture, or the humanities. One wonders if remedial education should be required prior to seminary admittance.

In the meantime, mainstream theological seminaries are in the midst of massive restructuring. Many are closing, while others are moving to online modalities. One must ask whether an online educational experience is sufficiently substantive and formative to produce teacher-leaders. Online classes should be a boon for lay leadership. It is not clear that they can form the leaders the church will need in the future.

Beyond Sunday Morning

At the Trinity Forum in 2023, Curtis Chang reported, "We've heard this so often from pastors. 'Look, I get my people one hour on Sunday. Fox News gets them for twelve hours a week.'"[18] His point was that pastors perceive that the church has ceded spiritual formation to secular forces. The church needs to respond in two ways. First, it needs to think through and commit itself to a mix of practicable spiritual exercises that are capable of holding and directing distracted members' attention. These practices need to be appropriate to the analogue world in which we live and the online world in which we increasingly reside. Second, mainstream Protestants need to compete in the marketplace of ideas and reinforce the church's message throughout the week.

There continues to be something indispensable about gathering with other believers for public worship on a weekly basis. It allows people to, as it were, "touch grass." It grounds people in a congregation that should care about the community in which it finds itself. Mainstream Protestants need to become stricter about their personal Sabbath observance, even as they create worship opportunities for people who must work on Sunday and improve the quality of their in-person offerings to meet the higher expectations people have developed since the proliferation of digital media.

When I served a congregation in New Jersey, we had an excellent response to a 5:00 p.m. Saturday service. It was developed with the help of parents whose kids participated in Sunday morning sports and attracted new members who worked Sundays. Unsurprisingly, regular Sunday morning worshipers did not feel the need for the service and were not fully committed to it. The stiffest resistance came from staff who did not want

18. Chang, "Why (and How)," para. 15.

to tie up their Saturday nights. Delivering the sermon Saturday night was a tremendous boost to Sunday morning preaching.

People find encouragement and accountability when they regularly engage in spiritual practices together. This is particularly true of daily prayer and explains the power of monastic communities. At my last call, I led a live online spiritual group that met weekdays at 8:00 a.m. for seven minutes. I greeted people as we gathered online, read a daily lectionary passage, offered a short, off-the-cuff reflection, and prayed the daily morning prayer. People direct-messaged prayer requests and concerns. It was particularly enriching for me. Some people who found this online community returned to Sunday worship and active church membership. We regularly had over a dozen live views, several of which represented more than one person. Over the course of a day, the short videos garnered thirty-five to forty views.

During the pandemic, a fellow pastor led amazing evening meditations. She clearly devoted a lot more time to preparation than I did. Her meditations were rich, digestible, and short. I still don't know how she maintained the pace. When the pandemic receded, she stopped. We all missed them. These were not the intimate gatherings of a small group on Facebook Live, but they reached more people. Her example makes me think that there may be value in coordinating with top communicators to create online time-boxed meditations that are responsive to Scripture and the events of the day.

These experiments in online ministry suggest that there may be a digital way to bring back communal gathering and accountability and help distracted people engage in regular spiritual disciplines. As with new approaches to Christian education, denominational institutions need to adapt.

Finally, mainstream Christians need to create new media outlets to responsibly communicate their values and vision with their members and the world. They should find ways to update organs like *The Christian Century* and *Christianity Today*, present them in new modalities, and market them so they have a prominent presence in the crowded online public square.

Renewal

None of these things will be possible if people don't want them. This suggests that the first step mainstream Protestants must take is to become intentional about seeking the spiritual renewal of the church. Until members are grasped by a theocentric vision of God's goodness and appreciate why

Christian faith is important, they will not be committed to the church's distinctive vision, and the church will lack the energy and resources it needs for the challenges that lie before it.

In my experience, talking about spiritual renewal of the mainstream Protestant churches provokes resistance. Mainstream church members associate renewals, revivals, and awakenings with forms of evangelicalism that are coercive, ignorant, excessively emotional, unaccountable, nativist, and socially regressive. We have enough of that already.

Yet US church history is full of awakenings that have been associated with progressive social reform.[19] The First Great Awakening (1740–1776) emphasized personal faith and equality in the eyes of God.[20] It is credited with laying the theological and moral groundwork for the revolutionary ideals of liberty, natural rights, and civic virtue. The Second Great Awakening (1800–1830) is associated with the abolition movement, temperance, women's rights, education, and institution building. The earlier-mentioned neo-orthodox renewal contributed to the New Deal, the Just and Durable Peace Conferences that shaped the post-World War II global order, and the civil rights movement. It also informed the post-World War II church boom.

It is important to remember that every renewal movement was intentional. None happened by accident. Each entailed innovation that was historically unique. All had a thick theological focus. Each invited people to faith in Christ and to seek God's rule. A theocentrically focused renewal movement could temper the tendency of modern evangelicalism to reduce the gospel to a cure for anxieties about mortality. It could expand members' concerns, leading them out of the self-absorption that our culture encourages, to embrace God and God's world. If we want these movements to have theological integrity, moral purpose, and adequate systems of accountability, responsible leaders need to step forward.

People do what they want to do. If people want true renewal and reform, it will require a work of the Holy Spirit. God alone gives renewal. As the nation abandons republican virtue, reneges on its civil rights commitments, and shows signs of entertaining hatreds many of us assumed had been buried in the past, the values of the church increasingly stand in stark contrast with the broader culture. The time to seek renewal has come.

19. Smith, *Revivalism and Social Reform.*

20. McLoughlin, *Revivals, Awakenings, and Reform.*

Bibliography

A Puritan's Mind. *The Westminster Larger Catechism*. Edinburgh: Assembly of Divines at Westminster, 1648.

Adams, James Luther. *Voluntary Associations: Socio-Cultural Analyses and Theological Interpretation*. Chicago: Exploration, 1986.

Adams, John. "Letter from John Adams to Massachusetts Militia, 11 October 1798." National Archives. https://founders.archives.gov/documents/Adams/99-02-02-3102.

———. "Letter from John Adams to Thomas Jefferson, 6 May 1816." National Archives. https://founders.archives.gov/documents/Adams/99-02-02-6595.

Advisory Committee for Social Witness Policy. "Report on Drug Policy Reform: Putting Healing Before Punishment." General Assembly of the Presbyterian Church (USA), 2018. https://pcusa.org/sites/default/files/2024-12/Putting-Healing-Before-Punishment-2018.pdf.

Ahlstrom, Sydney F. *A Religious History of the American People*. New Haven, CT: Yale University Press, 1972.

Allen, Diogenes. "The Witness of Nature." *Faith and Philosophy* 1.1 (1984) 27–43.

Allen, Joseph. *Love and Conflict: A Covenantal Model of Christian Ethics*. Lanham, MD: University Press of America, 1994.

Akerman, Anthony Maria. "Against Christian Nationalism: A Catholic Response to Stephen Wolfe." Josias, Aug. 19, 2024. https://thejosias.com/2024/08/19/against-christian-nationalism-a-catholic-response-to-stephen-wolfe/.

Applebaum, Anne. *Twilight of Democracy: The Seductive Lure of Authoritarianism*. New York: Doubleday, 2020.

Aquinas, Thomas. "Part II–II, Question 26, Vol. III." *Summa Theologica*. Translated by Fathers of the English Dominican Province. Allen, TX: Christian Classics, 1981.

Arendt, Hannah. *The Origins of Totalitarianism*. New York: Mariner Classics, 2024.

Argo, Nicole, and Hammad Sheikh. "The Belonging Barometer: The State of Belong in America (Revised Edition)." Over Zero and the American Immigration Council, June 2024. https://www.americanimmigrationcouncil.org/wp-content/uploads/2025/01/thebelongingbarometer_revisededition_june2024_1.pdf.

Aristotle. *Nicomachean Ethics*. Translated by Robert C. Bartlett and Susan D. Collins. Chicago: University of Chicago Press, 2012.

Bibliography

Associated Press. "Two Pennsylvania Judges Ordered to Pay $200m to Kids-for-Cash Scandal Victims." *Guardian*, Aug. 17, 2022. https://www.theguardian.com/us-news/2022/aug/17/pennsylvania-judges-kids-for-cash-damages-ciavarella-conahan.

Augustine. *The City of God*. Book 20. Translated by William Babcock. Hyde Park, NY: New City, 2013.

———. *Enchiridion on Faith, Hope, and Love*. Edited by Philip Schaff. Grand Rapids: Eerdmans, 1993.

———. "Letter to Boniface." In *Nicene and Post-Nicene Fathers*, Vol. 1, edited by Philip Schaff, 553. Translated by J. G. Cunningham. Buffalo, NY: Christian Literature, 1887.

Aurelius, Marcus. *Meditations of the Emperor Marcus Antoninus*. Book 6. Translated by Arthur Spenser Loat Farquharson. Oxford: Oxford University Press, 1944. Online ed. https://en.wikisource.org/wiki/The_Meditations_of_the_Emperor_Marcus_Antoninus/Book_6.

Baard, Rachel. *Sexism and Sin-Talk: Feminist Conversations of the Human Condition*. Louisville: Westminster John Knox, 2019.

Baltzell, Digby. *The Protestant Establishment: Aristocracy and Caste in America*. New York: Random House, 1964.

Belz, Herman. "Abraham Lincoln and the Natural Law Tradition." Witherspoon Institute, 2011. https://www.nlnrac.org/american/lincoln.html.

Berg, Thomas C. *Religious Liberty in a Polarized Age*. Grand Rapids: Eerdmans, 2023.

Berman, Harold J. *Law and Revolution: The Formation of the Western Legal Tradition*. Vol. 1. Cambridge, MA: Harvard University Press, 1983.

Berman, Joshua. *Created Equal: How the Bible Broke with Ancient Political Thought*. New York: Oxford University Press, 2008.

Beyerlein, Kraig. "The Effect of Religion on Blood Donation in the United States." *Sociology of Religion* 77.4 (2016) 408–35.

Bickerton, James. "Texas Secessionists Win GOP Backing for Independence Vote: 'Major Step.'" *Newsweek*, June 12, 2024. https://www.newsweek.com/texas-secession-takes-major-step-gop-backs-vote-1911678.

Blakely, Curtis R., and Vic W. Bumphus. "Private and Public Sector Prisons—A Comparison of Select Characteristics." *Federal Probation: A Journal of Correctional Philosophy and Practice* 68.1 (2004). https://www.uscourts.gov/sites/default/files/68_1_5_0.pdf.

Bluford, Robert Jr. *Living on the Borders of Eternity: The Story of Samuel Davies and the Struggle for Religious Toleration in Colonial Virginia*. Mechanicsville, VA: Historic Polegreen, 2004.

Bonhoeffer, Dietrich. *Letters and Papers from Prison*. Translated by Reginald Fuller. New York: MacMillan, 1953.

Bonnema, David. "Christian Hope Requires Us to Ask: What May Be?" Presbyterian Outlook, Sept. 16, 2025. https://pres-outlook.org/2025/09/christian-hope-requires-us-to-ask-what-may-be/.

Boswell, James. *The Life of Johnson LL. D: Comprehending an Account of His Studies and Numerous Works*. London: Charles Dilly, 1791.

Boyd, Julian P., et al, eds. *The Papers of Thomas Jefferson*. Princeton: Princeton University Press, 1950.

Bray, Samuel L., and Drew N. Keane, eds. *The 1662 Book of Common Prayer*. International ed. Westmont, IL: IVP Academic, 2021.

Breitenberg, Harold Jr. "To Tell the Truth: Will the Real Public Theology Please Stand Up." *Journal of the Society of Christian Ethics* 23.2 (2003) 55–96.

Brunner, Emil. *The Divine Imperative.* Translated by Olive Wyon. Philadelphia: Westminster, 1937.

Burtchaell, James Tunstead. *The Dying of the Light: The Disengagement of Colleges and Universities from their Christian Churches.* Grand Rapids: Eerdmans, 1998.

Calhoun, Craig, et al. *Degenerations of Democracy.* Cambridge: Harvard University Press, 2022.

Calvin, John. *Institutes of the Christian Religion.* Edited by John T. McNeill. Translated by Ford Lewis Battles. Philadelphia: Westminster, 1960.

———. *Institutes of the Christian Religion.* Translated by Henry Beveridge. Grand Rapids: Christian Classics Ethereal Library, 1845.

Case, Anne, and Angus Deaton. *Deaths of Despair and the Future of Capitalism.* Princeton: Princeton University Press, 2020.

Chamberlain, Will, et al. "National Conservatism: A Statement of Principles." Edmund Burke Foundation, June 25, 2022. https://nationalconservatism.org/national-conservatism-a-statement-of-principles/.

Chang, Curtis. "Why (and How) Pastors Should Help Churches Develop the Mind of Christ on Cultural Issues." Redeeming Babel, Mar. 30, 2023. YouTube video, 1:28:10. https://redeemingbabel.org/why-and-how-pastors-should-help-churches-develop-the-mind-of-christ-on-cultural-issues/#:~:text=Well%2C%20what%20does%20that%20do,Who%20saw%202016%20happen?.

Cherniss, Joshua L. *Liberalism in Dark Times: The Liberal Ethos in the Twentieth Century.* Princeton: Princeton University Press, 2021.

The Christian Century. "About Us." https://www.christiancentury.org/about.

Churchill, Winston S. "The Sinews of Peace: Speech by Winston S. Churchill, Prime Minister of the United Kingdom at the Westminster College, Fulton, Missouri, USA." NATO, Mar. 5, 1946. https://www.nato.int/en/news-and-events/events/transcripts/1946/03/05/the-sinews-of-peace?selectedLocale=.

Coalter, Milton J., et al., eds. "The Presbyterian Presence: The Twentieth Century Experience." *Church History* 63.3 (1994) 514.

Cohen, Elliot. "The U.S. Needs Soldiers, Not Warriors." *Atlantic*, Jan. 21, 2025. https://www.theatlantic.com/ideas/archive/2025/01/us-needs-soldiers-not-warriors/681380/?gift=kMZm5pSulgle9VdUoAJadI7vsty1EtDpH11_O6ei_5w.

Collier, Robert. "Family Demands the Truth: New Inquiry May Expose Events that Led to Pat Tillman's Death." *San Francisco Chronicle*, Sept. 25, 2005. https://www.sfgate.com/news/article/FAMILY-DEMANDS-THE-TRUTH-New-inquiry-may-expose-2567400.php.

Compton, John W. *The End of Empathy: Why White Protestants Stopped Loving Their Neighbors.* London: Oxford University Press, 2020.

Cook, Martin L. "Soldiering: Can Christians Serve in the Armed Forces?" *Christian Century*, July 4, 2001. https://www.christiancentury.org/article/soldiering.

Corwin, Edward S. "The Higher Law Background of American Constitutional Law." *Harvard Law Review* 42.2 (1928) 149–85.

Cotton, John."Christian Calling." In *The Puritans: A Sourcebook of Their Writings*, Vol. 1, edited by Perry Miller and Thomas S. Johnson, 319–26. New York: Harper Torchbooks, 1963.

Croucher, Shane. "California Secession Has 'No Credibility'—but the Anger Is Real." *Newsweek*, Feb. 1, 2025. https://www.newsweek.com/california-secession-has-no-credibility-anger-real-2022646.

Curry, David C. K. "The Gutting of the Liberal Arts: At Public Universities like SUNY Potsdam, the Humanities Are Being Hollowed Out." Chronicle of Higher Education, Apr. 8, 2024. https://www.chronicle.com/article/the-gutting-of-the-liberal-arts.

Daniller, Andrew. "Americans Take a Dim View of the Nation's Future, Look More Positively at the Past." Pew Research Center, Apr. 24, 2023. https://www.pewresearch.org/short-reads/2023/04/24/americans-take-a-dim-view-of-the-nations-future-look-more-positively-at-the-past/.

Davis, James Calvin. *The Moral Theology of Roger Williams: Christian Convictions and Public Ethics.* Louisville: Westminster John Knox, 2004.

Dawkins, Richard. *River Out of Eden: A Darwinian View of Life*. New York: Basic, 1995.

———. *The Selfish Gene.* 30th anniversary ed. London: Oxford University Press, 2006.

Deane, Claudia. "Americans' Deepening Mistrust of Institutions." Pew Charitable Trusts, Oct. 17, 2024. https://www.pew.org/en/trend/archive/fall-2024/americans-deepening-mistrust-of-institutions.

Deneen, Patrick J. *Regime Change: Toward a Postliberal Future.* New York: Penguin, 2021.

Descartes, René. *Descartes Selections.* Edited by Ralph M. Eaton. New York: Charles Scribner's Sons, 1927.

Diamond, Larry. "Facing Up to the Democratic Recession." *Journal of Democracy* 26.1 (2015) 141–55.

———. *Ill Winds: Saving Democracy from Russian Rage, Chinese Ambition, and American Complacency.* New York: Penguin, 2019.

Dickens, Charles. *A Christmas Carol: A Ghost Story of Christmas.* Project Gutenberg eBook, March 4, 2018. https://www.gutenberg.org/files/46/46-h/46-h.htm.

Dionne, E. J. Jr. "Keynote Address." In *Finding a New Voice: The Public Role of Mainline Protestantism*, edited by David Devlin-Foltz, 12–13. Washington, DC: Aspen Institute, 2001.

———. *Souled Out: Reclaiming Faith and Politics After the Religious Right.* Princeton: Princeton University Press, 2008.

———. "Theologies of Democracy in a New Century." Yale Divinity School *Reflections* (Fall 2007) 10–15.

Dionne, E. J. Jr., et al. "The End of White Christian America." Brookings Institution, July 11, 2016. https://www.brookings.edu/wp-content/uploads/2016/06/20160711_white_christian_america_transcript.pdf.

Dreisbach, Daniel L., et al., eds. *The Founders on God and Government.* Lanham, MD: Rowman & Littlefield, 2004.

Durham, W. Cole, and Elizabeth A. Sewell. "The Virginia Founders and the Birth of Religious Liberty." In *Lectures on Religion and the Founding of the American Republic*, edited by John W. Welch and Stephen J. Fleming, 117–52. Salt Lake City: Brigham Young University Press, 2003.

Edwards, Jonathan. *Ethical Writings.* Edited by Paul Ramsey. The Works of Jonathan Edwards 8. New Haven, CT: Yale University Press, 1989.

———. "Sermon 8—the Spirit of Charity the Opposite of a Selfish Spirit." Puritan's Mind. https://www.apuritansmind.com/puritan-favorites/jonathan-edwards/sermons/charity-and-its-fruits-sermon-8/.

Elazar, Daniel J. *Covenant and Commonwealth: From Christian Separation Through the Protestant Reformation*. Covenant Tradition in Politics 2. New Jersey: Transaction, 1996.

———. *Covenant and Constitutionalism: The Great Frontier and the Matrix of Federal Democracy*. Covenant Tradition in Politics 3. New Jersey: Transaction, 1998.

———. *Covenant and Polity in Biblical Israel: Biblical Foundations and Jewish Expressions*. Covenant Tradition in Politics 1. New Brunswick, NJ: Transaction, 1995.

———. "Recovenanting the American Polity." Jerusalem Center for Public Affairs, 1997. https://dje.jcpa.org/articles2/recovampol.htm.

Elazar, Daniel J., and John Kincaid, eds. *The Covenant Connection: From Federal Theology to Modern Federalism*. New York: Lexington, 2000.

Epictetus. *Discourses*. Vol. 1. Translated by W. A. Oldfather. Cambridge, MA: Harvard University Press, 2000.

ESPN. "Saints Bounty Scandal." Feb. 26, 2013. http://www.espn.com/nfl/topics/_/page/new-orleans-saints-bounty-scandal.

Fackre, Gabriel. "Was Reinhold Niebuhr a Christian?" First Things, Oct. 1, 2002. https://www.firstthings.com/article/2002/10/was-reinhold-niebuhr-a-christian.

Feldscher, Karen. "USAID Shutdown Has Led to Hundreds of Thousands of Deaths." Harvard T. H. Chan School of Public Health, Nov. 20, 2025. https://hsph.harvard.edu/news/usaid-shutdown-has-led-to-hundreds-of-thousands-of-deaths/.

Field, Laura K. *Furious Minds: The Making of the MAGA New Right*. Princeton: Princeton University Press, 2025.

Finkel, Eli J., et al. "Political Sectarianism in America: A Poisonous Cocktail of Other, Aversion, and Moralization Poses a Threat to Democracy." *Science* 370.6516 (2020) 533–36.

Finkel, Jay. "The Narcissistic Dynamics of Submission: The Attraction of the Powerless to Authoritarian Leaders." *American Journal of Psychoanalysis* 82 (Aug. 2022) 384–404.

Ford, Paul Leicester, ed. *The Works of Thomas Jefferson*. New York: G. P. Putnam & Sons, 1904.

Franklin, Benjamin. *The Records of the Federal Convention of 1787*. Vol. 3. Edited by Max Farrand. New Haven, CT: Yale University Press, 1937.

Freedom House. "Freedom in the World 2019: Featuring Special Release on United States." Feb. 4, 2019. https://freedomhouse.org/article/new-report-freedom-world-2019-featuring-special-release-united-states.

Frist, Bill. "Youth Mental Health Is Worsening: 'Connectedness' Is the Key." Forbes, May 6, 2024. https://www.forbes.com/sites/billfrist/2024/05/06/youth-mental-health-is-worsening-connectedness-is-the-key/.

Fry, Richard, and Kim Parker. "Rising Share of U.S. Adults Are Living Without a Spouse or Partner: On Key Economic Outcomes, Single Adults at Prime Working Age Increasingly Lag Behind Those Who Are Married or Cohabiting." Pew Research Center, Oct. 5, 2021. https://www.pewresearch.org/social-trends/2021/10/05/rising-share-of-u-s-adults-are-living-without-a-spouse-or-partner/.

Fukuyama, Francis. *The End of History and the Last Man*. New York: Free, 1992.

———. *Liberalism and Its Discontents*. New York: Farrar, Straus and Giroux, 2022.

Galinato, Gregmar, and Ryne Rohla. "Do Privately-Owned Prisons Increase Incarceration?" *Labor Economics* 67 (Dec. 2020) 101908. https://www.sciencedirect.com/science/article/abs/pii/S0927537120301123.

Gaustad, Edwin S. *A Documentary History of Religion in America.* Vol. 1. Grand Rapids: Eerdmans, 1982.

Gershman, Sally. "Alexis de Tocqueville and Slavery." *French Historical Studies* 9.3 (1976) 467–83. https://doi.org/10.2307/286232.

Ghiselin, M. T. *The Economy of Nature and the Evolution of Sex.* Berkeley: University of California Press, 1974.

Goldman, Joe, et al. "Democracy Hypocrisy: Examining America's Fragile Democratic Convictions." Democracy Fund, Jan. 4, 2024. https://democracyfund.org/idea/democracy-hypocrisy/.

Gorie, Euan D. C. "A Failed Utopia: John Witherspoon's History of a Corporation of Servants." *Journal of Scottish Thought* 14.1. (2025). https://doi.org/10.57132/jst.377.

Graeber, David. "On the Phenomenon of Bullshit Jobs: A Work Rant." Aug. 2013. https://davidgraeber.org/wp-content/uploads/2013-On-the-phenomenon-of-bullshit-jobs-A-work-rant.pdf.

Graybill, Stephen. *Rediscovering Natural Law in Reformed Theological Ethics.* Grand Rapids: Eerdmans, 2006.

Gregory of Nyssa. "Gregory of Nyssa—in Ecclesiasten Homiliae—the Start of Homily IV." Translated by Rev. Andrew Maguire. Early Church Texts. https://earlychurchtexts.com/public/gregoryofnyss_ecclesiastes_slavery.htm.

Greenberg, Sarah B. "Between Covenant and Contract: Jewish Political Thought and Contemporary Political Theory." *Religion and Contemporary Political Theory and Practice* 14.11 (2023) 1352.

Grotius, Hugo. *The Rights of War and Peace.* Book 1. Edited by Richard Tuck. Indianapolis: Liberty Fund, 2005.

Gurri, Martin. *The Revolt of the Public and the Crisis of Authority in the New Millennium.* San Francisco: Stripe, 2018.

Gushee, David P. *Defending Democracy from Its Christian Enemies.* Grand Rapids: Eerdmans, 2023.

Gustafson, James M. *Ethics from a Theocentric Perspective.* Vol. 1. Chicago: University of Chicago Press, 1981.

———. *Intersections: Science, Theology, and Ethics.* Cleveland: Pilgrim, 1996,

———. "Theology Confronts Technology and the Life Sciences." *Commonweal* 105.12 (1978) 386–92.

Haidt, Jonathan, and Greg Lukianoff. "The Polarization Spiral: How the Right's Monomania and the Left's Great Awokening Feed Each Other." Persuasion, Oct. 29, 2021. https://www.persuasion.community/p/haidt-and-lukianoff-the-polarization.

Harvard Public Opinion Project. "Harvard Youth Poll." Harvard Kennedy School Institute of Politics, Dec. 4, 2025. https://iop.harvard.edu/youth-poll/51st-edition-fall-2025.

Hatfield, Alyssa. "Varsity Blues Scandal Explained: Lawyers Provided a Behind-the-Scenes Understanding of How the Admissions Scam Worked." Boston College Law School Magazine Online, Dec. 5, 2023. https://lawmagazine.bc.edu/2023/12/varsity-blues-sandal-explained/.

Heller, Nathan. "The Bullshit-Job Boom." *New Yorker*, June 7, 2018. https://www.newyorker.com/books/under-review/the-bullshit-job-boom.

Helmstetter, Craig, and Terrence Fraser. "Poll: Majority of Americans Endorse Democracy, Younger Generations Skeptical." MPR News, Jan. 18, 2023. https://www.mprnews.org/story/2023/01/18/poll-majority-of-americans-endorse-democracy-younger-generations-skeptical.

Herberg, Will. *Protestant, Catholic, Jew: An Essay in Religious Sociology.* Chicago: University of Chicago Press, 1983.

Heschel, Abraham Joshua. *The Insecurity of Freedom: Essays on Human Existence.* New York: Farrar, Straus and Giroux, 1966.

Hetherington, Marc J. *Why Trust Matters: Declining Political Trust and the Demise of American Liberalism.* Princeton: Princeton University Press, 2004.

Hill, Faith. "20-Somethings Are in Trouble." *Atlantic*, Apr. 26, 2024. https://www.theatlantic.com/family/archive/2024/08/young-adult-mental-health-crisis/679601/.

Holland, Tom. *Dominion: How the Christian Revolution Remade the World.* New York: Basic, 2021.

Hollenbach, David. *The Common Good and Christian Ethics.* Cambridge: Cambridge University Press, 2002.

Horowitz, Jake, et al. "Local Spending on Jails Tops $25 Billion in Latest Nationwide Data." Pew Charitable Trusts, Jan. 2021. https://www.pew.org/-/media/assets/2021/01/pew_local_spending_on_jails_tops_25_billion.pdf.

Huff, Toby. *The Rise of Early Modern Science: Islam, China, and the West.* Cambridge, MA: Harvard University Press, 2017.

Hunter, James Davison. *Democracy and Solidarity: On the Cultural Roots of America's Political Crisis.* New Haven: Yale University Press, 2024.

Hunter, James Davison, and Carl Desportes Brown. *The Vanishing Center of American Democracy.* Charlottesville, VA: Institute for the Advanced Studies in Culture, 2016.

Hutson, James T. *Religion and the Founding of the American Republic.* Washington, DC: Library of Congress, 1998.

Illing, Sean. "Everything's a Cult Now: Derek Thompson on What the End of Monoculture Could Mean for American Democracy." *Grey Area* (podcast). Vox, Apr. 28, 2024. https://www.vox.com/the-gray-area/24133960/america-cult-internet-culture-end-monoculture-communication-tribalism.

Iyengar, Shanto, et al. "The Origins and Consequences of Affective Polarization in the United States." *Annual Review of Political Science* 22.129 (2019) 129–46.

Jacobs, Stephen Andrew. "The Scientific Consensus on When Life Begins." *Issues in Law and Medicine* 36.2 (2021) 221–33.

Jefferson, Thomas. *The Life and Selected Writings of Thomas Jefferson.* Edited by Adrienne Koch and William Peden. New York: Penguin, 1998.

Johns Hopkins Bloomsburg School of Public Health. "Two New Studies Provide Broadest Evidence to Date of Unequal Impacts of Abortion Bans." Feb. 13, 2025. https://publichealth.jhu.edu/2025/two-new-studies-provide-broadest-evidence-to-date-of-unequal-impacts-of-abortion-bans.

Johnson, James Turner. *Sovereignty: Moral and Historical Perspectives.* Washington, DC: Georgetown University Press, 2014.

Jones, Jeffery M. "Record Low in U.S. Satisfied With Way Democracy Is Working." Gallup, Jan. 5, 2024. https://news.gallup.com/poll/548120/record-low-satisfied-democracy-working.aspx.

Jones, Robert P. *The End of White Christian America.* New York: Simon & Schuster, 2017.

Jones, Seth G., and Catrina Doxsee. "The Tactics and Targets of Domestic Terrorists." Center for Strategic and International Studies, July 30, 2020. https://www.csis.org/analysis/tactics-and-targets-domestic-terrorists.

Kagan, Robert. *Rebellion: How Antiliberalism Is Tearing America Apart—Again.* New York: Alfred A. Knopf, 2024.

Kant, Immanuel. "Answering the Question: What is Enlightenment?" In *Kant: Political Writings*, edited by H. S. Reiss, 54–60. 2nd ed. Translated by H. B. Nisbet. Cambridge: Cambridge University Press, 1991.

Kass, Leon R. *The Beginning of Wisdom: Reading Genesis.* New York: Free, 2003.

Kayata, Erin. "Can a President Eliminate Mail-In Voting by Executive Order?" Northeastern Global News, Aug. 18, 2025. https://news.northeastern.edu/2025/08/18/mail-in-voting-donald-trump-voting-machines/.

King, Martin Luther Jr. *A Testament of Hope: The Essential Writings of Martin Luther King Jr.* Edited by James Melvin Washington. San Francisco: Harper & Row, 1986.

———. "Remaining Awake Through a Great Revolution." Commencement Address for Oberlin College, Oberlin, Ohio, June 1965. https://www2.oberlin.edu/external/EOG/BlackHistoryMonth/MLK/CommAddress.html.

Kleinfeld, Rachel. "The Rise of Political Violence in the United States." *Journal of Democracy* 32.4 (2021) 160–76.

———. "The Rising Tide of Political Violence: An Attempted Assassination of Trump Is Part of a Global Trend." Foreign Affairs, July 19, 2024. https://www.foreignaffairs.com/united-states/rising-tide-political-violence.

Kleinfeld, Rachel, and David Solimini. "What Comes Next? Lessons for the Recovery of Liberal Democracy." Democracy Fund, Oct. 31, 2018. https://democracyfund.org/idea/what-comes-next-lessons-for-the-recovery-of-liberal-democracy/.

Krakauer, Jon. *Where Men Win Glory: The Odyssey of Pat Tillman.* New York: Vintage, 2010.

Lewis, C. S. *Mere Christianity.* London: HarperCollins, 1952.

Lewsey, Fred. "Faith in Democracy: Millennials Are the Most Disillusioned Generation 'in Living Memory.'" University of Cambridge, Oct. 2020. https://www.cam.ac.uk/stories/youthanddemocracy.

Licona, Thomas. *Educating for Character: How Our Schools Can Teach Respect and Responsibility.* New York: Bantam, 1992.

Lilla, Mark. "Blame It On the Reformation." New Republic, Sept. 13, 2012. https://newrepublic.com/article/107211/wittenberg-wal-mart.

———. *The Stillborn God: Religion, Politics, and the Modern West.* New York: Alfred A. Knopf, 2007.

Linker, Daimon. "The Democratic World Is Losing Its Ability to Self-Govern." *Week*, Sept. 4, 2019. https://theweek.com/articles/862624/democratic-world-losing-ability-selfgovern

Lipka, Michael. "How Highly Religious Americans' Lives Are Different from Others." Pew Research Center, Apr. 12, 2016. https://www.pewresearch.org/short-reads/2016/04/12/how-highly-religious-americans-lives-are-different-from-others/.

Little, David. "Religious Liberty." In *Christianity and Law: An Introduction*, edited by John Witte Jr. and Frank S. Alexander, 249–70. New York: Cambridge University Press, 2008.

Lloyd, Vincent W. *Black Natural Law.* New York: Oxford University Press, 2016.

Long Term Trends. "Home Price to Income Ratio." https://www.longtermtrends.net/home-price-median-annual-income-ratio/.

Lopez, German. "A Federal Report Just Confirmed It: For-Profit Prisons Are More Dangerous than Public Ones." Vox, Aug. 12, 2016. https://www.vox.com/2016/8/12/12454410/private-prisons-violence-investigation.

Luce, Edward. *The Retreat of Western Liberalism.* New York: Atlantic Monthly, 2017.

Luther, Martin. *Lectures on Genesis: Chapters 31–37*. Luther's Works 6. Edited by Jaroslav Pelikan and Hilton C. Oswald. Translated by Paul D. Pahl. St. Louis: Concordia, 1970.

MacComb, Samuel. "The Optimism of the Christian Religion." *Biblical World* 28.1 (1906) 34–38.

Madison, James. "Memorial and Remonstrance against Religious Assessments, [ca. 20 June] 1785." Founders Online, National Archives. https://founders.archives.gov/documents/Madison/01-08-02-0163.

———. *Writings*. New York: Library of America, 1999.

Mai, Chris, and Ram Subramanian. *Price of Prisons 2015: Examining State Spending Trends, 2010–2015*. New York: Vera Institute of Justice, 2017.

Manchester, Margaret. "A Family 'Much Afflicted with Conscience': The Verins and the Puritan Order." *Journal of Family History* 42.3 (2017) 211–35.

Mark, Joshua J. "Enuma Elish—The Babylonian Epic of Creation—Full Text." World History Encyclopedia, May 4, 2018. https://www.worldhistory.org/article/225/enuma-elish---the-babylonian-epic-of-creation---fu/.

Marsden, George M. *The Soul of the University: From Protestant Establishment to Established Non-Belief*. New York: Oxford University Press, 1994.

Marx, Karl. *Economic and Philosophic Manuscripts of 1844*. Translated by Martin Milligan. Amherst, NY: Prometheus, 1988.

Marx, Karl, and Friedrich Engels. *Basic Writings on Politics and Philosophy*. New York: Anchor, 1959.

Mathewes, Charles. "On Using the World." In *Having: Property and Possession in Religious and Social Life*, edited by William Schweiker and Charles Mathewes, 189–221. Grand Rapids: Eerdmans, 2004.

Maussen, Marcel. "A Post-Colonial Reading of Alexis de Tocqueville's Writings on Slavery and Its Aftermaths." *Ethnicities* 23.6 (2023) 801–21.

May, William F. *Beleaguered Rules: The Public Obligations of the Professional*. Louisville: Westminster John Knox, 2000.

———. *Testing the National Covenant: Fears and Appetites in American Politics*. Washington, DC: Georgetown University Press, 2011.

McIntosh, John Rattray. *The Popular Party in Scotland, 1740–1780*. Glasgow: University of Glasgow, 1989.

McLoughlin, William G. *Revivals, Awakenings, and Reform: An Essay on Religion and Social Change in America, 1607–1977*. Chicago: University of Chicago Press, 1978.

Mendenhall, George E. "Ancient Oriental and Biblical Law." *Biblical Archaeologist Reader* 17.2 (1954).

———. "Covenant Forms in Israelite Tradition." *Biblical Archaeologist Reader* 17.3 (1954) 49–76.

Merton, Robert K. "The Puritan Spur to Science." In *The Sociology of Science: Theoretical and Empirical Investigations*, edited by Norman W. Stohrer, 228–53. Chicago: University of Chicago Press, 1979.

Midgely, Mary. *Beast and Man: The Roots of Human Nature*. London: Routledge: 1995.

———. *Evolution as a Religion*. New York: Routledge, 2002.

Miller, Perry, and Thomas Johnson, eds. *The Puritans: A Sourcebook of Their Writings*. Vol. 1. New York: Harper Torchbooks, 1963.

Miller, Richard B., ed. *War in the Twentieth Century: Sources in Theological Ethics*. Louisville: Westminster John Knox, 1992.

Miller, Tim. "Derek Thompson: Negativity Bias." *Bulwark Podcast*, May 30, 2024. https://www.thebulwark.com/p/derek-thompson-negativity-bias.

———. *Why We Did It: A Travelogue from the Republican Road to Hell.* New York: Harper, 2022.

Millies, Stephen. "What Is Catholic Integralism? One of the Oldest Ideas in Christianity Has Come to Renewed Prominence." *US Catholic*, Oct. 14, 2019. https://uscatholic.org/articles/201910/what-is-catholic-integralism/.

Moltmann, Jurgen. *The Crucified God: The Cross of Christ as the Foundation and Criticism of Christian Theology.* New York: Harper & Row, 1974.

Morgan, Edmund S., ed. "William Perkins on Callings." *Puritan Political Ideas, 1558–1784.* Indianapolis: Hackett, 2003.

Mounk, Yascha. *The Great Experiment: Why Diverse Democracies Fall Apart and How They Can Endure.* New York: Penguin, 2022.

———. *The People vs. Democracy: Why Our Freedom Is in Danger and How to Save It.* Cambridge: Harvard University Press, 2018.

Mounk, Yascha, and Roberto Stefan Foa. "The End of the Democratic Century: Autocracy's Global Ascendance." Foreign Affairs, Apr. 16, 2018. https://www.foreignaffairs.com/articles/2018-04-16/end-democratic-century.

Mueller, David L. "Roger Williams on the Church and Ministry." *Review and Expositor* 55.2 (1958) 165–81.

Mullen, David. "Weld County Resident's 'Crazy Idea' Has Spiraled into Full-On Movement." Denver Gazette, Feb. 4, 2021. https://www.denvergazette.com/2021/02/04/weld-county-residents-crazy-idea-has-spiraled-into-full-on-movement-7ee9d774-6657-11eb-b6ac-77573986361c/.

Murphy, Chris. "The Spiritual Unspooling of America: A Case for a Political Realignment." New Republic, Dec. 12, 2023. https://newrepublic.com/article/177435/chris-murphy-case-political-realignment-economics.

Murray, John Courtney. *Religious Liberty: Catholic Struggles with Pluralism.* Louisville: Westminster John Knox, 1993.

National Archives. "Declaration of Independence: A Transcription." https://www.archives.gov/founding-docs/declaration-transcript.

National Association of Realtors "First-Time Home Buyer Share Falls to Historic Low of 21%, Median Age Rises to 40." Nov. 4, 2025. https://www.nar.realtor/newsroom/first-time-home-buyer-share-falls-to-historic-low-of-21-median-age-rises-to-40.

NCHS Press Room. "U.S. Uninsured Rate Drops by 15% since 2020." CDC National Center for Health Statistics, June 24, 2025. https://www.cdc.gov/nchs/pressroom/releases/20250624.html.

Nelson, Eric. *The Hebrew Republic: Jewish Sources and the Transformation of European Political Thought.* Cambridge, MA: Harvard University Press, 2011.

Newman, Nic. "Overview and Key Findings of the 2025 Digital News Report." Reuters Institute, June 17, 2025. https://reutersinstitute.politics.ox.ac.uk/digital-news-report/2025/dnr-executive-summary.

The New York Community Trust. "Donor Biography: George W. Merk." Jan. 1, 2004. https://thenytrust.org/news/george-w-merck/.

Niebuhr, Reinhold. *The Children of Light and the Children of Darkness.* New York: Charles Scribner's Sons, 1960.

———. *Faith and History.* New York: Charles Scribner's Sons, 1949.

———. *The Irony of American History.* Chicago: University of Chicago Press, 2008.

———. *Moral Man and Immoral Society.* New York: Charles Scribner's Sons, 1932.

———. *The Nature and Destiny of Man.* Vol. 1. New York: Charles Scribner's Sons, 1964.

———. *The Nature and Destiny of Man.* Vol. 2. New York: Charles Scribner's Sons, 1964.

Niebuhr, H. Richard. *The Purpose of the Church and Its Ministry.* New York: HarperCollins, 1956.

———. *Radical Monotheism and Western Culture.* Louisville: Westminster John Knox, 1960.

———. *Theology, History, and Culture.* Edited by William Stacy Johnson. New Haven, CT: Yale University Press, 1996.

———. "Utilitarian Christianity." *Christianity and Crisis* 4.12 (1946) 3.

———. "War as the Judgment of God." In *War in the Twentieth Century: Sources in Theological Ethics,* edited by Richard B. Miller, 47–55. Louisville: Westminster John Knox, 1992.

Origen. *Contra Celsus.* Translated by Henry Chadwick. Cambridge: Cambridge University Press, 1980.

Ottati, Douglas F. *A Theology for the Twenty-First Century.* Grand Rapids: Eerdmans, 2020.

Packer, George. *Last Best Hopes: America in Crisis and Renewal.* New York: Farrar, Straus and Giroux, 2021.

Paine, Thomas. "Agrarian Justice." Social Security Administration. https://www.ssa.gov/history/paine4.html.

———. *Collected Writings: Common Sense, the Crisis, and other Pamphlets, Articles, and Letters.* New York: Library of America, 1995.

———. *The Writings of Thomas Paine—Vol. 1 (1774–79): The American Crisis.* Edited by Moncure Daniel Conway. New York: G. P. Putnam's Sons, 1894.

Pannenberg, Wolfhart. *Systematic Theology.* Vol. 3. Translated by Geoffrey W. Bromiley. Grand Rapids: Eerdmans, 1998.

Pape, Robert A. "January 2023 Survey Report: New Insight into Support for Political Violence from the Right and Left." Chicago Project on Security and Threats, Jan. 30, 2023. https://cpost.uchicago.edu/publications/new_insight_into_support_for_political_violence_from_the_right_and_left/.

Parker, Theodore. *Ten Sermons of Religion.* Boston: Crosby, Nichols, 1853.

Pascal, Blaise. *Pensees.* Translated by John Bennett. N.p.: Early Modern Texts, 2017. https://www.earlymoderntexts.com/assets/pdfs/pascal1660_3.pdf.

Patel, Faiza. "Trump's Orders Targeting Anti-Fascism Aim to Criminalize Opposition." Brennan Center for Justice, Oct. 9, 2025. https://www.brennancenter.org/our-work/research-reports/trumps-orders-targeting-antifascism-aim-criminalize-opposition.

Paz, Octavio. "Reflections: Mexico and the United States." *New Yorker,* Sept. 17, 1979.

Penn, William. *The Select Works of William Penn.* Vol. 3. London: William Philips, 1825.

Pew Research Center. "Public Trust in Government: 1958–2023." Pew Research Center, Sept. 19, 2023.

Philpot, Daniel. *Revolutions in Sovereignty: How Ideas Shaped Modern International Relations.* Princeton: Princeton University Press, 2001.

Picketty, Thomas. *Capital in the Twenty-First Century.* Cambridge: Belknap, 2014.

Pierson, George Wilson. *Tocqueville in America.* Baltimore: Johns Hopkins University Press, 1938.

Pinker, Stephen. *The Better Angels of Our Nature: Why Violence Has Declined.* New York: Penguin, 2012.

Plato, Edith Hamilton, and Huntington Cairns, eds. *Euthyphro.* Princeton: Princeton University Press, 1961.

Pluralism Project. "A Three Religion Country?" Pluralism Project at Harvard University, 2020. https://pluralism.org/a-three-religion-country%3F.

Porter, Jean. *Nature as Reason: A Thomistic Theory of the Natural Law.* Grand Rapids: Eerdmans, 2004.

———. *See Natural and Divine Law: Reclaiming the Tradition for Christian Ethics.* Grand Rapids: Eerdmans Press, 1999.

Postman, Neil. *Amusing Ourselves to Death: Public Discourse in the Age of Television.* New York: Penguin, 1985.

Presbyterian Church USA. "The Church's Foundational Principles for Governance." Office of the General Assembly, Dec. 1, 2010. https://pcusa.org/resource/churchs-foundational-principles-governance.

———. "Historic Principles of Church Order." In *The Constitution of the Presbyterian Church (U.S.A.), Part II: Book of Order 2023–2025.* Louisville: Office of the General Assembly, 2023.

———. "The Westminster Confession of Faith." In *The Book of Confessions: Study Edition, 6.001–6.178.* Louisville: Office of the General Assembly, 2016.

———. "The Scots Confession." In *The Book of Confessions: Study Edition*, 3.01–.30. Louisville, KY: Office of the General Assembly, 2016.

Public Religion Research Institute (PRRI). "Survey: Three Quarters of Americans See Democracy at Risk in 2024 Election: As Tensions Rise in a Divided America, One Third of Republicans Say Patriots May Have to Resort to Violence." Oct. 24, 2023. https://prri.org/press-release/survey-three-quarters-of-americans-see-democracy-at-risk-in-2024-election/.

———. "Threats to American Democracy Ahead of an Unprecedented Presidential Election." Oct. 25, 2023. https://prri.org/research/threats-to-american-democracy-ahead-of-an-unprecedented-presidential-election/.

Putnam, Robert. *Bowling Alone: The Collapse and Revival of American Community.* New York: Simon & Schuster, 2000.

Rauch, Jonathan. *The Constitution of Knowledge: A Defense of the Truth.* Washington, DC: Brookings Institution, 2021.

———. *Cross Purposes: Christianity's Broken Bargain with Democracy.* New Haven, CT: Yale University Press, 2025.

Rauschenbusch, Walter. *Christianity and the Social Crisis.* Louisville: Westminster John Knox, 1992.

———. *Christianizing the Social Order.* New York: MacMillan, 1912.

Rawls, John. *Political Liberalism.* New York: Columbia University Press, 1993.

Reeves, Richard V., and Christopher Pulliam. "Middle Class Marriage Is Declining, and Likely Deepening Inequality." Brookings Institution, March 11, 2020. https://www.brookings.edu/articles/middle-class-marriage-is-declining-and-likely-deepening-inequality/.

Rifkin, Ira. "Liberal Religion's Sharp Decline Closes Reform Jewish Seminary: How About Some Elite News Ink?" Get Religion, Apr. 19, 2022. https://www.getreligion.org/getreligion/2022/4/18/liberal-religions-broad-shrinkage-closes-reform-jewish-seminary-how-about-some-elite-news-ink.

Rink, Dieter. "Environmental Policy and the Environmental Movement in East Germany." *Capitalist, Nature, Socialism Journal* 13.3 (2002) 73–91.

Roberts, Alexander, and James Donaldson, eds. *The Ante-Nicene Fathers: Apostolic Fathers, Justin Martyr, Irenaeus*. Vol. 1. Translated by Rev. S. Thelwall. Grand Rapids: Eerdmans, 1988.

———. *The Ante-Nicene Fathers: Tertullian*. Vol. 3. Translated by Rev. S. Thelwall. Grand Rapids: Eerdmans, 1988.

———. *The Ante-Nicene Fathers: Lactantius, Venantius, Asterius, Victorinus, Dionysius, Apostolic Teaching and Constitutions, Homily, and Liturgies*. Vol. 7. Translated by Rev. S. Thelwall. Grand Rapids: Eerdmans, 1988.

Roberts, Raymond R. "Keep the INF Treaty." Unbound, May 3, 2019. https://justiceunbound.org/redeeming-realism-keep-the-inf-treaty/.

———. "Lamentations 3." *Interpretation* 67.2 (2013) 196–98.

———. "Renewing Public School Teaching as a Christian Vocation." *Presbyterian Outlook* 179.15 (1997) 9–10.

———. *Whose Kids Are They Anyway?: Religion and Morality in America's Public Schools*. Cleveland: Pilgrim, 2002.

Robinson, J. H. *Readings in European History*. Boston: Ginn, 1905.

Roof, Wade Clark, and William McKinney. *American Mainline Religion: Its Changing Shape and Future*. New Brunswick, NJ: Rutgers University Press, 1987.

Schaetzel, Shane. "Bring Back the Confessional State." Real Clear Catholic, Jan. 20, 2021. https://realclearcatholic.com/2021/01/20/bring-back-the-confessional-state/.

Schuurman, Douglas J. *Vocation: Discerning Our Callings in Life*. Grand Rapids: Eerdmans, 2004.

Seligman, Adam B. *The Idea of Civil Society*. New York: Free, 1992.

Shull, Thomas. "Americans May Be Turning Against Representative Democracy Along with Commitment to Democratic Values." Unpopulist, Apr. 18, 2024. https://www.theunpopulist.net/p/americans-may-be-turning-against.

Siedentop, Larry. *Inventing the Individual: The Origins of Western Liberalism*. Cambridge, MA: Belknap, 2014.

Silberman, James, and Dusty Devers. "The Statement on Christian Nationalism and the Gospel." Edited by William Wolfe et al. Statement on Christian Nationalism, May 23, 2023. https://www.statementonchristiannationalism.com.

Simons, Menno. "The Foundation of Christian Doctrine." In *The Complete Works of Menno Simon*. Vol. 1. Elkhart, IN: John F. Funk & Brother, 1871.

Simpson, James. *Permanent Revolution: The Reformation and the Illiberal Roots of Liberalism*. Cambridge, MA: Belknap, 2019.

Sloan, Douglas. *Faith and Knowledge: Mainline Protestantism and American Higher Education*. Louisville: Westminster John Knox, 1994.

———. "Faith and Knowledge: Mainstream Protestantism and American Higher Education." *Journal of Church and State* 38.4 (1996) 922–23.

Smith, Adam. *The Theory of Moral Sentiments*. Edited by Ryan Patrick Hanley. London: Penguin Classics, 2010.

Smith, Christian, and Melinda Lundquist Denton. *Soul Searching: The Religious and Spiritual Lives of American Teenagers*. New York: Oxford University Press, 2005.

Smith, Huston. *The World's Religions: Our Great Wisdom Traditions*. San Francisco: Harper San Francisco, 1991.

Smith, Timothy L. *Revivalism and Social Reform: American Protestantism on the Eve of the Civil War*. Baltimore: Johns Hopkins University Press, 1980.

Snyder, Timothy. *On Tyranny: Twenty Lessons from the Twentieth Century.* New York: Tim Duggins, 2017.

Stackhouse, Max. "Godly Cooking: Theological Ethics and Technological Society." First Things, May 1, 1991. https://firstthings.com/godly-cooking-theological-ethics-and-technological-society/.

———. "The Moral Roots of the Corporation." *Theology and Public Policy* 5.1. (1993) 43–55.

———. *Public Theology and Political Economy: Christian Stewardship in Modern Society.* New York: University Press of America, 1991.

Stanford, Libby. "Litter Boxes in Schools: How a Disruptive and Demeaning Hoax Frustrated School Leaders." *Education Week*, Nov. 29, 2022. https://www.edweek.org/leadership/litter-boxes-in-schools-how-a-disruptive-and-demeaning-hoax-frustrated-school-leaders/2022/11.

Stuntz, William J. *The Collapse of American Criminal Justice.* Cambridge: Harvard University Press, 2011.

Taylor, Charles. *A Secular Age.* Cambridge, MA: Belknap, 2007.

———. *Sources of the Self: The Making of the Modern Identity.* Cambridge: Harvard University Press, 1989.

Thompson, Derek. "No One Knows What Universities Are For." *Atlantic*, May 8, 2024. https://www.theatlantic.com/ideas/archive/2024/05/bureaucratic-bloat-eating-american-universities-inside/678324/.

———. "The True Cost of the Churchgoing Bust." *Atlantic*, Apr. 3, 2024. https://www.theatlantic.com/ideas/archive/2024/04/america-religion-decline-non-affiliated/677951/.

Thompson, Ernest Trice. *The Spirituality of the Church: A Distinctive Doctrine of the Presbyterian Church in the United States.* Richmond, VA: Presbyterian School of Christian Education, 1961.

Thornwell, James Henley. *Collected Writings of James Henley Thornwell.* Edited by B. M. Palmer and J. B. Adger. Richmond: Whittet & Shepperson, 1875.

Tillich, Paul. *The Interpretation of History.* Translated by N. A. Rasetzki and Elsa L. Talmey. New York: Charles Scribner's Sons, 1936.

Tocqueville, Alexis. *Democracy in America.* Vol. 1. New York: Vintage, 1990.

Tolstoy, Leo. *Anna Karenina.* Translated by Rosamund Bartlett. Oxford: Oxford University Press, 2017.

Tracy, David. *The Analogical Imagination: Christian Theology and the Culture of Pluralism.* New York: Crossroad, 1991.

Travis, Merle. "Sixteen Tons." Recorded Aug. 8, 1946, track 2 on *Folk Songs of the Hills*, Capitol Records, 1947, 78 rpm.

Troeltsch, Ernest. *The Social Teachings of the Christian Churches.* Louisville: Westminster John Knox, 1992.

Troutner, Timothy. "The Integralist Mirroring of Liberal Ideals." Church Life Journal, Mar. 8, 2019. https://churchlifejournal.nd.edu/articles/the-integralist-mirroring-of-liberal-ideals/.

Ture, Kwame, and Charles V. Hamilton. *Black Power: The Politics of Black Liberation.* New York: Random House, 1967.

Tveit, Jon, and J. P. Barnas, eds. "What Is the Josias?" https://thejosias.com/about/.

USAFacts. "How Much Do States Spend on Housing Prisoners?" Oct. 31, 2025. https://usafacts.org/articles/how-much-do-states-spend-on-prisons/.

Vallier, Kevin. *All the Kingdoms of the World: On Radical Alternatives to Liberalism.* New York: Oxford University Press, 2023.

Vedantam, Shankar. "How Private Prisons Affect Sentencing." National Public Radio, June 28, 2019. https://www.npr.org/2019/06/28/736875577/hidden-brain-how-private-prisons-affect-sentencing.

Vermeule, Adrian. "Beyond Originalism." *Atlantic*, Mar. 31, 2020. https://www.theatlantic.com/ideas/archive/2020/03/common-good-constitutionalism/609037/.

Voskuil, Dennis N. "Reaching Out: Mainstream Protestantism and the Media." In *Between the Times: The Travail of the Protestant Establishment in America, 1900–1960*, edited by William R. Hutchison, 72–92. New York: Cambridge University Press, 1989.

Wagner, Emma, et al. "What Drives Health Spending in the U.S. Compared to Other Countries?" Peterson Center on Healthcare, Aug. 2, 2024. https://www.healthsystemtracker.org/brief/what-drives-health-spending-in-the-u-s-compared-to-other-countries/.

Waldstein, Edmund. "Integralism and the Logic of the Cross." Church Life Journal, Mar. 19, 2019. https://churchlifejournal.nd.edu/articles/integralism-and-the-logic-of-the-cross/.

WallBuilders. "Lesson 4: American Founding and Federal Era (1785–early 1800s)." Sept. 27, 2023. https://wallbuilders.com/resource/lesson-4-american-founding-and-federal-era-1785-early-1800s/.

Wallis, Jim. *America's Original Sin: Racism, White Privilege, and the Bridge to a New America.* Grand Rapids: Brazos, 2016.

Walzer, Michael. "Notes on a Dangerous Mistake." *Liberties Journal* 4.2 (2024). https://libertiesjournal.com/articles/notes-on-a-dangerous-mistake/.

———. *Thick and Thin: Moral Argument at Home and Abroad.* South Bend, IN: University of Notre Dame Press, 1994.

Warren, Heather. *Theologians of a New World Order: Reinhold Niebuhr and the Christian Realists 1920–1948.* New York: Oxford University Press, 1997.

Washington, George. "From George Washington to the Hebrew Congregation in Newport, Rhode Island, 18 August 1790." Founders Online, National Archives. https://founders.archives.gov/documents/Washington/05-06-02-0135.

Weber, Max. *From Max Weber: Essays in Sociology.* Translated by H. H. Gerth and C. Wright Mills. New York: Oxford University Press, 1946.

Wedgewood, Ralph. "Hierocles' Concentric Circles." Academia. https://www.academia.edu/46912801/Hierocles_Concentric_Circles.

White, Lynn Jr. "The Historical Roots of Our Ecologic Crisis." *Science* 155.3767 (1967) 1203–7.

Wilkin, Robert Louis. *Liberty in the Things of God: The Christian Origins of Religious Freedom.* New Haven, CT: Yale University Press, 2019.

Williams, Peter W. *America's Religions: From Their Origins to the Twenty-First Century.* Chicago: University of Illinois Press, 2015.

Williams, Roger. *On Religious Liberty: Selections from the Works of Roger Williams.* Edited by James Calvin Davis. Cambridge, MA: Belknap, 2008.

Wills, Gary. *Under God: Religion and American Politics.* New York: Touchstone, 1990.

Wilson, Doug, et al. "Transcript: Interview with Doug Wilson on Christian Nationalism." Christ Over All, Oct. 18, 2023. https://christoverall.com/article/concise/transcript-interview-with-doug-wilson-on-christian-nationalism/.

Wilson, E. O. *On Human Nature.* Cambridge: Harvard University Press, 1978.

Winright, Tobias. *Serve and Protect: Selected Essays on Just Policing.* Eugene, OR: Cascade, 2020.

Wintemute, Garen J., et al. "Views of American Democracy and Support for Political Violence: First Report from a Nationally-Representative Survey." MexRxiv, July 19, 2022. https://www.medrxiv.org/content/10.1101/2022.07.15.22277693v1.

Witt, John Fabian. "How to Save the American Experiment." *New York Times*, Oct. 6, 2025. https://www.nytimes.com/2025/10/06/opinion/politics/how-to-save-the-american-experiment.html.

———. *The Radical Fund: How a Band of Visionaries and a Million Dollars Upended America.* New York: Simon & Schuster, 2025.

Witte, John, ed. *Christianity and Human Rights: An Introduction.* Cambridge: Cambridge University Press, 2010.

Witte, John Jr., and Frank S. Alexander, eds. *Christianity and Law: An Introduction.* New York: Cambridge University Press, 2008.

Wolfe, Stephen. *The Case for Christian Nationalism.* Moscow, ID: Cannon, 2022.

Wolfe, Stephen, et al. "Transcript: Interview with Stephen Wolfe on Christian Nationalism." Christ Over All, Oct. 20, 2023. https://christoverall.com/article/concise/transcript-interview-with-stephen-wolfe-on-christian-nationalism/.

Wong, Scott, et al. "People Are Scared to Death: Members of Congress Fear for Their Safety After Charlie Kirk Assassination." NBC News, September 11, 2025. https://www.nbcnews.com/politics/congress/congress-scared-charlie-kirk-assassination-canceling-events-rcna230632.

Zubovich, Gene. *Before the Religious Right: Liberal Protestants, Human Rights, and the Polarization of the United States.* Philadelphia: University of Pennsylvania Press, 2022.

Subject Index

www.ingramcontent.com/pod-product-compliance
Lightning Source LLC
LaVergne TN
LVHW050633100826
845148LV00011B/1853

* 9 7 9 8 3 8 5 2 5 1 4 2 1 *